THE
HORNET
FILE

By Lewis G Cooper

For Leo Hoek
hoping it stirs
some pleasant memories.
thanks for your contribution

[signature]

An Air-Britain Publication

Copyright 1992 by Lewis G Cooper

Published in Great Britain by

Air-Britain (Historians) Ltd
1 East Street, Tonbridge, Kent

Sales Dept: 5 Bradley Road, Upper Norwood, London SE19 3NT

Correspondence to:

J.J.Halley, 5 Walnut Tree Road,
Shepperton, Middlesex, TW17 ORW
and not to the Tonbridge address

ISBN 0 85130 202 5

Printed by Hollen Street Press Limited
141/3 Farnham Road, Slough, Berks.

Contents

Introduction 5

Design and Development Flight Testing 7

Hornet Production and Flight Testing 15

Hornet Trials at A. & A.E.E., Boscombe Down 19

N.5/44 Sea Hornet 27

Sea Hornet NF.21 Conversion 29

Sea Hornet Trials at A. & A.E.E., Boscombe Down 31

The Church Fenton Wing 39

The Linton-on-Ouse Wing 55

Far East Air Force 77

Royal Air Force Training and Support Units 91

Sea Hornet Squadrons 95

Royal Navy Second Line Squadrons and Support Units 113

Production 119

Individual Hornet Histories 121

Individual Sea Hornet Histories 131

Type Data 143

Abbreviations 145

Acknowledgments 147

INTRODUCTION

That an in-depth study of de Havilland's Hornet should be written is beyond question. There can be little doubt that the Hornet reached a zenith in piston-engined aircraft design for high performance fighter aircraft. Speeds approaching 500 m.p.h. were attained during initial flight tests from Hatfield although prototype RR915 was beset by annoying buffet problems which persisted almost throughout the entire flight test programme. Subsequent revelations at A.&A.E.E. concerned directional problems, cured by adding a dorsal fin.

On issue to squadrons, the early F.I version lacked reliable gun sights, serviceability was below average and deliveries proved to be sluggish. Single-engine landings were to become routine, while coolant pump failures and throttle synchronisation difficulties compounding problems for squadron maintenance crews.

Despite some failings, all former pilots, without exception, have expressed considerable enthusiasm for the Hornet - a "Pilot's Aeroplane". Aerobatics were considered a joy to perform, thanks to an excellent reserve of power and good all-round view. All mentioned the added bonus of handed engines, which effectively cancelled out take-off swing, and its superb single-engine performance.

The advent of jet fighters abruptly terminated any possibility of the Hornet becoming the RAF's standard long-range fighter; only four home squadrons were equipped. Early Meteors had inferior speed performance at all heights, poor range and short endurance.

A later change of role for the Hornet to low-level intruder on defence exercises resulted in numerous surprise attacks on airfields. Operating at extreme low level, R.A.F. and F.A.A. pilots were almost invulnerable to interception by defending jets. Fighter-to-fighter combat with Griffon-Spitfires or Sea Furies was another matter due to the Hornet's larger turning circle and heavier ailerons. Protracted steep dives in early F.Is from high altitude during interception exercises was often to result in "porpoising", causing some concern to pilots.

In later service, Hornets and their naval counterparts began to suffer internal decomposition. Some R.A.F. examples flew many hundreds of hours of highly-stressed, incessant diving attacks on sorties in Malaya. Tropical conditions, combined with regular high "G" manoeuvres, proved too much for the structure. Compared with the life expectancy of wartime Mosquitoes, some early production F.3s had a comparatively long service life, having previously equipped U.K.-based squadrons before being ferried out to Malaya.

RR919, the second prototype Hornet (via P. Jarrett)

DESIGN & DEVELOPMENT FLIGHT TESTING

F.12/43 HORNET FIRST PROTOTYPE RR915

Preliminary design studies for a private venture, twin-Merlin fighter were commenced toward the end of 1941, several other projects being shelved. Attention now focussed on the D.H.103 with design work under the control of W.E. Bishop, assisted by A.G. Peters who acted as design co-ordinator. Work started at on a full size mock-up which was carefully screened from prying eyes.

In January 1943 the completed mock-up was duly inspected by a visiting delegation from the Ministry of Aircraft Production, followed by an agonising delay lasting five months. Permission was eventually received to proceed with the construction of two prototypes under Specification F.12/43. This specification outlined a requirement for a single-seat, twin-engined, long range day fighter and was virtually written around the existing D.H. design.

Dated 5 October 1943, Specification F.12/43 included a reference to the existence of a new "Slimline" version of the Merlin, specially designed by Rolls-Royce to accommodate low drag cowlings, known as RM14SH or Merlin 130. Propellers were to be of fully feathering/reversible pitch design with a future provision for counter-rotating types.

Extracts from the original specification F.12/43 are listed as follows:

Operational Requirements: Proviso of optimum performance at 22,000 feet; high rate of climb; good fighting manoeuverability, especially in the rolling plane; high speed and long range. Maximum speed as high as possible, (consistent with a high rate of climb and manoeuvrability) and not less than 480 m.p.h. at 22,000 feet. The rate of climb not less than 4,400 ft/min from ground level to 22,000 feet.

Manoeuverability: Turning circle was to be as small as possible with provision for a maximum lift position on the flap control.

Endurance: Permanent tankage was required for: Five minutes at max. take-off power; plus fuel for max. power climb to 22,000 feet; plus fifteen minutes at max. level speed at 20,000 feet; plus 1,000 miles range in still air at best economical cruising speed at 20,000 feet.

Armour protection: Required from astern against German MG151 and 20 mm ammunition. From ahead against German MG131 and 13 mm ammunition. Later provision was required against German MG151 and 20 mm ammunition should this become necessary.

Engine performance: There was to be no hesitation in engine power during combat manoeuvres and suitable equipment to prevent cut-outs when the aircraft was subjected to negative g.

Protection from the elements: Since the Hornet was destined for service in the Far Eastern theatre of war, stringent requirements stipulated the following conditions; should the aircraft be allowed to stand in the open for long periods under tropical conditions, either inland or near sea, it was essential that wooden components did not become seriously affected. Class 1A treatment was recommended.

Tropicalisation: The first and all subsequent production aircraft were required to be entirely suitable for tropical operations and equipped with an efficient cooling system.

The official decision to proceed with construction of two prototypes resulted in rapid progress with RR915, the first aircraft. The fuselage halves were ready for mating in the assembly jig towards the end of 1943.

Construction methods were similar to those adopted for the Mosquito, apart from the introduction of composite Alclad/wooden bonding. Alclad sheet was used for the tail unit and wing leading edges. Highly stressed areas utilised reinforcements of additional Dural stringers, wing undersurfaces subject to high tensile loads were constructed of Alclad sheet/Dural stringers. The upper wing surfaces were composed of double thickness ply with the wing spars beefed up by plywood booms cemented to Dural "L" section extrusions. Alclad/wood joints were joined by a radical bonding agent known as Redux adhesive, recently developed by Aero Research Ltd.

Induction intakes were located in wing leading edges and positioned outboard of engines and ducts to superchargers provided with rotary valves which automatically operated Vokes filters when the undercarriage was lowered.

Wing radiators combined cooling facilities for engine coolant and the supercharger intercoolers. Unlike the Mosquito, engine cowlings were completely free of intake ducts. During construction, RR915 was given regular centre of gravity checks and the weight was closely monitored. Initial weight estimates were found to be well within target figures.

Rolls-Royce delivered the first two Merlin 130 engines which were installed on 25 April 1944, initial engine runs commencing on 20 July.

Preliminary Pilots' Notes were issued on 23 July with copies issued to various departments, including Geoffrey de Havilland Jnr., Sir Geoffrey de Havilland and Mr. R.E. Bishop, Chief Designer.

The estimated take-off distance to unstick at 14,500 lb AUW was 340 yards, compared with 450 yards for the original Mosquito. A swing to starboard was expected due to the greater engine power and slipstream effect. Provision was made for use of higher grade 150 fuel. The initial rate of climb was provisionally estimated at 3,700 ft./min.

It was assumed that the Hornet would have a somewhat flatter landing approach than the Mosquito, approximating 1:7.5 with flaps set at forty-five degrees and undercarriage lowered.

Temporary speed limits were imposed for lowering of flaps (150 m.p.h.) and undercarriage (180 m.p.h.). Special emphasis was placed on the general increase in slipstream effect over the Mosquito and directional stability was considered as inferior.

Previous wind tunnel tests had indicated the possibility of a break-away of airflow from nacelles, although thought unlikely to cause tail buffet. This prophesy was later confirmed throughout later tests.

Estimated maximum speeds were a remarkable 501 m.p.h. at high altitude and 431 m.p.h. at sea level. Single engine safety speed was expected to be 150 m.p.h. using full rudder or 185 m.p.h. using only trimming tabs. Speed limitations were based on the Hornet's limiting Mach Number of 0.75 at 5,000 feet giving a maximum IAS of 475 m.p.h.

All-up weight for initial taxying trials and first flight was 14,100 lb which included a full fuel load of 347 gallons, giving a wing loading of 39 lb/sq.ft. Empty weight was expected to be 11,100 lb. Original estimates were to prove remarkably accurate, having been calculated at 12,089 lb with a later project estimate of 11,950 lb. These figures compared well with an actual 11,957 lb obtained during final weighing, i.e. within 7 lb.

RR915 FLIGHT TEST PROGRAMME

SUMMARY OF FLIGHT TESTS 1-152

After initial taxying trials and first short hops, RR915 was wheeled out for its first flight on 28 July 1944, with Geoffrey de Havilland Jnr. at the controls. Three short test flights were carried out between 28-31 July, totalling two hours twenty-five minutes.

Some faults were discovered including:
    (a) It was almost impossible to raise the undercarriage without applying some negative g.
    (b) Ailerons were found to be "super heavy" due to incorrect gearing.
    (c) There was extreme tail buffeting which increased at high speed and was considered worse than similar buffet on the prototype Mosquito.
    (d) It was impossible to lower the tail for a three point landing. A gentle nose-up trim occurred when flaps were lowered at thirty-five degrees; at 35-45 degree settings, a sharp nose-down tendency existed. This could

Second prototype RR919 with bomb racks and lowered Fowler flaps (BAe)

not be counteracted by using the elevators although at 25-39 degrees setting it was possible to lower the tail satisfactorily.

(e) The Chassis lever was judged to be positioned too close to the engine control rods and the solenoid refused to disengage.

(f) A modified flap lever gate was required and needed to be installed as soon as possible.

(g) Flap operation was too slow.

(h) Engine ignition switches needed to be re-positioned on port side of cockpit.

(i) Cockpit ventilation was unsatisfactory due an insufficient supply of air. There was considerable noise from the ventilator. A stream of air into the pilot's face would counteract the effects of sun's rays.

(j) The cockpit heater worked in wrong fashion; winding the controls should STOP hot air.

(k) Manual operation of radiator flaps resulted in rapid movement which was too fast for accurate settings.

(l) It was difficult to anticipate take-off swing due to the port engine responding faster than starboard due to different settings in calibrated boost capsules.

(m) Stalling characteristics could not be fully investigated on account of spring tab ailerons (fitted subsequent to first hops) riding upwards just before the onset of stall. Tugging on ailerons at this point indicated possible tip stall.

(n) Lowering the undercarriage caused a slight nose-down trim.

(o) Single engine safety speed on either engine appeared to be about 165 IAS at full boost, ascertained with undercarriage and flaps raised, engine idling in fine pitch.

(p) With ailerons in their current configuration it was difficult to make any assessment of lateral stability, although the Hornet may be more stable than the Mosquito and appeared to take on bank more quickly after applying rudder.

(q) It was impossible to obtain a longitudinal phugoid; this was deferred until resolution of tail buffet problems.

(r) The chassis was somewhat harsher than the Mosquito although with the tail damper in operation it seemed quite acceptable.

(s) It was impossible to open the cockpit sliding canopy in flight, due possibly to suction causing the two locating pins to press up tightly.

(t) The seat tilting gear did not operate correctly.

(u) Both Merlins were very bad on opening throttles; these problems were reported to Rolls-Royce.

(v) High petrol pressures (21 lb) were also contained in the report to Rolls-Royce.

At this phase in the Hornet's flight test programme it was decided to enlist the services of Geoffrey Pike in a bid to eradicate the initial teething problems.

On the evening of 9 August, RR915 took off for the fifth test, a twenty-minute flight with the tailplane set at two degrees negative incidence to assist in getting the tail down for landing. On becoming airborne it became evident that there was insufficient downward elevator movement for safe flight due to decrease of the tail angle. The prototype was flown around at low speed before landing at Hatfield.

Due to the unsafe tailplane setting it proved impossible to carry out a check on re-set ailerons during the sixth test although they were found to be lighter than on previous tests.

It was impossible to bring the aircraft slowly to the stall for an accurate assessment of stalling speeds with any degree of accuracy due to wing root flow breakaway which spoiled the effects from the elevators. These effects showed some commonality with the Mosquito, although they were more pronounced.

Stalling characteristics were mild and were generally similar to the Mosquito, although the warning was indicated by a pronounced tugging of the ailerons. Various flap settings were used but had little effect on the stalling qualities. Aileron tugging started at 123 IAS with flaps and undercarriage raised and this increased in intensity up to the stall with tail buffet at 120 IAS. The clean stall occurred at about 110 IAS and 85 IAS with wheels and flaps down. Geoffrey Pike carried out the seventh test, generally agreeing with previous criticisms. During the course of a half-hour flight, he experienced considerable discomfort due to heat and a lack of sufficient fresh air. Vibrograph readings taken indicated that previous airscrew vibration appeared to have faded away.

An eighth test lasting half-an-hour was made on the same day for some circuits and landings using various flap settings. At a twenty-degree setting it was just possible to get the tail down - trying hard - but it was impossible at increased setting.

Between 11-16 August, eleven test flights were carried out by Geoffrey de Havilland after RR915 had been fitted with the original aileron torsion bars and an increased mechanical gear ratio. There was a decided improvement in aileron control through the whole speed range, i.e. from stalling up to 360 IAS. The ailerons tended to float upwards by about one inch at the stall without harmful effect. Full movement could be applied at 300 IAS, despite a slight tendency for loads to lighten between 300-360 IAS.

Cockpit environment was found to be improved following the sealing of endwing ribs and extractors situated on upper wing surfaces.

Level speed tests were carried out at 8,000 feet using 18 lb boost at 3,000 r.p.m. which resulted in a corrected true airspeed of 432 m.p.h.

Mr. Wilkins, flight test observer, accompanied the test pilot for the tenth test. The next flight was of short duration due to a collapsed tailwheel plunger. Test No.12 was flown by Geoffrey de Havilland, who reported an improvement in aileron control from stall to 360 IAS although aileron upfloat was more noticeable on approaching the stall.

Tests from No.13 were now concentrated on solving tail buffet with observations of wool tuft behaviour on the insides of engine nacelles and adjacent wing surfaces. Mr. Bishop, Chief Designer, checked flow patterns from a formating aircraft and found the flow to be smooth over nacelles and wing undersurfaces at 280 IAS. Mr. Plumb acted as flight test observer on some tests.

The fifteenth flight almost ended in disaster when Geoffrey Pike suffered a semi-collapse due to oxygen starvation during level speed tests. To make matters worse, severe elevator overbalance commenced at 30,000 feet. Pike's problems were not eased by the loss of four gallons of engine coolant from the port engine. The prototype eventually made a single-engine landing back at Hatfield.

During a further test on buffet, observer J. Wimpenny noticed streams of vapour streaming back from the Merlins in a turbulent wake which was striking the tailplane.

Three tests were made by Geoffrey Pike in a fresh attempt to check the superchargers in MS gear and attaining the rated altitude were found to be incorrectly calibrated.

Four-foot strips were added to elevator trailing edges in an attempt to cure elevator overbalance, although the control loads were slightly heavier.

After tests of full MS supercharging, Geoffrey Pike commenced rated altitude trails, followed by two additional flights by Geoffrey de Havilland who discovered that the prototype was 1,000 feet below anticipated full throttle height in FS gear and 400 feet down in MS gear.

Results from full throttle speed tests are listed below:

FS gear:
29,000 ft. 3,000 r.p.m. +11.8 lb. boost TAS 482 m.p.h.
27,000 ft. 3,000 r.p.m. +14.1 lb. boost TAS 486 m.p.h.
23,800 ft. 3,000 r.p.m. +17.8 lb. boost TAS 489 m.p.h.

MS gear: 17,000 ft. 3,000 r.p.m. +12.2 lb. boost TAS 456 m.p.h.
15,000 ft. 3,000 r.p.m. +14.2 lb. boost TAS 458 m.p.h.

at the respective full throttle heights:

FS Gear: 4,600 ft. 3,000 r.p.m. +18 lb. boost Corr. TAS 491 m.p.h.
MS Gear: 12,690 ft. 3,000 r.p.m. +18 lb. boost Corr. TAS 460 m.p.h.

Tests 24-28 were flown by Geoffrey Pike for re-check on tail buffet, whose presence was confirmed by vibrograph readings. The Hornet was flown alongside a formating Mosquito for the observation of wool tuft behaviour around the engine nacelles which had been extended and increased in length by one foot. Some minor improvement at 280 IAS became evident. Flow was found completely smooth over the top wing and nacelle extensions. Wing chord was extended aft and inboard of the extended nacelles with trailing edges set at right angles to the fuselage. The increased wing chord had no effect in eliminating tail buffet. Subsequent vibrograph readings during another flight confirmed a lack of success.

Tests 29-31 were concerned with checks on elevator angles with extended wing chord, trailing down more evident than hitherto.

Second prototype RR919 in flight (via P. Jarrett)

Further tests were carried out in order to establish revised figures for boost levels and intake efficiency with tropical filters faired over. On the next three tests the wing chord extensions were removed and stalling tests carried out with tropical filters faired over. Stalling behaviour became less pleasant with tail buffet occurring 4 m.p.h. nearer to the stall and was accompanied by a wing drop. A revised elevator tab gearing had no appreciable effect on the presence of high stick forces during landings.

Plans for fitting vertical tails to the engine nacelles were curtailed due to excessive elevator overbalance at speeds above 300 IAS due to present tab gearing. Other nacelle modifications consisted of fitting fish tails to the ends of engine nacelles, later tested with no sign of improvement.

Geoffrey de Havilland, with J.C. Wimpenny as observer, carried out tests for recording elevator movements during landings when five degrees were found to have been lost due to stretch in the control circuit. Landings were made using twenty and thirty degree flap settings with wool tufts showing that the wings remained largely unstalled, i.e. until the final phase of hold off when the stall commenced, followed by an immediate touch-down.

On 31 August, Geoffrey de Havilland treated the works to an aerobatic display during a rehearsal for next day's visit by Air Chief Marshal Sir Charles Portal and Sir Wilfrid Freeman.

Test 39 involved stalling trials which were abandoned when Geoffrey Pike and his observer were almost overcome by an influx of petrol fumes.

RR915 was fitted with extended radiator flaps and modified radiator backplates, tail buffet becoming slightly worse after a careful test to 365 IAS. Investigations into continuing buffet and vibration accounted for tests 42-44 during which J.C. Wimpenny accompanied Geoffrey de Havilland for wool tuft observations. Stalling tests were made with the leading edge intakes faired over which failed to show any improvement. Test observer J. Wimpenny was joined by I. Lyon for test 44 when both carried out their tasks in somewhat cramped conditions behind the pilot.

Tests 45-53 were concentrated on the main problems persisting since commencing the flight test programme; nacelle flow breakaway; landings and stalls with comparisons between split and Fowler flaps and rated altitude trials with filters in operation. With Fowler flaps positioned at twenty degree setting, it became just possible to lower the tail for a landing, not quite possible at thirty degrees and impossible at forty-five degrees. The aircraft was difficult to bring to the stall on account of wing root breakaway and ineffective response from elevators.

Comparative tests were made with re-fitted split flaps, throughout a full range of settings when elevator stick loads were lighter, although the pilot's arm was working at a bad mechanical angle when easing stick hard back for a landing. By now it had become just possible to lower the tail with flaps over their full range with little to spare. Additional tests made with well-tufted nacelles did little except confirm the previous findings of increased turbulence on wing undersurfaces and inner nacelles as flow approached the trailing edge position.

The flight test observer confirmed that feathering either propeller made no difference, nor did the closing of radiator flaps. On the other hand, opening the radiator flaps halfway to climbing position resulted in the complete break away of airflow aft of the air exit. This affected both wings and nacelles and additional wool tufting over a distance of one foot either side of the tailplane made no difference around the tail region. A subsequent rated altitude test was abandoned due to failure of starboard oil temperature thermometer.

Tests 55-62 were devoted to trials of fixed flap extensions between fuselage sides and normal flaps and tail buffet investigations using modified radiator bottom entry lips and diving tests.

In Tests 60-62, several carefully judged landings were made with the fixed flap extensions set at twenty to thirty degrees, and one at forty-five degrees, without noticing any improvement in lowering the tail.

During Tests 56-59 there were indications of a virtual disappearance of tail buffet; however propeller tip interference was more evident and found rather disturbing by both pilots.

Diving tests were carried out by Geoffrey Pike and Geoffrey de Havilland, commencing with Test No.60 on 16 September 1944, when some shake developed which affected the entire aircraft on approaching 340-350 IAS at 15,000 ft. Observations by Mr. Hadwin indicated the presence of either aileron or wing flutter. The shake was found extremely unpleasant by both pilots, further dives being ruled out. Strips were fitted to elevator trailing edges to cure hunting which only succeeded in making fore-and-aft stick movements more jerky. Total time flown by RR915 had reached 34 hrs.45 min.

Tests 63-71 were concerned with investigations into buffet, aileron flutter, the fitting of a larger tailplane and suction around canopy. Both pilots were unanimous in feeling that one type of buffet had been mostly cleared up, only to discover other forms which probably originated from the outsides of nacelles. Some confusion was caused by two separate types of buffet transmitted to the stick when a progressive reduction in buffet had revealed propeller tip interference. Mr. J. Wimpenny confirmed an improvement underneath wings and nacelles but nothing similar over the nacelles.

Elevator horns were removed for Test 69, flown by Geoffrey de Havilland, who reported a deterioration in longitudinal stability and tightening up during turns. Longer engine nacelles were re-fitted without any improvement in buffeting

Tests 72-101 (28 September to 13 October 1944) brought total flying hours up to 53.30 and were mainly concerned with attempts to solve buffet.

Opposite rotating propellers were fitted and landings made at various flap settings. Merlin No. 190372 was installed on 2.10.44.

Modified flat-sided nacelles were fitted and the wing chord extended between the fuselage and nacelles without any sign of improvement.

Paddle-blade propellers were installed which resulted in tip/fuselage interference reaching near acceptable limits, despite the port propeller being seriously, aerodynamically out of balance. Some alarming propeller surge was experienced due to a fault in the governor.

Landings improved with the tail coming down quite satisfactorily when using a twenty degree flap setting. The increased elevator chord made no apparent improvement although modifications to radiator under-lips did show promise.

Tests 102-109 involved investigations into elevator buffeting, propeller tip/fuselage interference and take-off swing. A new tail cone was fitted. Trials using the new handed propellers became protracted due to severe vibration from starboard propeller at around 2,400 r.p.m., possibly caused by faulty reduction gear. Severe propeller surge continually interfered with the programme and occasional instances of feathering and oil leaks resulted in two single-engine landings. Buffeting and propeller tip interference were acceptable up to 400 IAS.

With opposite-rotating propellers fitted, rudder control on take-off was barely adequate but general handling was greatly improved without any tendency for a port wing to drop at unstick. Directional trim was not affected with no rolling on application of power at low airspeeds. A greater nose-down tendency occurred during dives although this had always been present from the beginning of the flight test programme.

Tests 110-126 (1 to 15 November 1944) were concerned with investigations into stability, airscrews, rudder flutter, the effects of a new ventral fin, position error calibration and general handling at various c.g. positions.

The paddle blade propellers were replaced by narrow bladed type as previous experience of the former type had indicated poor governing.

RR915 became unpleasant in turns at certain c.g. positions and was less stable in dives after the installation of opposite-rotating propellers, requiring a substantial pull force on stick. Geoffrey Pike was to encounter severe rudder flutter during dives to 440 IAS at 10,000 feet.

The Hornet flight test programme was destined to show a considerable improvement, following consultations with Mr. Collar of R.A.E., when it was decided to increase both mass balance and static balance by 21%. These measures had an immediate effect of eliminating flutter up to limit of 450 IAS.

Meanwhile, trials with the ventral fin had proved disappointing without having any effect on additional stability or controllability during the take-off run.

Tests 127-139 between 21 November to 2 December

First prototype RR915 showing split flaps, September 1944 (via R. Stymes)

1944 involved further investigations into the effects of changing over handed engines (Merlin 131 R.R. No.190374 was installed on 28 November 1944), longitudinal stability and operation of inching radiator flap controls.

Propellers now revolved in a downward direction toward the fuselage and this immediately improved rudder control on the take-off run. Earlier propeller tip/fuselage interference also diminished; some slight vibration was ultimately traced to a failure of the port reduction gear bearing.

Stability in dives was considered generally similar to that encountered using unhanded propellers with a slight loss in longitudinal stability. Tests 140-146 between 15 and 29 December 1944 were concerned with longitudinal stability at various c.g. positions which brought the total number of flying hours to 75.55. Duties were shared between Geoffrey Pike and Geoffrey de Havilland.

On Test 140, Geoffrey de Havilland dived the prototype to 400 IAS, having commenced from a trimmed speed of 300 IAS and experienced a neutral stick force. Turns of five g were made at 10,000 feet, flying at 300-320 IAS. From a lower speed of 170 IAS some positive stick force became evident at two g, tighter turns were not achieved due to the amount of wing root flow breakaway.

Geoffrey Pike flew the aircraft to 420 IAS from trimmed speed of 320 IAS at 12,000 feet and experienced a neutral stick force at 420 IAS.

Sustained turns at four g resulted in a neutral stick force with some tightening-up on attaining five g. During climbing at 25 lb boost, the aircraft became very unstable when both pilots concluded that the aircraft felt "OK" at

normal cruising speeds and in high speed flight but still remained a border-line case.

An inertia weight was installed in the elevator control system, Geoffrey Pike flying the prototype with the c.g. position at 0.33 AMC. From a trimmed speed of 320 IAS, the aircraft was dived again to 420 IAS which resulted in a slight nose up tendency. A stick force of 1-2 lb was recorded. The aircraft remained very unstable at climbing speeds and power settings. Following inspection by Rolls-Royce, Derby, one of the original Merlin 130 engines was installed on 19 January 1945, with the second engine remaining at Derby for modifications.

Accounts for this phase of flight test programme for RR915 are concluded with further extracts from Experimental Pilot's Test Records which cover Tests 147-152 from 3 to 9 February 1945.

Geoffrey de Havilland carried out Test 147 on 3 February 1945 in the prototype, now fitted with a modified tail with its span increased by 6 inches (5% more area), larger (6.5%) elevator horns and the c.g. set at 0.33 AMC. Tests flights took place at 10,000 feet in order to obtain comparisons. For Test No.148 a balance weight for the elevator circuit was mounted half-way along the fuselage. Turns of 5g were executed without any signs of the previous stick force reversal. Turns of three g were flown near the ground when the stick force felt unpleasantly heavy, which required re-trimming. On Test 149 the aircraft felt satisfactory and a neutral stick force of 3g was recorded, followed by reversal at 4g. The aircraft continued to be unstable when climbing, which was not considered to be serious.

Test 150 was made with the elevator balance tab gear ratio increased to 0.3:1 from 0.1:1. There was some gain

RR915 ready for engine runs at Hatfield prior to painting (BAe)

in stability with a neutral stick force occurring at 4g instead of 3g as in the previous test.

Test No.151 indicated that stick forces were OK near ground at c.g.position 0.27 AMC.

Test No.152 was an attempt to make a high altitude dive which was then abandoned due to a fluctuating Mach Number indicator.

It is known that one Merlin 131 was returned to Derby for repairs on 18 July 1945. RR915 was allotted to de Havillands on 20 September 1946 for further development flying, eventually being sold to D.H. Hatfield on 10 September 1947 against Contract 12/Sales/29926/DA1 21A, at the end of a rigorous flight test programme, only to suffer the fate of being scrapped.

RR919, the second prototype spent some time at Hatfield where it was engaged on drop tank and 500 lb bomb carriage trials from 6 November 1944. Details of trials at Boscombe Down are contained in the section devoted to the handling and armament trials.

Right: Hornet cockpit layout

Hornets and Mosquitoes on the production line at Hatfield. PX236 in foreground. (D.H. photo)

HORNET PRODUCTION AND FLIGHT TESTING

Firm orders were received for 60 Hornet F.Is from Contract 3235 in the serial range PX210-PX253 and PX273-PX288. de Havilland established a production line at Hatfield, the first production F.I, PX210, making its first flight on 1 February 1945. Despite increased service load, top speed of production aircraft remained impressive at 472 m.p.h. at 22,000 feet with an initial rate of climb of 4,000 ft/min.

In common with the Mosquito, other roles were envisaged which included a PR.II photo-reconnaissance variant. Three F.Is were modified accordingly, acting as prototypes, and consisted of PX216, PX220 & PX249, the latter aircraft later becoming the first Hornet to be fitted with a dorsal fin. All three Hornets were devoid of armament and equipped with rear fuselage cameras, although only PX216 was destined to remain in P.R. configuration. Large orders for the PR.II (Contract No.5129) were largely cancelled following the end of the Japanese war, only six PR.IIs, VA962-VA966, being completed.

Despite having long range and high performance, the PR.II was, in effect, competing with de Havilland's own

Mosquito PR.34 which carried a navigator and was also capable of similar high performance.

The newly formed Aero Flight Test Department at Hatfield assumed additional responsibilities for various problems with production Hornets, Sea Hornets and Vampires. Among the aircraft held over for development were two Sea Hornets, NF.21 PX239 for position error measurements and F.20 TT202, a "rogue" aircraft which suffered from airframe buffet during dives to Mach 0.7. A.J.Fairbrother, a flight test observer, went aloft in TT202 on several occasions, seated in the rear fuselage to observe (through a rear blister in a service bay door) tufted flow over the sides of nacelles and lower inner wing surfaces. In addition, PR.22 TT187 suffered from aileron flutter, subsequently cured by minor changes to mass balances.

Longer range requirements for Far East Hornets led to a proposal to fit 200-gallon drop tanks, the first pro-production set being manufactured at the end of 1947. The general reliability of emergency tank jettison and fuel transfer systems left much to be desired. Some concern was caused by a possible serious asymmetric fuel state, although preliminary ground testing proceeded without incident. The ultimate full-dress flight test is described later in some detail, an indirect result of fuel transfer difficulties.

Before the final Hornet F.I had left the production line, de Havillands followed on with Contract 3235 (serial range PX289-PX315, PX328-PX369 and PX383-PX398) for the manufacture of the F.III version, which possessed increased range and offensive capability. The internal fuel capacity was increased from 360 to 450 gallons and provision made for two outboard 200-gallon drop tanks or two 1,000-lb bombs, with two attachment points for R.P. projectiles.

Contracts for PX399-425, PX440-PX487 and PX501-PX530 were cancelled, although these reductions were somewhat offset by later Contracts 3630 and 5045, covering serial ranges WB870-WB889, WB897-WB912, and WF954-WF962, WF966-WF979 respectively. A final order for 12 F.IVs was incorporated in contract No.5045 covering 12 aircraft, serial ranges WF968-WF979.

The Hornet F.IV differed from F.III only by the installation of a vertical F.52 camera, the original 60-gallon fuel tank being replaced by a 46-gallon tank in order to make space. All aircraft in the WB and WF serial ranges were manufactured at de Havilland's Chester factory. The four 20 mm cannon armament was retained.

Eleven F.IIIs were converted to F.IVs by Airwork at Gatwick:

PX293 (ex-19 Sqn.); PX296 (ex-64 Sqn.); PX299 (ex-Linton Conversion Flight); PX301 (ex-19 Sqn.); PX304 (ex-65 Sqn.); PX334 (ex-64 Sqn.); PX337 (ex-65 Sqn.); PX344 (ex-64 Sqn.); PX346 (ex-64 Sqn.); PX352 (ex-65 Sqn.); PX362 (ex-Linton Station Flight).

The production line at Chester was pre-occupied with Sea Hornet orders, resulting in serious delays to deliveries for the R.A.F. The first F.3s (a change from Roman to Arabic numbers took place in 1948), WB870 and WB871, were not delivered to Nos.27 and 10 Maintenance Units until 24 November 1950. The trickle of deliveries was to seriously affect No.33 Squadron in Malaya, now in the process of discarding its troublesome Brigands. As a stop-gap, some surplus hand-picked Hornets from M.U.s were ferried out to F.E.A.F. after being overhauled and subjected to shake-down trials.

Production testing did not pass without incidents. Noteworthy was Sqn. Ldr. H.J. Greenland's experience in PX315 when on 7 September 1946, the Hornet's flap bracket fractured. PX315 over-ran the airfield and overturned, trapping him inside the cockpit. At the time of the accident, Geoffrey de Havilland was taxying out in the ill-fated DH.108, abandoning his flight in order to supervise rescue operations.

Hornet F.I PX210 at Boscombe Down, March 1945 (via P. Jarrett)

PX275 with both propellers fully-feathered, November 1946. (via P.Jarrett)

Sqn.Ldr. Greenland's second accident was in PX362 on 6 November 1946, memorable in that it involved the aileron control becoming jammed during take-off. The Hornet was airborne for less than two minutes, its port wing tip and partially retracted undercarriage contacting the ground before crash-landing. On examination it was discovered that a workman's spanner had jammed the aileron control box. Following repairs and checks, PX362 was finally cleared for delivery on 9 January 1947, although this aircraft eventually developed "rogue" characteristics!

PX290, the second production F.III became a further casualty whilst undergoing trials with braking propellers at de Havilland's Propeller Division. On 30 July 1947, PX290 swung on landing at Hatfield when the undercarriage collapsed; the aircraft was subsequently delivered to 54 MU by road and classed as Cat.E.2 (write-off).

PX383 flown by Geoffrey Pike* was engaged on flight clearance trials for carrying two 200-gallon drop tanks. Shortly after taking off on 28 February 1949, he encountered a serious asymmetric flight problem when the boost control failed on the starboard Merlin and in attempting to lighten the load only one drop tank successfully jettisoned. Control now became impossible; Pike headed out to open country, successfully abandoning the aircraft which crashed a mile from RAF Barkway, Royston, Herts.

Attempts to interest the Air Forces of Australia and Argentina came to nought, despite both countries sending pilots to Hatfield for flight evaluations.

* Known respectfully as 'Isa' by ground engineers owing to his frequent opening remark on leaving the cockpit of the first prototype: "I suggest...."

Hornet I flying at Radlett Show, February 1946

Hornet F.IIIs PX297 and PX396, the latter with additional fin area (British Aerospace photos 2572 and 3260D

HORNET TRIALS AT A. & A.E.E., BOSCOMBE DOWN

Armament and handling trials.

The second Hornet prototype, RR919 was flown to Boscombe Down on 18 November 1944 for trials lasting until 23 May 1945. It was fitted with Fowler flaps, unmodified elevators and lacked opposite rotating propellers. Prior to delivery, the second prototype had flown three hours and forty-five minutes during maker's trials at Hatfield.

Trials at A & A.E.E. were to become rather protracted due to unproven firing mechanisms and the existing firing units. RR919 was grounded for a considerable period owing to various airframe defects.

Gaining access to various engine components was to prove difficult, especially to remove the magnetos and two outer sparking plugs. Problems arose when attempting to locate engine bearer nuts and exhaust system lower securing nuts.

Operation of the press-button for the sliding canopy came in for some criticism from pilots. The port gun panel suffered some damage during gun firing, caused by blast and vibration. A heavier gauge replacement was requested. Air firing on four sorties was marred by link stoppages occurring within the exits, due to a momentary slack developing in the ammunition feed. Links tended to accumulate in the combined ejector hopper for the inboard guns which resulted in slack feed stoppage. In all, some twenty-four air firings were carried out under all flight conditions, including negative g. A total of 15,041 rounds was expended.

In a bid to solve this problem, separate link chutes were designed and fabricated at Boscombe Down, based on the well-proven type used on the Hawker Tempest. The gun door was provided with suitable exits. As the trials progressed, it became evident that gun recoil was

excessive when on the twenty-fourth air firing a six-inch long crack developed in the port outer gun mounting flange.

Firing during dives at forty degrees resulted in expended links being carried back up to the tailplane, damaging both sides. Some links were later discovered inside the gun bay. Judging by the airflow, indicated by oil leaks, it was discovered that the majority of links were being directed toward the port side of the tailplane. It was considered that a different flow pattern would result once counter-rotating propellers had been installed.

RR919 was returned to Hatfield for the installation of a new blast tube panel and fitting of a G.M.II gun sight. On return from Hatfield it was found that:

(a) no gun control unit had been fitted;
(b) connecting wires were hanging loose;
(c) cables from the Ranging Control Unit to Ranging Pulley had been fitted in reverse order;
(d) there was excessive flexibility between the gun sight bracket and cockpit coaming;
(e) no sun screen for the gun sight had been installed.

The existing GGS restricted forward view so D.H. proposed to install a stay for the sight bracket on top of the windscreen. Pilots at Boscombe were to comment on the inconvenience of operating throttles with the Range Control Unit fitted to the starboard throttle.

Navigation tests were carried out on 27 February 1945 using a Pioneer Magnesyn Remote Indicating Compass with a repeater mounted inside the cockpit.

Gun heating tests commenced on 30 June 1945 and were to last until 1 July, three air shoots being made

PX329 at the R.A.F. Display in 1950

between 30,000-35,000 feet. On the first, only two guns had fired a full load of ammunition when the port outer suffered a stoppage due to a lightly-struck round. The starboard outer gun also stopped firing after a slack feed developed in the ammunition belt.

Thermometers were then strapped to each gun and another air firing was carried out after allowing temperatures to stabilise. After the last air firing, it was considered unlikely that stoppages were caused by lower than normal temperatures.

The radiator flaps could be set to any position between fully open and fully closed and tests were made using the half-open setting, whereas production Hornets were fitted with two-position flaps i.e. either closed with a two-and-a-half inch gap or fully open.

During the latter part of trials, RR919 flew a further ten hours and forty-five minutes.

PX210, the first production Hornet F.I arrived at Boscombe Down on 28 February 1945 for handling trials, fitted with Merlin 130/131 engines driving opposite-rotating propellers, split landing flaps and modified elevators.

The second production F.I, PX211, underwent comprehensive handling and stability trials between September and October 1945. The aircraft was found lacking in certain respects, especially in longitudinal stability and suffered from a tendency for the rudder to move to full travel of its own accord during a sideslip. *

Engine failure characteristics were considered as dangerous. A larger tailplane was deemed necessary on all later production aircraft, in addition to the proposal for fitting a new dorsal fin to improve directional

* The revelations concerning tendencies of rudder locking and related asymmetric problems were the direct result of expert diagnosis by Jan Zurakowski, later confirmed by Cyclops Brown.

An underside view of RR919 shows the radiator layout (via P. Jarrett)

The Hornet PR.II prototype at Boscombe Down in November 1945 (via P. Jarrett)

behaviour.

Test pilots at Boscombe Down had confirmed that in the event of engine failure, unless immediate action was taken the aircraft would quickly enter a vertical dive with the rudder held immovably over at full travel towards the dead engine. Tests at air speeds below 155 knots with high power settings indicated that the wing with the dead engine developed extreme sideslip and dropped through ninety degrees. Unless remedial action was taken within two seconds, recovery required throttling the remaining engine. Height loss during recovery amounted to about 1,500 feet.

The minimum safety speed for single engine failure on take-off was 155 knots IAS. In order to minimise the vicious characteristics, it was recommended that maximum power for take-off was only to be used when necessary. At maximum take-off power, the power loading was extremely low at four-and-a-half pounds per BHP. When flying on instruments it was considered advisable to keep airspeed above 160 knots IAS.

Under normal fighter aircraft loading, the Hornet F.I failed to meet the standards of acceptability, having a low value of stick force/g in the region of two pounds.

Zurakowski never let an opportunity pass by without giving the staff a display which usually included single-engine aerobatics. Unconfirmed reports indicate that "Zura" also carried out "Meteor-style Cartwheels" in early Hornets.

PX217 arrived at Boscombe Down on 27 June 1945, following maker's trials at Hatfield, and flew a further 150 hours whilst at A. & A.E.E. It was joined by PX218 on 3 July 1945 for a period of intensive flying trials. Unfortunately, it lacked a considerable number of modifications which had become due on reaching flying sixty hours. Throughout these trials, 150 grade fuel was used by both aircraft. The "Boscombe Down Boffins" considered the Hornet to be a highly developed aircraft from the engineering standpoint, although somewhat complicated when compared with contemporary fighters.

In all, 128 dives were made to limiting speed. Some sixty-six grass landings and 117 runway landings were made over the trial period. PX218 suffered a tailwheel tyre-burst after twenty-one grass and thirty-one runway landings. The port undercarriage torque link had been incorrectly assembled, limiting the amount of travel for shock absorber.

Services: Most unserviceability of the hydraulics systems on both aircraft was caused by the engine-driven pump. Only one failure occurred in the air. Pilots' reports contained complaints about the presence of hydraulic fluid inside the cockpit. This was later traced to a leak from an oil filler cap which was passing through two slots in the filler neck and past screw threads.

The pilot of PX217 was compelled to use the emergency hand pump when both undercarriage and flaps failed to retract. There were instances when undercarriage lights failed to illuminate. The position indicators on PX218 gave continuous trouble when red lights failed to go out and promptly illuminated when the aircraft was under high g. On five occasions the indicators had shown that the legs were not locked down. When the green lights failed to glow, the undercarriage was, in fact, securely locked. The reason for a series of irritating problems was ultimately traced to incorrectly adjusted micro-switches. Strangely, no similar problems were experienced with PX217.

All pneumatic, de-icing and oxygen systems performed faultlessly throughout the trial period, although some concern was expressed on the performance of the existing radio installation which was considered to have a poor range and somewhat prone to reception interference.

Heating and ventilating systems: The heating system seemed to provide an ample supply of hot air to the pilot's left side, leaving his right-hand side and feet cold. The cockpit became noticeably hot at low altitudes with inadequate ventilation.

Airframe: Defects were present on PX218 with dope peeling and a break-up of jointing compound above the wing roots and undersurfaces of the cannon bay panel. Fabric had started to lift off in bubbles due to the effects of the hot sun. There were instances of plywood deterioration, although this was not considered serious. PX218 was returned to Hatfield, where the compound was stripped away and replaced by a new finish using only tape at wing/fuselage joints. This measure proved successful in withstanding exposure to all weathers. For reasons unknown, PX217 was not affected.

Some minor damage to PX217 was caused when the leading edge of the port flap fouled the underwing skin on the trailing edge. Local repairs were carried out on site.

Mod. H.105 was issued for strengthening the rudder mass balance weight.

Flying controls: These proved to be trouble-free throughout the trial period.

Power plants: Considerable unserviceability was caused by five engine changes during 140 hours flying and by investigations into reports of engine vibration. Two were directly attributable to engine faults, two by suspected defects and one (on PX218) when serious damage was caused by a loss of coolant to the starboard engine when a connecting hose was pulled off. A similar instance had occurred on the port engine of PX217 although, fortunately, this was discovered before any damage was caused.

Reasons for the failures lay with the relative movement between engine and airframe and a shortness of hose connections. Longer coolant hoses with two Jubilee clips were fitted to PX217 and no further trouble was experienced.

The first engine change on PX218 followed only eight hours flying, due to a bolt fracture in the lower reduction gear casing. The bolt was eventually located inside the crankcase which involved removing the Merlin from the engine bearers. Suitable modifications were soon carried out.

The next engine change came after fifty hours after reports of some fluctuations in r.p.m. and boost/oil pressures, traced to a broken inlet valve spring on Number Two cylinder.

PX217 suffered a severe blowback and lost power when flying at max. boost and r.p.m. which succeeded in buckling the air intake and blowing away the Vokes filter. Although the Merlin was found to be free from

PX293 front view shows the cannon layout (via P. Jarrett)

damage after strip inspection, it was considered prudent to fit new type spark plugs before attempting further tests.

The fifth engine change occurred following the discovery of a serious oil leak; however, no defects were actually found. During a test in PX217 the pilot found it was impossible to close the starboard throttle and the engine was shut down before landing. A throttle butterfly had seized inside the throttle chamber due to adverse wear. Instances occurred with both engines of PX217 cutting out when the aircraft was dived from 33,000 feet to 24,000 feet, which proved impossible to trace to any particular fault. Fuel warning lights lit up, indicating a drop in pressure in spite of the booster pumps being switched on. Fuel pressure gauges were installed on fuel lines although there were to be no further instances of cut-outs during subsequent flights.

The D.H. Hydromatic propellers provided trouble-free operation, apart from some instances of r.p.m. fluctuations.

After 139 hours exhaust stubs for "A" block on Number Two cylinder were found to have broken away, hanging on by one stud. Another exhaust stub had fractured and nuts for the remaining stubs were missing.

Engine throttle synchronisation difficulties which had plagued PX218 were ultimately traced to grease (instead of oil) being packed in the differentials.

PX217 made an unscheduled single-engine landing due to a fractured throttle universal joint when power dropped off, then abruptly increased to full power, despite throttle adjustments.

Ignition: The port magneto on PX218 cut out after the contact breaker housing filled with oil. There were no instances of faults with PX218 but a number were experienced on PX217, including an incident when the magneto switches failed to switch off the engine due to faulty connections.

Air intake trunks were to suffer cracks on five occasions, with one causing serious damage.

PX221 arrived at Boscombe on 30 November 1945, principally for weight and loading data tests. Tare weight was 12,097 lb compared with 11,938 lb previously estimated at Hatfield. At max. permitted landing weight of 16,145 lb. Carbon monoxide tests were made up to the last 1,000 feet of a climb to 20,000 feet without any traces of contamination. Five minutes of flying in combat conditions and thirty minutes at maximum cruise also failed to indicate recordable contamination.

PX218 returned to Boscombe for cabin heating and ventilation tests from 14 May to 1 June 1945, all flown at 35,000 feet. Temperatures inside the cockpit indicated that additional ventilation was necessary whilst operating under tropical conditions. Conversely, under extremes of cold, more heat was required even when wearing flying boots. It was recommended that additional ventilators be fitted inside the cockpit.

Responsibility for Hornet tropical trials was taken over by a Wing Commander at Air Ministry, pilots being Flt.Lts. Groves and Macready. Both were eventually attached to the Intensive Flight Development Section at Boscombe Down to gain Hornet flying experience, PX217 and PX218 being used for twelve hours of familiarisation.

Meanwhile, PX227 and PX228 had arrived at Pershore, only to be returned to Hatfield for a complete wiring change. After a frustrating delay, PX227, flown by Groves, set out for Istres, flying time being limited to one-and-a-half hours due to lack of long-range ferry tanks. Navigational aids were almost non-existent, requiring accurate dead reckoning navigation. The lightweight VHF sets were found incapable of more than ten miles range.

A split tyre on PX227 at Bordeaux resulted in Groves sending an urgent requisition to Air Ministry which was duly ignored. A personal message was relayed which resulted in a delay of three weeks before the spare tyre was delivered from the U.K. After arriving at Habbaniya, Iraq, on 22 May, a fitter managed to break a copper pipe during servicing, delaying departure until 3 July. Grove's troubles were not yet over; when within 200 miles of Mauripur, the large R.A.F. base near Karachi, he was forced to shut down one engine. On landing, Macready in PX228 ran off the hard-standing on to soft sand, the swing causing an accumulation of sand inside the tail-wheel compartment which effectively prevented castoring. As a consequence, both under-carriage legs suffered damage, necessary repairs being carried out by de Havilland representatives who had been kept waiting in India since July 1945.

After arriving at Karachi, Groves joined Macready in an endeavour to locate spares which had been shipped out in advance. Much to their dismay, they discovered that a crate clearly marked "Hornet Spares" had in fact been despatched to Australia, nobody in authority being aware of their purpose for the trials!

During the last of six flights in PX227, Groves indulged in a few aerobatics and discovered that both radiators had pulled over from their mountings. After making further enquiries about availability of spares, Groves was told by the Wing Commander, Technical Branch, "not to be a nuisance". The trials programme was further hindered by a complete lack of interest

Hornet PX227 on tropical trials at Palam, July 1947

PX312, the Hornet F.III prototype, with extended fin and flaps lowered

and liaison by the RAF Technical Branch in India, most of whom were only concerned with returning to the U.K. for demob. Leaving Macready to continue trials, a by-now-disillusioned Groves joined the dash for demobilisation, sailing for the U.K. The schedule for tropical trials included six weeks at Karachi, Khartoum and Singapore.

PX223 arrived at Boscombe on 21 August 1946 for trials of the four 20 mm cannon/GGS Mk.IVB installation which lasted from August to October 1946. A second aircraft, PX348, arrived on 24 October and allotted away on 13 November.

Trials commenced on 21 August were to suffer delays due to aircraft unserviceability and manpower shortage. Prior to the start of trials, D.H. had been requested to eliminate gun sight vibration and make improvements to the range control which was positioned on the throttle box.

To assist de Havilland, arrangements were made for D.H. engineers to use firing butts at A. & A.E.E. in order to obtain vibration records. New gun sight brackets were designed and fitted to both aircraft, PX223 being fitted with a vibration damper.

The non-availability of a GGS Mk.IVB resulted in the installation of Mk.IID Series III, similar to the Mk.IVB but lacking a built-in range control. PX223 was not fitted with a modified throttle box and the sights could only be used as fixed sights.

PX348 was fitted with a GGS Mk.IVB together with a modified throttle box which differed from the original design by the incorporation of a range control on the inboard throttle knob.

The GGS installation was considered as the best compromise for satisfying existing requirements for the view ahead, crash hazard and sighting, i.e. without major re-design of the Hornet's nose.

Gun Sight vibration was persistent, although it still proved possible to hold reasonable aim whilst firing.

PX223 fired nearly 11,000 rounds, although it tended to suffer from petty unserviceability, being replaced by PX348 for the remainder of trials. Three pilots carried out air shoots who had previously been involved with tests on PX223. All agreed that vibration was, if anything, worse when guns were fired. When using the range control with throttles closed, a likely condition when overtaking a target, the pilot's fingers fouled the cockpit coaming. This problem had been pointed out in a letter dated 23 August; however the necessary modifications were not incorporated in PX348.

Poor visibility through the windscreen during rain proved to be a real handicap to accurate sighting and persisted for some time after entering clear conditions. Due to the windscreen becoming translucent, it was recommended that a clear view panel should be provided.

During the trial period, three pilots from Fighter Command and the Fleet Air Arm were allowed to fly the Hornet and it was well liked by all on account of its excellent handling qualities, good all-round vision from the cockpit and good single-engine performance. Take-offs and landings were considered as straightforward. On the debit side some concern was expressed on slight fore-and-aft instability when climbing and there was some difficulty in trimming the Hornet to fly hands and feet off for any length of time.

PX312 arrived on 30 June 1947 for brief handling trials associated with drop tanks and included jettison tests, the results being considered as suitable for service use.

Additionally, it was considered that the existing bungee should be removed from the elevator circuit - provided pilots were warned about the rapid increase of stick force needed to recover from trimmed dives on approaching limiting speed. Owing to aileron buffet and dive recovery characteristics, it was recommended that limiting speed with drop tanks fitted be reduced from 305 to 290 knots.

PX312 returned to Boscombe Down for the completion of handling trials. Stick force/g loads were considered as too high for a fighter aircraft at all c.g. positions, forces becoming excessive at the approach of limiting speed. Elevator trimming was far too sensitive, making accurate trimming difficult. Rudder locking could be induced whilst climbing and in cruising flight, although the rudder would free itself should speed or bank be increased.

PX249 arrived on 11 December 1947 for checks on spinning characteristics which followed maker's spinning trials at Hatfield. The case of an engine failure occurring under instrument flying conditions had been considered particularly dangerous, as unless immediate corrective action was taken the aircraft would reach a stage where recovery would become difficult.

In an attempt to improve behaviour, a dorsal fin was fitted to PX249, which extended about eight feet forward of the fin. The standard Hornet fin was retained. Brief handling tests were made to assess the effects. Whilst a tendency still existed for the rudder to move over, no locking was evident. The most noticeable effect of the dorsal fin occurred during asymmetric flying when the rate of yaw decreased with a corresponding reduction in foot loads. Control was effected by using the rudder alone, it being unnecessary to throttle back on the live engine. Assuming that the pilot was slow in taking corrective action and allowed the aircraft to enter a dive, recovery was considered as relatively simple.

The introduction of a dorsal fin had also resulted in an improvement of rudder and directional characteristics.

On completion of trials it was strongly recommended that similar dorsal fins be retro-fitted to all existing Hornets and that production aircraft should to be modified accordingly. As a consequence, modification kits were circulated to all Hornet squadrons.

Hornet F.3 PX393 arrived on 1 July 1949 for clearance trials for R.P.s and bombs. Trials with Mk.8 R.P.s resulted in some damage to ailerons and mainplanes when lower rear saddles were forced off by R.P. contact. Single-tier installations (with drop tanks fitted) proved satisfactory.

After repairs to ailerons, PX393 developed flutter and was returned to Hatfield for investigation, delaying trials for six months.

Deflected air around the drop tanks was tending to affect the lower tiers on the double-tier R.P. installation. R.P.s fired during dives at 290 knots at a thirty-degree dive angle caused a starboard inner R.P. to strike and fracture the front upper saddle fins, piercing an aileron. Following further discussions, it was agreed that henceforth, No.8 Mk.II saddles be used when firing R.P.s. Only single-tier rockets were to be fitted when drop tanks were carried

Final clearance trials were commenced on 15 November 1950 and lasted until February 1951. During the second sortie, an inner acorn was damaged whilst firing eight sixty-pound R.P.s. On the fifth sortie, flown at 400 knots in a forty-degree dive, several adaptors came loose. In a later dive to 400-410 knots, the starboard inner adaptor was torn away and an outer saddle bent backwards. This resulted in further recommendations that single-tier R.P.s should be fired before releasing bombs; conversely bombs should be released before discharging double-tier R.P.s.

From 20-23 February 1951, brief handling trials were made with dives to limiting speed and the aircraft trimmed at 19,000 feet. Dives to 415 knots required a push force of 65 lb, releasing the control column and resulting in a gradual build-up of g force on the accelerometer to about two-and-a-half g. Some vibration set in at 320 knots which caused slight movement of R.P.s, pitot head and ailerons. The dive recovery was effected by a 25 lb pull force at 2g.

PX385 commenced acceptance trials during September and October 1951, using 100-gallon drop tanks as incendiary bombs. These were filled with ninety gallons of F.T.F. (Flame Thrower Fluid). Handling proved difficult at speeds below 150 knots. It was concluded that drop tanks that were released in the "Safe" condition would not ignite, although any attempt to land with a hang-up would be hazardous.

Following the installation of towing equipment at Boulton Paul in PX336, trials were commenced for towing a 30-foot-long banner and an R.F.D. Winged Target. The Winged Target was a double-fuselage monoplane of 26 feet wingspan, and just over 16 feet in length, each fuselage fitted with a keelboard. Construction was mainly of pine for wing ribs and fuselage formers. A 800-foot tow line was used with a take-off distance of some 633 yards. Landing with a target in tow involved a long straight approach using quarter flap at 1,500 feet at 115/130 knots, decreasing to 110/115 knots on touch down of target. A "Talk Down" technique was employed via an observer from a ground transmitter. Towing the banner required a 524 yard take-off run using a snatch technique, 700 feet of braided nylon rope making up the tow line. These trials began in October 1951 and lasted until February 1952.

PX347 arrived on 30 August 1950 for trials with the F.52 camera. During one sortie flown at 300 m.p.h. at 200 feet, the external window cover was jettisoned, dropping cleanly away and found to be repairable. A climb to 30,000 feet for taking photographs was entirely successful with no traces of condensation on lens or window. The F.52 installation proved difficult and arduous to fit and the existing alternative F.24 camera was unsuitable for conditions in the Far East.

The first hooked Hornet, PX212, during deck landing trials aboard HMS Ocean, 10 August 1945 (via P.Jarrett)

PX214 converted to Sea Hornet F.20 with folding wings (via Bruce Robertson)

The de Havilland N.5/44 Sea Hornet

Deck Landing Trials at R.A.E. and on HMS *Ocean.*

Following an RAF order for the Hornet F.I, the Admiralty expressed a keen interest for a naval version, suitably strengthened and fitted with folding wings, arrester hook and accelerator gear. During late 1944, another tailor-made specification (N.5/44) was issued to cover the construction of prototypes. For this purpose a standard Hornet F.I, PX212, was taken from the production line for partial conversion to the first F.20 prototype. Although lacking folding wings, PX212 was fitted with an arrester hook, allowing the Navy to commence deck landing trials without undue delay. Heston Aircraft succeeded in having the aircraft ready for flying on 19 April 1945, with delivery to R.A.E. on 10 May 1945.

On 11 May 1945, Lt. Cdr. Eric Brown flew the aircraft for the commencement of preliminary deck-landing trials, using the dummy carrier deck at Farnborough, and completed the programme by mid-May.

The next few months were spent on handling trials and deck landing assessment. Elevator response at low approach speeds was not considered effective enough from small stick movements and the heavy, ineffective ailerons were unacceptable for carrier landings.

Forward view was assessed as excellent during the final approach at 100 knots. Lateral control during turbulence left much to be desired as did throttle movement which was considered as not sufficiently coarse at low boost settings. Changes in the flap control to a three-position type were recommended to assist easy selection by the pilot in event of a baulked landing or wave-off.

Within a short time, de Havillands had fitted PX212 with aerodynamically nose-balanced ailerons which automatically increased the movement from seven to seventeen degrees. The new installation proved to be a considerable improvement and resulted in lightness and effectiveness over the entire speed range. At airspeeds below 130 knots, however, they became more sluggish. Lt.Cdr. Brown concluded that the new ailerons were just acceptable for use in the forthcoming carrier deck-landing trials.

Sea Hornet F.20 TT186 at Radlett for the S.B.A.C. show in September 1946 (via P. Jarrett)

On 4 August 1945, PX212 was flown to Arbroath for a series of A.D.D.L.s, before Brown departed for Ayr to sample PX230, which was the back-up aircraft (later converted to Prototype NF.21 under Specification N.21/45).

PX230 was fitted with enlarged throttle handgrips which allowed the addition of GGS control knobs. During a series of ADDLs there was a tendency for engines to suffer a rich cut on take-off unless cleared beforehand. Approach speeds were varied from 82 to as low as 78 knots, although the lower speed resulted in aileron twitch and a high sink rate.

On 10 August 1945, Lt.Cdr. Brown in PX212 carried out the first landing at sea aboard HMS *Ocean* then sailing off Ailsa Craig. Touch-down on *Ocean's* deck coincided with the exact hour of the announcement of the end of the Japanese war. No problems were encountered on take-off or landing with the run regarded as unbelievably short and free from swing.

Further trials continued on 11 August 1945, despite a failure of the hydraulic pump. The emergency hand pump was used for the remainder of the trials. Lt.Cdr. Brown preferred to continue using PX212 due to his deep dislike of the unconventional layout for GGS control knobs on the throttles of his reserve aircraft.

Following a series of take-offs and deck landings (made without the provision of a crash barrier), PX212 was flown back in the evening to Farnborough. PX230 also flew down to R.A.E., arriving on 11 September 1945 before returning to Hatfield on 17 August.

After the successful conclusion of deck-landing trials, type accelerator proofing was carried out using PX214 which had been delivered to R.A.E. in January

1946. Trials were made up to an overload weight of 18,200 lb and became the first launches for a twin-engine aircraft from an accelerator (tail down) catapult. Overload landings were made up to a maximum weight of 17,700 lb.

On 28 January 1946, Lt.Cdr. Brown made two demonstration take-offs using the accelerator, solely for the benefit of the Third Sea Lord, and finished off the proceedings with an aerobatic display.

Meanwhile, PX212 had been fitted with a new Lockheed damper to the arrester hook, specifically for checking efficiency when entering arrester gear installed at Farnborough. After completing these trials, PX212 was flown to S.T.U., Ford, and handed over on 9 February.

Six months later TT186, the first production F.20, made its initial flight from Hatfield and had incorporated all the required modifications as requested by Lt.Cdr. Brown. TT186 was fitted with slotted flaps, a new dorsal fin and camera windows in both sides of rear fuselage.

Sea Hornet F.20, TT191, was flown to Farnborough for a prolonged programme which involved assessments on the practicability of executing single-engine carrier deck-landings.

On 18 October 1948, NF.21 VV434, the fifth production aircraft, arrived at R.A.E. for Type Arresting Proofing and was later despatched to Lee-on-Solent on 20 October 1948. TT191 arrived at Farnborough on the same day for a three-month stay, often in use by Lt. Cdr. Brown for aerobatic displays to visiting top brass.

Arrester barrier trials were carried out at Farnborough from June 1947 by Hornet PR.II VA964 which had been earlier been used for other trials.

SEA HORNET NF.21 CONVERSION BY HESTON AIRCRAFT LTD

By 1945, an urgent naval requirement existed for a high-performance, long-range night fighter which would supersede the Fleet Air Arms's Firefly NF.Is, this leading to the issue of Specification N.21/45. To satisfy this need, a Sea Hornet F.20, PX230, was delivered to Hatfield for conversion to the first prototype NF.21 and fitted with a separate, heated, observer's compartment. Provision was made for nose-mounted ASH radar. The Merlin 134/135 engines were fitted with flame-damping exhausts.

PX230, with the unpopular Corliss throttles, had been a reserve aircraft for preliminary deck-landing trials aboard H.M.S. *Ocean*. It was complete with arrester hook although it was without the dorsal fin and had non-folding wings. The Navy lacked a fully navalised Sea Hornet and as a consequence Heston Aircraft were entrusted with the design and modification work. The small design team at Heston was under George Cornwall, Chief Designer. Included in the project were manufacture of accelerator hooks, arrester gear and wing folding mechanism. The second prototype PX239 was delivered complete with a new dorsal fin and was fully navalised at Heston.

Several types of nose radomes were subjected to trials before the definitive thimble nose profile was finally adopted, a practical if somewhat ugly configuration.

Due to the restricted space within the Sea Hornet's slender wing, component sizes needed to be kept to an absolute minimum, consistent with strength requirements. Use of light alloys currently available was ruled out due to inadequate strength properties, whereas there was a natural reluctance to employ steel. This was partly due to a severe weight penalty; however a compromise was reached following direct liaison with J. Booth Ltd. who agreed to a suggestion to use zinc/aluminium alloy, similar to the proven DTD 363 sheet and fully capable of being forged. Known later as DTD 363 (modified), this

material was to be used extensively on later aircraft at Heston. Despite no evidence of failure, other manufacturers ran into serious problems with stress corrosion.

Shortly after arriving at Heston, the Sea Hornet was positioned inside the hangar where Eric Barraclough, Technical Liaison Engineer, confronted "Chief Chippy" Ted Hagell, instructing him to commence sawing off the outer wings. After considerable persuasion, the incredulous Hagell finally agreed to the somewhat drastic measure - provided someone else did the marking out.

Design of the wing folding mechanism and power unit was allotted to Messrs. Harvey, Champneys and Clift.

Another requirement lay with the provision of a retractable pilot's headrest, fitted to provide head support for the pilot during the fierce initial g encountered during accelerator launches.

Designer Eric Barraclough succeeded in developing a metal spray for the wooden undersides of fuselage which acted as an aerial, orthodox types being ruled out on account of drag penalty. The thin coating of zinc/tin and copper proved to be a complete success, prompting favourable comment from R.A.E. who proceeded to develop the process for other radio applications.

Reports had been received which mentioned problems with adverse wear on arrester hooks by carrier deck cables and these were solved by Sydney Foster who introduced the "Colmony" process which was successful in retarding abrasive wear. The arrester gear itself consisted of an "A" frame connected to the rear fuselage by two massive forgings bolted to the main rear fuselage structure whose reinforced longerons provided the required strength to withstand extra loads in rapid deceleration.

All work in hand was successfully completed in around six months, involving a tremendous effort by the small team at Heston.

Sea Hornet F.20s TT189 (above) and TT191 (below) were tested at Boscombe Down (Photos courtesy P Jarrett and British Aerospace respectively)

Sea Hornet NF.21 VV430 (D.H. photo 3445F via P Jarrett)

SEA HORNET TRIALS AT A. & A.E.E., BOSCOMBE DOWN

Sea Hornets were tested by C Flight. Known test pilots were Lt.Cdr. H.C.N. Goodhart, Lt.Cdr. P.S. Wilson, Lt. K.R. Hickson.

Test Aircraft:

PX219 (3 March 1947 to 31 July 1947) Handling and safety trials for Mk.8 type 10 R.P. installation. Initial impressions were generally favourable, view over the nose considered as excellent, allowing low level R.P. attacks and 40 degree dives to be made with good accuracy. Flight manoeuvrability and steadiness in dives resulted in the Sea Hornet being assessed as a good gun platform. A forty-degree limit on dive angle was recommended to prevent pilots exceeding a 350-knot limiting speed at all-up weight of 17,000 lb.

During March to May 1947, brief handling trials were carried out with eight 60 lb R.P.s. when the aircraft was found to be easy and pleasant to fly and stalling characteristics well liked by Boscombe pilots. Brief tests were concerned with the aircraft's behaviour with c.g. at most aft position. After being trimmed for level flight, no stick force was necessary to maintain 350 knots IAS when a limited number of R.P.s were carried.

PX219 had been delivered complete with "A" frame arrester hook, Type 90 IFF and Mk.8 zero-length R.P. Projectors. During tests, elevator control loads were not found positive at limiting diving speed. The stick lacked a self-centering action when ailerons were operated and stick released.

PX222, Hornet F.I, arrived 21 January 1947 for night suitability trials and was flown at night for assessment of flying qualities, including cockpit illumination. Conditions at the time of test were seven-tenths cloud with no wind. Special attention was paid to the forward view and amount of exhaust flame visible to the pilot under simulated deck landing approach conditions. The flame damping exhaust shrouds were comprised of four "Fish Tail" manifolds with louvred shrouds mounted on each side of the engines. No gyro gunsight had been fitted inside the cockpit.

The aircraft was flown straight and level at heights between 300-400 feet over a pre-determined course and the following conclusions were made: The cockpit dimmer switches on the starboard side of cockpit were situated too close together for efficient operation, especially when wearing gloves; the port side switch was hidden by the throttle quadrant; the flap indicator was not illuminated with no illumination whatsoever for the main fuel cocks; the gyro horizon proved difficult to see when the pilot's seat was raised; once a gyro gunsight was installed it would become even more difficult.

The Hornet presented no difficulty during take-off, in flight or when landing. No lighting reflections were visible in cockpit hood or windscreen and there was a satisfactory absence of glare from the exhausts. All instruments and operating levers were ready to hand except the gyro horizon.

The view ahead for landing was restricted by flame dampers and the amount of flame actually visible during simulated deck landings was minimal and unlikely to cause temporary blindness to the pilot. No comparisons could be made between a standard F.I owing to no previous trials using standard exhaust installation.

PX230 Sea Hornet NF.21 Prototype. Following conversion to a night fighter, this aircraft arrived at Boscombe Down on 24 April 1947 for trials which included stick force/g tests. On 16 May 1947, Lt. Hickson was diving the aircraft on an air test from 12,000 feet to 5,000 feet at 480 m.p.h. and during recovery the port engine detached from the wing. Controls became ineffective and the NF.21 entered an inverted spin. Hickson succeeded in abandoning the aircraft, suffering only minor injuries.

PX239 Sea Hornet NF.21. (April to December 1948) Handling trials were carried out with and without 100-gallon drop tanks. On 26 August 1948, the aircraft suffered failure of port engine, resulting in a single-engine landing. Carbon monoxide contamination tests were made on 13 October 1948. A week later, whilst investigating trim changes with radiator shutters selected in various positions, the aircraft was put into a dive to limiting speed, shutters in "automatic". With the onset of "porpoising" and a nose-up change of trim, Lt.Cdr. Wilson re-trimmed the aircraft after noting a 65 lb push force. On turning the elevator trimming wheel, the aircraft yawed violently to starboard with rudder pedals locked hard over. Rudder trim had not been applied during the dive and despite the sudden movement of the rudder at limiting speed, no structural failure had occurred. After landing it was found that during rigging both elevator and rudder turnbuckle adjusters were positioned in parallel. In consequence, applying elevator trim transmitted full trim to the rudder. Lt.Cdr. Wilson was both amazed and extremely thankful that the airframe had withstood the high loads.

On 21 October 1948 stick force/g tests were made during untrimmed dives. Criticism was made concerning the observer's cockpit. As with other Sea Hornet variants it was recommended that due to the appearance of aileron buffet above 290 knots IAS with drop tanks fitted, limiting speed be reduced to 260 knots above 10,000 feet.

Sea Hornet PR.22 prototype TT187 at Boscombe Down, October 1947

Sea Hornet T.22 prototype TT187 (via Bruce Robertson)

Hornet F.I PX214 converted to the second prototype Sea Hornet is displayed at Heston

PX214 showing its folding wing mechanism (BAe)

The arrester hook arrangement on TT191 (via P. Jarrett)

Sea Hornet NF.21 second prototype PX239 (via P Jarrett)

During handling trials on 26 October 1948, the starboard intercooler boiled, which resulted in an immediate shut-down and single-engine landing. The aircraft was inspected in November by C Flight and found to have developed a crack in a housing for the undercarriage main hinge, wide enough to insert a small finger.

After completion of trials the aircraft was delivered to Yeovilton for ground instructional use as A2039.

TT186 (First production F.20). Service clearance trials were carried out from 19 July to 22 July 1949. These consisted of the firing of eight 3-in R.P.s with two 100-gallon drop tanks fitted. The R.P.s fired satisfactorily, although some damage was inflicted to some electrical connections on the rear of rocket posts. On the fourth test, further damage occurred to the leading edge of port mainplane after a saddle detached from the rocket motor.

TT187, Sea Hornet PR.22 Prototype arrived for general handling tests (July-October 1948). TT187 was delivered to Boscombe Down complete with modified elevators (10% horn balances) and flame-damping exhausts. The new exhaust system was considered to have a potential de-stabilising effect on longitudinal stability. Since the

PR.22 was designed to operate in a night role, photoflashes were mounted externally on light series carriers below the wings.

Owing to aerodynamic differences between the PR.22 and F.20, it became necessary to check handling characteristics which were generally found satisfactory apart from following points:

Rudder control was very light at high speeds; limiting speed with drop tanks should be 290 knots IAS up to 10,000 feet and 260 knots above 10,000 feet; there was some evidence of elevator oscillation, especially at low air speeds in bumpy weather, of sufficient magnitude to be considered disconcerting on entering cloud or when flying at night. Single-engine handling characteristics of the PR.22 were good, differing little from those of the NF.21 and were considered as satisfactory for the day/night reconnaissance role.

There was concern with elevator oscillations and self-stalling behaviour on approaching the stall, with flaps lowered and undercarriage down, was unfavourable. During some simulated deck landings, there were no problems - provided the aircraft was trimmed for a speed not in excess of 95 knots and approach speed maintained at 87 knots.

Asymmetric handling was judged as good with a recommended figure of 145 knots included in Pilot's Notes for the single-engine safety speed after take-off.

The lack of an aileron trimmer came in for criticism as did the rather high stick force/g figures, especially those when the c.g. was in a forward position. In view of the large amount of development flying already completed, and bearing in mind the aircraft's role, it was decided that existing figures be accepted.

TT188, Sea Hornet F.20, commenced clearance trials for bombs and pyrotechnics during October 1947. These were subsequently cancelled by the Ministry of Supply in view of the unsatisfactory results and adverse handling reports. In February 1948, TT188 was engaged in carbon monoxide contamination tests.

Handling trials with external stores indicated that basic Sea Hornet F.20 aircraft possessed quite different out-of-trim dive characteristics from those expected from the Hornet F.I, which was fitted with a revised elevator circuit. The trials were terminated after a canopy failure which caused considerable damage.

TT189, Sea Hornet F.20, 15 February 1949. Intensive flying trials 3 March 1949. Further intensive flying trials.

TT189 and **TT191**. (December 1948)
Both were used for clearance trials for the carrying of various offensive loads, including mines, bombs, depth charges and anti-submarine bombs. Other loads included; "Window" dispensers, photo-flashes, ASR equipment and reconnaissance flares.

Originally, TT248 was also involved in the trials programme until a collapse of the undercarriage resulted in TT189 acting as a replacement. Complete Bomb Carrier Units were then transferred to TT189, the trials being completed in March 1949.

TT190 Sea Hornet F.20. Commenced windscreen wiper trials on 4 March 1949 and was still on strength at A. & A.E.E. on 5 June 1950.

TT191 Sea Hornet F.20. Due to the non-availability of a fully-modified F.20 for these trials (November to December 1947), it was decided to use TT191 for checks on buffet at limiting speeds. On their completion it was recommended that special care be exercised with jettisoning drop tanks in level flight when carrying R.P.s. TT191 was also engaged with ASI/position error correction tests during March 1948.

During February to May 1949, speed/power measurements were made with the arrester hook removed

Sea Hornet TT186 in flight (B Ae photo)

Sea Hornet F.20 TT189 at Boscombe Down (via P Jarrett)

with results considered similar in most respects to the Hornet F.3. Other tests made included: flights without external stores with both drop tanks empty; with two 100-gallon drop tanks full and eight 60 lb R.P.s or two 1,000 lb bombs.

TT248 Sea Hornet F.20. Handling trials (November to December 1947) commenced for stick force/g tests with aft c.g. position at maximum permissible air speeds when figures were found to be excessive. The Bungee spring was removed from the elevator control circuit and proved to have a beneficial effect on longitudinal stability characteristics. During climbs at 155 knots, some difficulty was experienced at all heights with fore-and-aft trimming. Above 20,000 feet, releasing the stick after displacement resulted in a divergence into a dive or stall after 10 seconds. Flat turns in both directions when climbing resulted in rudder bar loads becoming light at half travel and full opposite aileron was needed to hold the wings level when applying full rudder.

Dives at maximum permissible climb power (radiator flaps closed) to 415 knots IAS caused an increased stick force of 35 lb and "wallowing" occurred at low altitude at 360-380 knots which was considered as a detriment to accurate aiming. "Porpoising" was evident during dives at various heights between 13-16,000 feet at 350 knots IAS. This did not always occur and tended to fade out below 10,000 feet.

Turns at high g required a 19-lb pull force on stick in a steady 3.6 G turn.

On delivery, TT248 was found to have ineffective ailerons which was most noticeable at low airspeeds during the landing approach. Examination revealed excessive slack in aileron control circuit which was promptly rectified. The ailerons were re-rigged by resident D.H. representatives.

After climbing to 29,000 feet, severe internal frosting affected the inside windscreen. During the descent the radiator flaps were closed and full cockpit heating selected without success. The entire windscreen and side panels had become coated with severe frosting, although the canopy itself was not affected.

Attempts to open the sliding canopy at 140 knots required a considerable effort by the pilot, who flew several circuits around Boscombe in a vain effort to clear the windscreen. The frost coating failed to clear until after landing.

Previous "Porpoising" was attributed to reaching a high Mach Number and not considered disconcerting to the pilot. During May and June, TT248 was fitted with a modified tailplane of 10% horn balance which effectively increased the span to nearly 19 feet. This modification resulted in a considerable improvement in stick free fore-and-aft stability. Stick force/g figures at moderate airspeeds, however, were still regarded as too high for a fighter aircraft.

In August and September 1948, new seven-pound inertia weights and 10% horn balances were installed on all Sea Hornet F.20 aircraft which were now considered as pleasant to fly. The stick force/g figures were considered as satisfactory at all altitudes.

October 1948 to January 1949. Handling trials were made with R.P.s, when aileron trimming was not sufficiently effective when slight lateral rocking occurred in dives. Several simulated carrier deck landings were made with the c.g. at a forward position. The tail could then be lowered to give a three point attitude by pulling back on the stick and cutting the throttles.

Asymmetric R.P. loading presented no difficulties under normal flight conditions. It was considered that deck landings could probably be made under these conditions. Due to ineffective trimming, a five-pound stick force was required to hold the wings level when carrying R.P.s. on one wing only and this became tiring. February to March 1949. Following repairs, handling trials were made with bombs with particular emphasis on asymmetric behaviour after a single bomb was dropped off during take-off. As a result, the recommended unstick speed (with 1,000 lb under one wing) was 120 knots. Even then full opposite aileron was needed and the wings could not be held level at lower than 120 knots.

Safe speed for landing appeared to be 140 knots and not considered as easy, despite using differential throttles and full opposite aileron at all times.

VV430, the first production Sea Hornet NF.21, flew in from R.R.E. Defford on 12 November 1948. Handling trials with bombs commenced on 12 December. In common with previous Sea Hornet trials, it lacked effective aileron trimming. Considerable vibration occurred on the outer wings when diving with external stores above 300 knots IAS. Accordingly, the recommended speeds were altered to; 275 knots at 20,000-25,000 feet and 300 knots between 15,000-20,000 feet.

Radio acceptance trials (18 November 1948 to 12 April 1949) were carried out and it was concluded that the Morse key should be re-positioned and the rear seat should be lowered to prevent the observer from assuming a bent attitude; maintenance of equipment in the radio bay was difficult owing to severe congestion - forty minutes were required to change a transmitter; replacement of fuses in the Modulator unit needed twenty times the normal length of time and was especially difficult when airborne.

In January 1949, A.S.I. and altimeter pressure corrections, followed by trials for climb and level speed performance; power analysis and specific air range (without external stores). Results of these performance tests indicated a maximum rate of climb from sea level to 9,200 feet of 2,515 ft/min. Time to service ceiling (32,400 feet) was a shade over twenty-five minutes. A maximum speed of 363 knots was attained with radiators flaps closed and a weight of 16,970 lb.

Over the altitude range, the level speed performance of the NF.21 was 25-30 knots TAS slower than the Hornet F.3 and 15-20 knots slower at maximum cruising power. The level speed performance of the single-seat F.20 at max. continuous cruising power was only marginally higher at 6 knots at 5,000 feet.

Conclusions:

Handling characteristics of the NF.21 in either day or night roles were considered generally satisfactory with or without drop tanks. Elevators were regarded as rather light for a night fighter with the c.g. at aft limit when drop tanks were fitted, assessed as satisfactory subject to a speed limitation of 290 knots IAS which prevented the onset of aileron buffet.

Some slight spiral instability made the aircraft unpleasant to fly with feet off rudder pedals and it was considered advantageous to secure an improvement. During flights in bumpy weather whilst climbing or at slow cruising speeds or in the glide, elevator oscillation proved sufficiently violent to pull the control column out of the pilot's hands. At higher airspeeds, the effects were not so pronounced; although they were not classed as dangerous every attempt was to be made for their elimination.

During out-of-trim dives, the aircraft was trimmed for level flight at climbing power before to diving when a push force of nineteen lb. was needed on the stick to hold the aircraft in dive at 415 knots IAS at 5,000 feet. On releasing the control column, the accelerometer reading registered about 4g.

On 23 June 1949, the canopy collapsed during a routine air test.

VW959 Sea Hornet NF.21. During March 1951, this aircraft was engaged in general handling trials with air/sea rescue containers fitted. Handling qualities were considered as indistinguishable from others when bombs were carried and found satisfactory up to 350 knots IAS. Earlier tests had resulted in aileron vibration at speeds above 300 knots.

Sea Hornet F.20

Sea Hornet NF.21

Hornet F.3 PX302 EB-D of No.41 Squadron (via Sqn Ldr H.H. Moon)

The Church Fenton Hornet Wing, Nos. 19 and 41 Squadrons

No. 19(F) Squadron

1946

Equipped with Spitfire L.F.XVIEs and based at Wittering, No.19 Squadron commenced a gradual transition to Hornets during October, becoming the second front-line fighter squadron to re-equip with the new fighter. A Mosquito T.III arrived during the middle of the month for twin conversion training.

The first Hornet F.I, PX246 (ex-64 Squadron) flew into Wittering on 10 October. On 28 November, pilots commenced ferrying the surplus Spitfires to Lyneham for open storage. W/O Vine became the first squadron pilot to solo the Hornet after period of dual in the Mosquito T.III.

W/O D.L. Hayward was among the band of 19 Squadron ex-Spitfire pilots and was formerly a Mustang pilot with 126 Squadron based at Hethel, Norfolk. He was soon to become a leading exponent of Hornet aerobatic flying. Following two periods of dual in the T.III, he was sent off on his first Hornet solo. On 25 November, a section of four Hornets set off for a low level cross-country exercise to Prestatyn - Hucknall-

Horsham St.Faith and return. Next day, W/Os D. Hayward, Whyte and F/Sgt. Inglis were detailed for height climbs; W/O Hayward succeeding in attaining 37,500 feet during an hour-long flight. At this altitude the Hornet's controls were nearly ineffective on attaining near-absolute ceiling.

No.19 Squadron was commanded by Sqn.Ldr. C.I.R. ("Duke") Arthur DFC & Bar, who remained with the squadron until August 1948. A cadre was quickly established; the majority of squadron pilots were N.C.O.s with wartime combat experience, although most lacked previous twin-engine flying time.

In December armed reconnaissance exercises were carried out, with some interceptions by Meteor IIIs and Vampires. The Hornets easily out-turned their opponents although matters were decidedly different during diving chases when some lack of control occurred at high Mach Numbers. This resulted in severe buffeting, pilots reporting stick shake and "porpoising" particularly evident in dives from high altitude. On 20 December, several aircraft carried out a formation cross-country exercise, flying at fifty feet.

1947

A formation flying exercise on 15 January was followed by a break for a tail chase. On the 22nd, the squadron formed up with other Hornets for a Group exercise which was flown at 25,000 feet, throttles wide open with 450 m.p.h. speeds being recorded. At this stage W/O Hayward's starboard Merlin gave up the struggle, forcing him to return to base. On the 21st, the T.III was flown down to the Rolls-Royce airfield at Hucknall to pick up some urgently needed engine spares. Two days later, it crashed on landing at Newton.

Severe wintry conditions in February seriously curtailed flying. Following some improvement in March, two flypast rehearsals were made. On the 28th, interceptions were made at 25,000 feet when W/O Hayward's aircraft suffered another failure of his starboard Merlin.

Operation *Rufus* was commenced on 12 April. Three days later the squadron flew all available aircraft in Battle formation. Operation *Rufus II* commenced on the 16th, lasting three days and consisted of flypasts led by Sqn.Ldr. Arthur with four F.Is in "vic" formation over the RAF Apprentice School at Halton. Among those watching the proceedings were the Chief of Air Staff, various Cabinet members and the Prime Minister. Between the 22nd and 24th, 19 Squadron commenced flying its Hornets to their new base at Church Fenton. F.Is PX226, PX248 and PX277 were delivered by W/O Hayward.

With little time in which to settle in, the squadron was deployed to Coltishall on the 28th for participation in Operation *Web Foot*. This exercise commenced on the 29th and involved four Hornets led by the C.O., with Flt.Lts. Donaldson, Higson and W/O Hayward as wingmen.

Shortly after arriving at Church Fenton, 19 Squadron ground staff began the task of repainting their Hornets in a distinctive pre-war 19 Squadron blue/white check layout. Several types of design included a wrap round check layout aft of fuselage roundel and, later, oblong patterns each side of fuselage roundels. At one period PX246 also sported chequered markings behind the spinners, similar to those adopted for 19 Squadron's post-war Mustangs. These attractive markings were soon abandoned, eventually appearing as a small motif on the fin.

On 3 May, a flypast was made over Sherbourne. Four days later a section of Hornets set off for a four-hour Continental cross-country flight to Westkapelle-Münster - Dortmund - Eindhoven - Westkapelle - Church Fenton.

Operation *Web Foot II* began on the 13th when 19 Squadron deployed to Coltishall as part of the Eastern Sector. Four aircraft were used, two providing top fighter cover. Two Hornets had to make forced landings, both due to engine failure. Another Continental cross-country flight was made on the 15th, via Bentwaters - Westkapelle - Dinant - Kohl - Münster - Church Fenton.

Hornet F.3 PX259 camouflaged at Church Fenton (via P. Jarrett)

Hornet F.3 PX387 QV-H (A. Pearcy)

In June, following several hours of intensive practice, 19 Squadron carried out a close formation display for the press. W/O Hayward performed some individual aerobatics for the assembled gathering.

The squadron flew in formation over Blackpool Airport on 23 July for the air display. Hornets became grounded shortly afterwards due to faulty engine bearers.

On the 30th, exercises were carried out with the Home Fleet, No.19 deploying several Hornets to RAF Chivenor from the 29th to the 31st on fleet patrol duties. The current shortage of aircraft resulted in borrowings from the Linton Hornet Wing. Their main duties consisted of providing fighter cover against approaching bombers.

During the first part of August preference was given to practise GCA let-downs at Bassingbourn. Flt.Lt. Donaldson's Hornet developed engine problems and while attempting a single-engine approach, one flap failed to lower. After overshooting, he successfully executed a landing without flaps.

On the 9th, W/O Hayward delivered a Hornet to Northolt for static display. The annual A.O.C.'s inspection occurred on the 15th, when the squadron put on a three-Hornet flypast. An aerobatic display made for his benefit by P.II. Dennis Hayward was hastily abandoned after a canopy failure, which caused Hayward to suffer ear injuries.

All Hornets were grounded during September owing to technical problems and a resulting modification programme. Several aircraft were flown to the servicing wing at Linton-on-Ouse to receive attention. On the 10th,

flying was eventually resumed.

"Pressure Pattern" navigation exercises were commenced, a prelude to more ambitious medium/low level exercises planned to the Middle East. Shortly afterwards, six F.Is left Church Fenton on the 21st, bound for Manston and staying overnight before obtaining clearance to Istres in Southern France. The Hornets set off in three pairs, arriving at Istres in time for lunch, where Flt.Lt. Donaldson's Hornet suffered a burst tyre. Shortly after departing for a refuelling stop at Elmas, Sardinia, Flt.Lt. Lord's aircraft went u/s due to a faulty cooling pump. A second night was spent at Castel Benito, outside Tripoli, before pairs began setting off for the final leg to Fayid in the Suez Canal Zone.

Most of the flying over desert regions occurred at heights ranging from 500-1,000 feet. Former "Blue Two", Flt.Lt. Ransley, recalls the uncomfortably high temperatures inside his cockpit during passage at low level over the Western Desert. During those far-off days, the sole navigation equipment had consisted of a compass plus a collection of dubious maps.

On the return flight a stop was made at El Adem for refuelling. A series of irritating serviceability problems were encountered by Red section due to bolts working loose on engine bearers. In some extreme cases, it was discovered that bolts had previously been filed down in attempts to eradicate fouling.

Blue section were now on the return journey, arriving at Elmas only to discover that Yellow section were still awaiting a replacement coolant pump. Inclement weather around Istres had compelled Red section to remain at Elmas for two days, resulting in a late arrival at Church Fenton on the 27th.

Church Fenton "Open Day" on the 20th included a flypast by three Hornets and individual aerobatics by a single aircraft. Mock attacks were made on three Lancasters of Bomber Command. W/O Hayward, squadron aerobatic pilot, performed a well-practised aerobatic display. His programme included upward and hesitation rolls, Cuban eights, stall turns and Immelmann turns. Slow flying and steep turns with "everything down" were flown within the airfield boundary.

Six Hornets were deployed on 8 October to Coltishall for exercises with Bomber Command in the fighter escort role. Keeping station with Lancasters and Lincolns at 18,000 feet was to prove difficult due to the vastly different cruising speeds. This was solved by constant weaving. The Hornets were pitted against Meteors from Tangmere and Horsham St.Faith. On the 24th, the T.III was collected from Hatfield, following a period of refurbishment.

In company with two Hornets of 65 Squadron, four aircraft from the squadron were detached to Stradishall on 10 November for escort duties at high and low level altitude. On the 11th, practice interceptions were made on Lancaster B.I (FE)s of No.35 Squadron, operating from RAF Stradishall. Just before noon, the Lancaster formation was approaching Stanford, Norfolk. Plt.Off. Steedman in PX284 was observed to appear from above the port quarter and pass under the rear-most Lancaster. Climbing steeply the Hornet struck Lancaster B.I (FE) TW647, on its starboard wing root. A large part of the Hornet's wing broke off, giving the pilot little chance of baling out. Seven members of the Lancaster crew (all from 115 Squadron) perished, although the captain managed to escape. One of the passengers aboard the ill-fated Lancaster was Sqn.Ldr. G.H. Humphreys, a former Battle of Britain pilot.

On the 13th and 14th, the squadron was engaged on high level escort duties with Lancasters of Bomber Command, protecting them against intercepting Meteors and Vampires. A fatal crash on the 21st involved PX233, flown by Plt.Off. Turner. After being briefed for cloud flying and single-engine landings, he eventually commenced an approach to Church Fenton with one engine feathered. Speed fell below critical level and during the subsequent overshoot the aircraft stalled, crashing a half-mile from the airfield.

Escort duties were carried out on the 25th for twenty-four bombers with Hornets drawn from 19 Squadron and the Linton Hornet Wing. Mock combats occurred against Spitfires and Meteors, when the Hornets acquitted themselves well, especially against the Meteors.

During December, flying became impossible due to arrival of severe wintry weather.

1948

On 8 January, Sgts. Hilliard and Harvey received dual instruction in the T.3. On the 14th and 15th, W/O Hay-

ward flew down to Odiham to give an aerobatic display. Bomber interceptions occurred on the 20th.

The temporary gun sight installations had been put to good use, permitting the squadron to carry out air-to-ground firing on the Holbeach firing range. Most pilots, however, found gun sights virtually useless, preferring to rely on the traditional ring and bead method for achieving accuracy. During the period 26th January to 12th February, squadron pilots commenced an instrument flying course using Harvards of No.41 Instrument Training Squadron, Church Fenton.

PX248 crashed on landing on 2 February. Further training was carried out on cine-camera exercises.

During March, P.I Taylor and P.I Sharples were given dual instruction in the T.3. Four Hornets intercepted a formation of USAF B-29s flying at 20,000 feet. Re-equipment with Hornet F.3s began on the 22nd when PX293 was delivered from Hullavington, closely followed by PX343 from Shawbury on the 23rd and PX347 on the 24th.

During April, endurance tests were carried out using the recently arrived F.3s and entailed four-hour flights at heights ranging from 2,000-10,000 feet. Several F.3s were air tested following maintenance checks at Linton. On the 12th, the squadron deployed to Coltishall to carry out strafing attacks on Paston firing range, returning to Church Fenton on the 17th.

On the 19th, PX250 crashed on landing. There were continued interceptions of USAF B-29s. By way of a change, on the 23rd interceptions were made on Royal Navy ships in the North Sea.

The squadron was engaged in air firing from 24 May at Armament Practice Station Acklington, where very low cloud and rain persisted inland from the coast. Clearer conditions over the sea allowed some firing to continue. The East coast main railway line ran past the airfield at Acklington, British Rail having chosen a particular day to run the *Flying Scotsman* non-stop between King's Cross, London, and Edinburgh. The landing approach being flown directly over the main line, Murphy's Law directing that a Hornet would clip the telephone wires between two signal boxes shortly before the train was due. The resulting hold-up was to cause red faces all round.

On 24 July, four Hornets led by the new C.O. (Sqn.Ldr. Woodward DFC & Bar) left Church Fenton on temporary detachment to West Malling for exercises next day with the Royal Observer Corps.

On August 2nd and 3rd, Pilot II Hayward performed two aerobatic displays over Boundary Park, Leeds. On the 4th, 9th and 10th, ground strafing was carried out on Paston Firing Range.

During the A.O.C.'s annual inspection on the 17th, Air Vice Marshal T.C. Traill CB OBE DFC was treated to a formation flypast.

Exercise *Dagger* commenced on 3 September with No.19 Squadron intercepting large formations of USAF B-29s at 31,000 feet flying direct from the USA. The squadron made their attacks in line, encountering the

British-based Hornet F.1s and Development Aircraft

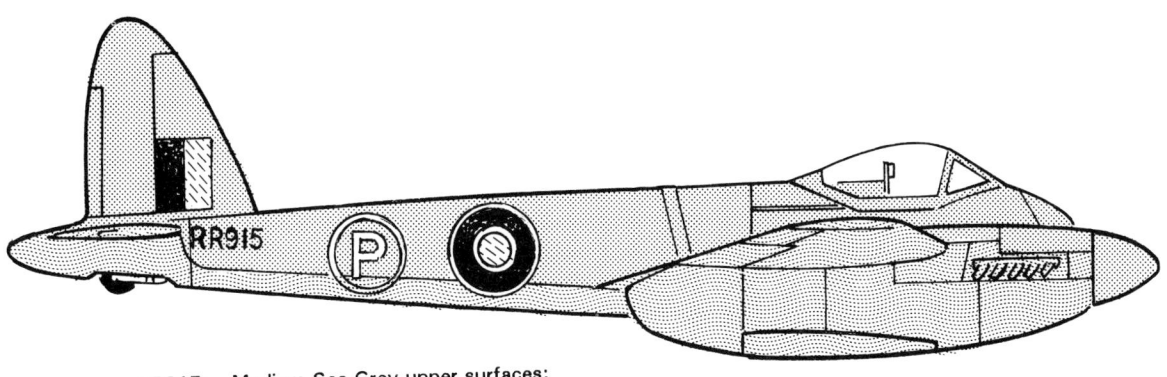

RR915: Medium Sea Grey upper surfaces;
yellow undersides

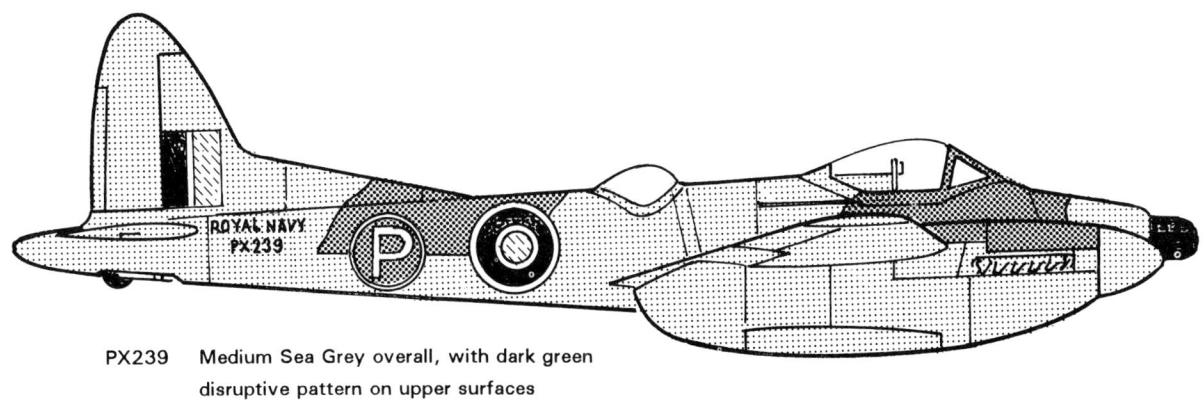

PX239 Medium Sea Grey overall, with dark green
disruptive pattern on upper surfaces

PX281 of No.226 O.C.U.
Medium Sea Grey upper surfaces; P.R. Blue undersides;
Sky spinners; black codes

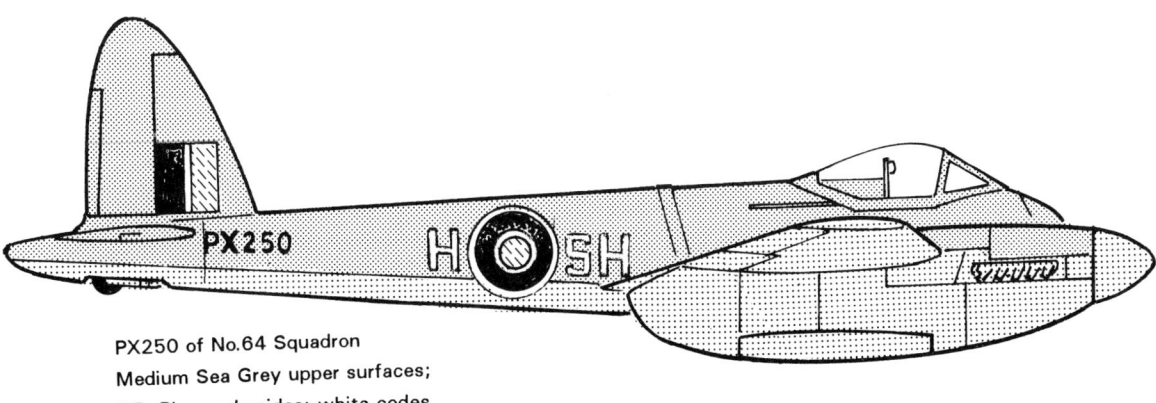

PX250 of No.64 Squadron
Medium Sea Grey upper surfaces;
P.R. Blue undersides; white codes

PX246 painted with No.19 Squadron's short-lived checker-board markings

PX347 QV-D after P.II Aitchison overshot on his second solo, 8 February 1949

massed wake from the American bombers which proved troublesome for accurate aiming. Scramble time from initial warning to becoming airborne was a creditable one minute forty-five seconds. Other interceptions were made on five R.A.F. Mosquito PR.34s flying at 25,000 feet.

On the 14th, battle climbs reached 30,000 feet and were followed by aerobatics. On the 15th, three Hornets, led by Sqn.Ldr. Woodward, represented part of the Battle of Britain flypast over London.

The annual Church Fenton Open Day had demonstrations of close formation flying and mock attacks on Lincolns. Hornets PX346, PX389 and PX390 were scrambled to intercept six high-flying Lancasters. Three others flown by Flg.Off. Starkins, P.II Hayward and P.II Taylor departed to perform individual aerobatic displays at Horsham St.Faith, Leeming and Finningley. On the 28th, several interceptions were made on formations of USAF B-29s.

Over several days, October 1st/8th, 15th and 28th, sections of Hornets made attacks on B-29s. On the 5th, a section departed from Church Fenton for the now routine "Continental" cross-country.

An Autumn exercise, code-named *Hedgehog*, commenced on the 24th and involved co-operation with the Royal Observer Corps. During the following day a short deployment was made to the Central Gunnery School at Leconfield to allow firing practice on the Skipsea firing range.

Flying became somewhat restricted in November due to a persistent fog layer, although some air firing was carried out on the 3rd at 30,800 feet. Several former Hornet pilots have commented on the difficulty of achieving accurate aiming while flying at high altitudes. Hornets were not regarded as very good gun platforms when firing at higher altitudes. On the 5th, a low-level cross-country exercise was flown over Scotland.

During 8 to 12 December, the squadron detached several aircraft to R.N.A.S. Culdrose for Exercise *Sunrise* on fleet interception duties. Flying became rather spasmodic due to inclement weather conditions.

1949

On 5th to 7th January, Pilot I Moss and Flg.Off. Starkings both received dual instruction in the Mosquito T.3. A long distance navigational exercise on the 9th to Fayid, Egypt, passed without incident, apart from two instances of mechanical defects. A Hornet flown by Flg.Off. Starkings made a single-engine landing at El Adem due to a faulty cooling pump. P.II Taylor also carried out an unscheduled landing in Sicily after having problems with his radio and a suspected fuel shortage. Despite these problems, all four Hornets, led by the C.O., succeeded in leaving Malta on the 18th, arriving at Church Fenton on the same day. This exercise resulted in a total of 18 hours flying, of which two were spent on instrument flying in cloud. Inclement weather in February severely restricted flying.

March witnessed the start of Exercise *Forth/Clyde* when Flg.Off. Barley's Hornet struck part of a tree during low-level intruding over R.N.A.S. Abbotsinch, Barley making a safe landing at Church Fenton.

On 12 April, F.3 PX332 arrived from No.10 Maintenance Unit, followed by PX349 from No.52 MU on the 26th which brought squadron strength to the required level.

In May the squadron flew across to A.P.C. Acklington, where all aircraft became grounded due to faulty gun supports which prevented any hope of air-to-air firing.

Exercise *Foil* commenced with 19 Squadron deployed to Linton-on-Ouse, sharing hangars and offices with 64 Squadron for ten days. One particular sortie involved an attack on London at 25,000 feet, although most flying was conducted at much lower levels, usually between 150-200 feet. Although lacking present day terrain-following radar and computerised bombing aids, low level intruding demanded high levels of concentration, accurate map reading and precise navigation. Even average sorties could last between two or three hours and there were occasions when Hornet pilots had been briefed to attack no fewer than seven targets during a single sortie. Despite the higher than average workload, these exercises were considered "great fun" by the participating pilots.

The annual Battle of Britain flypast on 15 September included a contingent from 19 Squadron led by the C.O., in company with Flt.Lt. Mills, Plt.Off. Czerwinski and Plt.Off. Tresize. In common with pilots from both Hornet Wings, the 19 Squadron quartet coped well with the very hazy conditions persisting around the London area.

The 17th was "At Home" day for Church Fenton, Sqn.Ldr. Woodward commencing proceedings by leading a formation flypast followed by a pass with one engine feathered on each aircraft. On the 20th, the squadron was detached to Linton-on-Ouse for participation in Exercise *Bulldog*. Low-level attacks were carried out on selected targets, including aerodromes and radar installations.

PX338 arrived on 18 October from No.10 M.U. The latter part of November found 19 Squadron pilots engaged on air-to-air and air-to-ground firing which was to last until 10 December. Formation flying and tail chases on the 20th virtually concluded the year's flying activities.

1950

Practice low flying, aerobatics and instrument procedures formed the main flying activity for the first fortnight of the new year.

The appropriately titled exercise *New Year* commenced on the 12th when in spite of poor visibility, no flights were cancelled. Another exercise in February, code-named *Pancake*, involved the squadron in low level intruding, all targets being located and attacked with good results.

March was mainly occupied with cine-camera exercises, air-to-ground firing and air-to-air firing.

In April the regular deployment was made to APS Acklington for air-ground firing. No.19 Squadron succeeded in breaking the Command record with an average score of 36.8%, Sqn.Ldr. Woodward achieved some distinction in obtaining highest individual score of 65%. Several shuttles were flown to Linton in the Mosquito T.3, VP351, to collect Hornets from the Servicing Wing.

May 1st was the start of Exercise *Stardust* and sector reconnaissances were flown. On the 12th, F.3 PX342 was forced to make a single-engine landing shortly after taking-off for an air test. On the 23rd, PX367 arrived from No.37 MU. The squadron was engaged on a formation night flying exercise, all aircraft showing navigation lights.

During the first fortnight of June there was constant practice in formation flying and cinegun exercises. On the 20th, 19 Squadron flew in Wing Formation before deploying to West Malling on the 24th and 25th for practice flypasts. On 3 July, the squadron was positioned at West Malling, performing flypasts over Farnborough on the 7th and 8th for the R.A.F. Display, accompanied by Hornets from Nos. 41, 64 & 65 Squadrons.

From August 10th to 31st, the squadron was detached to APS Sylt for air-to-air and air-to-ground firing practice, followed by bombing and discharging of R.P.s accounting for an average of 13 hours for each pilot, before returning to Church Fenton on 1 September.

A practice flypast was mounted on 5 September for the annual Battle of Britain air display, with further practice on the 12th. Between the 13th and 15th, Plt.Off Mitchell, a new pilot, spent several hours in practice low level aerobatics ready for the big day on the 16th when he gave displays over Hooton Park and Catterick.

The 12 Group exercise commenced on 5 October, when No.19's Hornet pilots were required to operate for nearly three hours at 12,000 feet. Within two days, a further large scale exercise was scheduled, code-named *Emperor*. Starting on the 7th, this exercise involved the squadron in sorties to Manston and Martlesham Heath. On the 10th, *Emperor* continued with Hornets directed to Sandwich and Rhyl. On the 11th, low level sorties were made to Horsham St.Faith and Newton. During the 14th, numerous targets had been selected, one sortie included intruding over airfields at Honiley, Wymeswold, Filton, Valley, Woodvale, Hooton Park and Church Fenton. On the 15th *Emperor* was now in the final phase with 19 Squadron F.3s engaged in low-level attacks on fighter airfields at Horsham St.Faith, Coltishall and West Raynham. A witness states that during the later phase of *Emperor*, Air Traffic Control at West Raynham had decided to inform the station, via intercom, that to all intents and purposes, *Emperor* was now over, congratulating the station personnel on their performance. No sooner had the message been relayed when several

A formation of Hornets from Church Fenton and Linton-on-Ouse at the Royal Air Force Display, 1950 (J.J. Halley)

low flying aircraft appeared on the horizon - Hornets! Quick off the mark, ground crews had already began towing the jets back to their hangars as the Hornets swept in. Giving orders to air traffic personnel for firing of Very cartridges, the embarrassed officer cursed the intruders over his loud hailer. On their return to base, the jubilant Hornet pilots promptly filed reports of the mass destruction of grounded jet fighters.

On the final day, P.I Moxon was in the act of intruding over Stradishall, only to be bounced by a flight of Meteors from a standing patrol at 2,000 feet. Caught in the slipstream from an overtaking Meteor, Moxon lost control at very low level, passing through some beech trees with his aircraft sustaining severe damage to both wing leading edges and radiators. His wingman, P.II Hayward, feathered one Merlin to escort Moxon's stricken Hornet back to Church Fenton where Moxon landed without further incident. Later inspection revealed that the radiator intakes contained beech nuts.

A section of four Hornets set off for Sylt on 30 November, only to encounter very low cloud over Germany and after about six hours flying they finally made landfall over the English coast to discover that they were almost fifty miles off track.

On December 18th and 19th, a section of Hornets, operating in pairs, flew to Gutersloh. The squadron received confirmation of its impending re-equipment with Meteors.

19 April 1950 was a sad day for P.I Watson who set off for his final Hornet flight, setting off on a low-level cross-country exercise, finally landing at Shawbury to hand over the aircraft to No.37 M.U.

Hornets equipping No.19 Squadron. Serial/Codes

Hornet F.1:

PX226 QV-A;	PX233 QV-K;	PX234 QV-D, C;
PX246 QV-A, -M;	PX248 QV-D, -E;	PX250 QV-G;
PX276 QV-F, -H;	PX277 QV-B, -F, -E, -P;	
PX278 QV-F, -E;	PX284 QV-H, -K.	

Hornet F.3:

PX293 QV-A;	PX294 QV-C;	PX301 QV-D, -C;
PX306 QV-G;	PX307 QV- ;	PX313 QV- ;
PX332 QV-D;	PX338 QV-B;	PX342 QV-E, -F;
PX343 QV-B;	PX346 QV-C;	PX347 QV-D;
PX349 QV-G, -H;	PX354 QV-J, -M;	PX363 QV-B;
PX367 QV-J;	PX387 QV-H;	PX389 QV-A;
PX390 QV-D, -F.		

Known Squadron Pilots: (1946-51)

Commanding Officers:

Sqn.Ldr. C.I.R. Arthur DFC & Bar, Sqn.Ldr. V.C. Woodward DFC & Bar, Sqn.Ldr. B.L. Duckenfield AFC.

Officers:

Flg.Off D. Auty, Flg.Off Barley, Flt.Lt. W.S.D. Bottrell, Flt.Lt. G.M. Donaldson, Flt.Lt. E.M. Higson, Flt.Lt. C.W.R. Lord,, Flg.Off R.N. Lowe, Flt.Lt. W.H. Mills, Flt.Lt. Miller, Flt.Lt. R.A. Ransley, Plt.Off W. Sharples, Flg.Off F.E. Smith, Flg.Off S. Sparkes, Plt.Off A. Steedman, Flg.Off P.R. Starkings, Plt.Off C.N.C. Mitchell, Plt.Off Turner, Flg.Off P.W.R. Varley, Flt.Lt. Williams.

N.C.O. Pilots:

Pilot I M. Cempel, Pilot I B. Czerwinski (later Plt.Off), Pilot II D.L. Hayward, W/O Hughes, Flt.Sgt. Inglis, Pilot II McTavish, Pilot I J. Moss, Pilot II W.A. Moxon, Pilot II K. Taylor, Pilot II G.O. Trezise, W/O J.H. Vine, Pilot I W. Walton, Pilot I W. Watson, W/O P.M. Whyte.

Hornet F.3 PX350 EB-Z of No.41 Squadron (P.Jarrett)

No.41(F) Squadron, RAF Church Fenton

No.41 Squadron was originally equipped with the formidable Spitfire F.21 and based at Wittering from 30 August 1946 until 16 April 1947, when a move was made to Church Fenton. Some four months later, their Spitfires were replaced by an assortment of Oxfords and Harvards. The squadron's role now changed to instrument flying training when it became No.12 Group Instrument Training Squadron.

1947

During August the squadron commenced essential instrument flying training for all Hornet pilots who were now required to obtain instrument ratings. Known as No.41 Instrument Training Squadron, former fighter pilots were acting as instructors/safety pilots. Sqn.Ldr. W Hoy DFC, AFC was C.O. and C.F.I. W/O Dowson, newly arrived on 65 Squadron, became the first Hornet pilot to complete the course, eventually staying on as an instructor, although he eventually returned to his beloved Hornets after a posting back to No.41 Squadron. The task of training all pilots in No.12 Group, Fighter Command, was to be completed during June 1948. Most of the Harvards and Oxfords were flown away. Hornets were to follow shortly. Pilot strength was for the squadron was maintained by an influx of experienced pilots from the Linton Hornet Wing.

1948

In June 1948, No.41 Squadron became the fourth and last home-based squadron to re-equip with Hornets, remaining under the command of Sqn.Ldr. W. Hoy, DFC, AFC, a former C.O. of No.25 Squadron with Mosquito NF.30s.

Initial deliveries of F.Is commenced with the arrival of PX231 (ex-226 OCU) and PX232 (ex-65 Squadron), both arriving on 6 June. Further aircraft were ferried to Church Fenton on the 9th, PX277 and PX278, (both ex-19 Squadron) and on the 16th, PX252 (ex-65 Squadron), which was delivered from Linton. The Hornets were considered second-hand and badly-used, requiring a great deal of attention by ground crews. Pilots were frustrated by lack of flying time but assisted the ground crews. A Mosquito T.3 was borrowed from Linton to provide check-outs and by the end of June all pilots had accomplished their first Hornet solos.

Several new pilots were posted to the squadron, including Pilot I Williams, previously with 64 Squadron, and latterly with the Ferry Training Unit flying the equally potent Tempest VI. On the 26th he ferried PX242 from Linton to Church Fenton.

Pilot II Dowson was due to re-commence Hornet flying after his stint of instrument flying instructing, this being delayed due to a fresh instructing requirement.

Some concern was caused by flap failures on F.1s when only one flap lowered, which could be a potential killer when flying in the circuit or during bad weather. Engine synchronisation difficulties plagued some aircraft which made accurate formation flying extremely difficult.

During July, as a change from routine, P.II Dowson was busy with air experience flights in Oxford PG943 for visiting R.O.C. personnel, no fewer than twenty passengers being carried within an hour.

On the 27th, the squadron was active with constant practice in formation flying and aerobatics. Several pilots flew to Hullavington to collect new aircraft, ferrying them to Linton for acceptance tests before issue to 41 Squadron. A centralised servicing system was now established at Linton which catered for both Hornet Wings. With immediate effect, all pilots were given instruction on servicing and daily inspections.

Instrument flying revision exercises began in August using Harvard FX459. Close formation flying kept the squadron occupied throughout the month. After being briefed for a low flying exercise, P.I Williams was obliged to return early in a recently delivered F.3 due to engine failure. Newly posted from 64 Squadron to 41 Squadron, Pilot II George was required to complete an Instrument Rating Course on Harvards with P.II Dowson as instructor. Trained during World War II in Rhodesia, P.II George flew the mighty P-47D Thunderbolt in the Far East, returning to the U.K. to join 19 Squadron, then equipped with Spitfire XVIs. He converted to the Hornet at No.226 Operational Conversion Unit at Bentwaters, serving briefly with 65 Squadron before a posting to Church Fenton. Squadron pilots were rather startled and to some extent amused when a solitary Hornet appeared in the circuit, finally landing with wheels up. The somewhat embarrassed occupant was a senior officer, specifically engaged on a lecture tour to emphasise to squadron pilots the urgent need to reduce the number of accidents caused by pilot error. On the 27th, Flt.Lts. Harvey and Robinson, with P.II George, made head-on and three-quarter rear attacks on U.S.A.F. B-29s.

Midway through his period of instructing, P.II Dowson was let loose with PX350, a recently-delivered F.3, for a 25,000 feet height climb. A previous detail on the 19th for low flying was "scrubbed" when PX252 went unserviceable. There were several B-29 and B-50 interceptions at 30,000 feet with their crews "less than happy" with a series of head-on attacks by 41 Squadron Hornets. Closing speeds were in the region of 600 knots. The tall fins of US bombers presented a real collision hazard to approaching fighters. B-29s were flown in large formations of 50+ aircraft and were easily detected when some distance away.

When flying on a parallel course to the B-29s, Hornet pilots needed to position their aircraft some 10-12 miles ahead before executing maximum rate 180-degree turns for classic head-on attacks. One former Hornet pilot E.V. George recounted: "Then things happened very quickly!" During any attack from a three-quarter position, the Hornets ran into considerable amounts of wake turbulence from the stepped up formation. As a result, the intercepting Hornets were tossed in all directions, which made accurate aiming extremely difficult. The squadron was declared fully operational for the forthcoming exercise, code-named *Dagger*.

Exercise *Dagger* commenced during September 3rd/4th. P.II Dowson was "Red II" whilst flying in the exercise and soon became engaged with incoming U.S.A.F. B-29s.

Sqn.Ldr. H.H. Moon arrived at Church Fenton to take over command of 41 Squadron.

On the 8th, a formation flying exercise was aborted after only 25 minutes due to a weather clamp. Re-equipment with F.3s continued at a slow rate, F.1s PX242, PX244, PX252, PX277 & PX278 being destined to soldier on for some months.

Essential practice for the forthcoming Battle of Britain Flypast kept 41 Squadron Hornets in the air for nearly two hours. P.I Williams in F.3 PX350 took his place in the formation on the traditional 15th. On the 18th, he set off in F.1 PX252 for a round flight to Hemswell, Binbrook and Coningsby, performing individual aerobatic displays. Pilot II George did his set piece over three airfields at Upwood, Wyton and Stradishall.

On the 23rd he had a narrow escape in PX308 after a period of cloud flying. After making two landings with overshoots, he approached at high speed, touching down half-way along the runway. On attempting to swing off the runway, his wheels ran into a ditch, causing the Hornet to pitch over on to its back. Lacking a crash pylon, George was forced to assume a crouched position inside the cockpit, before the rescue team arrived to cut away the fuselage. PX308 was one of a pair which were on a cloud flying exercise, both recalled owing to poor weather in the local area. The other Hornet was flown by P.II Watson who was instructed to divert to Wittering. During the hot summer months, it became routine for pilots to fly clad only with underclothes beneath their flying overalls, a fact which did not escape the Eagle eye of Wittering's Station Warrant Officer when Watson entered the Sergeant's Mess.

Pilot II Watson, (a former pilot with No.17 Squadron in Burma with Spitfire Marks VIII and XIV and with No.1 Squadron Spitfire Mk.21s) converted to the Meteor F.3 before Hornets. After studying Meteor Pilot's notes, he enquired about the procedure for single-engine failure; "shut down the other engine and glide in like a Spit" came the cheery reply.

His conversion to the Hornet consisted of twenty minutes dual in a Mosquito T.3 under the watchful eye of Sqn.Ldr. Page. After spending several happy years flying Hornets, Watson remained in the R.A.F. flying many types of aircraft, including all jets from Vampires to Javelins.

On the 28th the squadron continued their almost daily encounters with B-29s. Next day a section set off for a Continental cross-country exercise to Münster and Groningen. Several aircraft intercepted some Lincolns during interception exercises.

Over seven interceptions made during October were directed at incoming U.S.A.F. B-29s, accounting for ninety-minute-long sorties. During a later exercise, P.I Williams in PX232 was compelled to make an early return due to technical problems.

Operation *Hedge Hop* began on the 24th in co-operation with the Royal Observer Corps. On their return from a low-level sortie, Flt.Lt. Harvey, Flg.Off. Scholfield and P.I Williams all agreed that after almost three hours spent at zero feet, one could have too much of a good thing!

Several F.3s were delivered at this time, including PX350 and PX366. On the 18th, 41 Squadron carried out formation flying and cine-camera exercises. In the third week of the month, there were almost daily interceptions of U.S.A.F. B-29s. On the 20th, 41 Squadron Hornets searched for shipping within the firing range. Operation *Hedge Hop* took place on the 24th, which was followed by some air-to-air firing. A visit was made to the Central Gunnery School, Leconfield, on the 26th for air-ground firing on Skipsea range. Both squadrons of the Church Fenton Wing were engaged with B-29s on the 29th.

Sqn.Ldr. H.H. Moon, a former wartime fighter pilot flying Hurricanes, Spitfires, Typhoons and Tempests, took over command of the squadron.

Formation and sector attacks were flown on the 23rd. Next day P.II George, flying PX244, had the unenviable experience of having total engine failure at 8,000 feet and was faced with the daunting prospect of attempting a dead stick landing. After a forced landing in a field, his Hornet came to rest near Fox Hill Farm, near Derby. The starboard wing was badly damaged after striking a hedge and the Hornet was assessed as a write-off. The cause of this total engine failure was attributed to icing.

On 22 November, Flg.Off. Scholfield in PX366 suffered a bird strike which punctured the nose. On the same day, Flt.Lt. Robinson in PX277 flew into a flock of lapwings during take-off, two being caught in the radiators. On the 25th, four aircraft led by Sqn.Ldr. Moon set off for formation flying only to be diverted to West Raynham due to dense fog, where they were marooned for eight days. Flt.Lt. Harvey, flying an air test, was also caught out and forced to make a precautionary landing on a disused airfield near Grimsby.

Tests were made using "Canary", a type of radar used for identification purposes. Despite a fog warning on the 25th, the neighbouring squadron, No.19, despatched a pair of Hornets on a Continental cross-country exercise. No.41 had decided not to fly on this occasion until receiving orders from "above" dictating otherwise.

As a direct consequence, four Hornets were detailed for a formation cine-camera exercise. Flying over Yorkshire, now cloaked in thick fog, P.II Watson recalls seeing the steeple of York Minster protruding "'rocket-like" through the mist. Within a short time the pilots were given instructions to divert to West Raynham. All were clad in their usual attire of flying overalls over

underclothes. After landing, one of their number was promptly placed aboard a train to Church Fenton for the express purpose of picking up personal kit! The four pilots were marooned at West Raynham until 2 December.

Between December 3rd to 13th, B-29 interceptions occurred at frequent intervals, no less than eleven being carried out from the third day of the month. On the 9th, several Hornets flew down on deployment to R.N.A.S. Culdrose for an exercise, code-named *Sunrise*, scheduled to start next day. This particular exercise was in co-operation with Sea Hornets of No.801 Squadron, Culdrose, and also included a number of aircraft from No.19 Squadron to make up the required numbers. Hornets were scrambled on three occasions to intercept B-29s.

One of the few remaining F.1s, PX278, was ferried to Shawbury, its pilot returning to Church Fenton aboard Mosquito T.3 VT628. The week leading up to the Christmas period was mainly devoted to cine-camera exercises, air fighting and formation flying.

1949

Poor weather in January tended to restrict flying during latter part of month. On the 8th, PX366 was sent up for a weather test.

11th January: This particular day started badly, PX306 jumping its chocks and colliding with PX277. The spectacular ground prang was caused by an unfortunate mechanic forgetting to tighten the throttle clamping nut, prior to starting up, allowing the Merlin to quickly develop full power when 2,000 hp was unleashed. With one Merlin at full power, PX306, complete with its terrified Corporal, commenced a rapid and destructive ground loop. Hornet F.1 PX277 never flew again, being consigned to R.A.F. Leconfield as instructional airframe 6658M. PX306 finished up with nose pointing to the sky after breaking its back, a complete write-off.

Several scrambles were made to intercept B-29s. On the 19th, P.II Dowson succeeded in coaxing PX298 to 36,000 feet during a height climb.

Progressive re-equipment with F.3s continued during February with the arrival of PX308, PX314 and PX357. The fourth week of flying activity included cine-camera, air-to-ground firing and formation exercises. During the 6th to 11th, four Hornets were despatched on a Middle East cross-country, flying mostly at 18,000 feet in a trial of "Pressure Pattern" navigation. The route taken followed along roughly similar lines to that employed by other Hornet squadrons i.e. Church Fenton-Manston-Luqa-El Adem-Fayid, with a refuelling stop made at Istres.

On March 1st a reconnaissance was flown over the Firth of Forth, followed two days later by another over the Clyde area. On the 15th, the squadron indulged in a free-for-all "Tail Chase" and cine-camera exercises.

PX333 arrived from No.10 M.U. Mosquito T.3 VT628 departed on the 17th bound for the U.S.A.F. base

PX306 after running away at Church Fenton on 11 January 1949

at Sculthorpe. After landing, the passenger aboard the T.3, P.I Williams, was quickly briefed for a four-hour bombing mission in B-29 '364' to Heligoland, acting as an observer.

On the 24th, the squadron carried out air-to-ground firing on the Skipsea range.

Between April 7th and 9th, pilots carried out Gyro-Gunsight ranging and cine-camera exercises, followed on the 11th and 12th by B-29 interceptions.

On some occasions, the American bombers were assailed by the combined strength of both Hornet Wings, classic head-on attacks being pressed home, causing alarm to B-29 crews. The latter part of month was confined to air-to-air firing practice. The T.3 was in regular use providing dual checks for new pilots.

On 2 May, most activity was centred on air-to-air and air-to-ground firing. Air-to-air firing was directed at towed gliders. On the 19th, PX302 arrived from No.10 M.U.

In mid-June, several pilots were given simulated I/F using the station Oxford BG594. On the 20th, the squadron flew to Linton-on-Ouse on deployment in preparation for Exercise *Foil*. Radar installations became the main object of the initial wave of attacks on the 23rd. The first intruder attacks were made on the airfield at Horsham St. Faith.

Flt.Lt. Robinson and P.I Watson were briefed for low level intruding over Norfolk. Heading towards the East coast in thick cloud which extended down to near sea level, they began letting down slowly, breaking

through cloud at 200 feet. At this point they only narrowly avoided a USAF B-29 emerging from the overcast. On the 26th, low level attacks were carried out on Odiham and Horsham St.Faith, followed on the 29th by attacks on Newton airfield and Bardhill Radar Station. enjoyed the exercise, gaining valuable experience in intruder tactics. All were unanimous in agreeing that "intruding was the answer" as far as the Hornet was concerned.

One accident occurred during the first day of *Foil* when Flg.Off Haslam, No.2 to the C.O., was unlucky to strike the roof of a wooden hut whilst attacking Trimley Heath Power Station. One propeller was bent backwards under the wing, removing the undercarriage doors which in turn struck the tailplane causing further damage. Flg.Off Haslam flew back to Church Fenton on one engine, landing without incident. On the same day Flt.Lt. Robinson was compelled to feather his starboard engine after attacking the airfield at Horsham St.Faith, returning safely to Church Fenton.

Foil continued during July 2nd and 3rd, with Bardhill Radar Station, Bawdsey, Langford Grounds and Idlicote Hill as prime targets.

The first few days of July brought *Foil* to an end, much to the disappointment of squadron pilots who preferred to have carried on in their interesting role - indefinitely! On the 4th, the squadron departed from Linton to Church Fenton.

All Hornets were airborne on the 11th in a practice flypast for the A.O.C.'s inspection which was due on the following day.

Fuel consumption tests were carried out on 4 August, using several aircraft which were flown at various altitudes and power settings to ascertain the best combination for optimum fuel consumption, prior to an attempt to break the Gibraltar to London speed record.

On the 14th exercises were held with the R.O.C. On the 9th, Flg.Off Haslam made a rather heavy landing, resulting in a collapse of the landing gear. Flg.Off A.M. Andrews was posted to the squadron on 15 August.

On the 16th, Flt.Lt. T. Robinson, 41 Squadron's aerobatic exponent, was killed during rehearsals for the B.A.F.O. Air Demonstrations held at RAF Gutersloh. Flying PX363, his speciality consisted of two consecutive loops from ground level. On the day of the tragedy, cloud base was 5,000 feet and in endeavouring to avoid entering cloud base, his loop was tightened, the Hornet mushing in from the ensuing pull out. A possible cause of the accident was attributed to high g forces and temporary blacking out.

On the 23rd, Flg.Off. Andrews in PX333 was only slightly hurt during an emergency landing, his aircraft ending up half-submerged on a bank of the River Ouse at Acaster Malbis near York. Moments before the accident, Flg.Off Andrews had been engaged in single-engine flying, only to be forced into an unscheduled landing on a disused airfield. Unfortunately the airfield was covered with runway obstructions. After overshooting, the Hornet finished up careering across an adjoining field before entering the river.

Several aircraft were detached to Heligoland for live firing, making the flight from Church Fenton at low altitude. To quote one of the pilots engaged in air-to-ground firing: "anything was fair game - Great!"

Flt.Lt. Harvey became the squadron aerobatic pilot. His preferred "simple" display routine consisted of a take-off with flaps set in the high lift position, followed by a steep climb to 8,000 feet. Meanwhile, another Hornet provided spectators with a temporary distraction before Harvey entered a dive to over 450 m.p.h., feathering both engines on his way down. After pulling out of the dive at near ground level, the Hornet was climbed up for a loop to 4,000 feet, continued down again to ground level and flown parallel to the runway. The Hornet was put into a 180 degree turn and flown to a position directly adjacent to the main spectators' enclosure. Both engines were then successively unfeathered. By this time airspeed had decayed to about 180 m.p.h., although during the unpowered flight both propeller levers had been carefully pre-set in unfeather position and throttles set to start. After the previous silent approach, the spectators were clearly impressed by the consequent crackle and roar of both Merlins when they were re-started. His display routine was varied according to the location and audience, which usually included single-engine aerobatics.

September 1st to 5th was devoted to formation flying, cine-camera exercises and air-to-ground firing. A succession of aircraft movements included: 10th, PX357

flown down to Northolt, returning to Church Fenton; 12th, PX298 ferried to D.H. Propeller Division, Leavesden; 20th, PX300 arrived from 10 MU.

During the 25th and 26th, No.41 were actively engaged in Operation *Bulldog*, carrying out four-hour-long, low level sorties to Hope Cove, S.Devon, Beaulieu and airfields at Waddington and West Malling. PX314 returned early to be classed unserviceable on arrival at Church Fenton. On the 26th, *Bulldog* continued with flights of three hours duration.

Although the exercise had failed to produce the amount of flying expected, nevertheless valuable experience had been gained when operating under instrument flying conditions. Total Hornet monthly flying times amounted to 166.20 hours.

F.3 PX395 was added to squadron strength during October. Generally, it was a quiet month, apart from some air-to-ground firing.

Before departing from 41 Squadron, the C.O., Sqn.Ldr. Moon, flew on a routine Middle East navigation exercise, in company with Flg.Off. Hindle and Capt. Rhodarmer U.S.A.F. This long distance training exercise included the usual stops at Istres, Castel Benito and El Adem, with Fayid as the final destination.

In November, Sqn.Ldr. J. Wallace DSO, DFC took over command of the squadron. On the 8th, low-level cross-country flights were made over Scotland. During the 14th, the squadron deployed to Acklington for A.P.C. which lasted until the 29th and involved periods for lectures on sighting and weapon firing theory, followed by examinations. PX314 arrived on the 19th from No.10 M.U.

1950

Flying was not resumed until 6 January following Christmas leave, after which normal squadron exercises took place, mainly formation flying until the 12th, when together with the rest of the Wing, the squadron took part in Exercise *New Year*. In spite of extremely poor weather with visibility sometimes as low as 800 yards, all the targets were attacked as briefed. Continental cross-country flights resumed on 16 January. Flt.Lts. Harvey and Beasley completed the first, although it was originally intended to carry on with others on the following days. Bad weather over the Continent prevented further attempts. Following some sign of an improvement, two sections of Hornets set off, Flg.Off Haslam and P.II Watson being forced to return after an hour due to technical problems. P.I Williams and P.II George, however, successfully completed the exercise.

During a limited number of single-engine landings, Flt.Lt. Harvey was compelled to land at Linton with one engine feathered due to inlet valve failure. Three new pilots were given dual in the Mosquito, all eventually soloing on the Hornet; all were subsequently engaged on routine familiarisation exercises.

Exercise *Pancake* commenced on 21 February. After a protracted lull due to bad weather, Exercise *12 Bore*

PX333 skids into the River Ouse at Acaster Malbis on 23 August 1949 (photo courtesy Mrs. J. Williams)

was begun on 20th/21st March when the squadron was detached to Horsham St.Faith. A week later, firing practice was carried out at APC Acklington, ending on April 14th.

The squadron participated in Exercise *Stardust* on 30 April, which was mainly to consist of low-level cross-country formation flights.

June's activities were mostly formation flying practice in preparation for the forthcoming Farnborough Air Display. During July, 41 Squadron was engaged in formation flypasts as part of the Church Fenton Hornet Wing.

During August, the squadron detached to APC Sylt for live firing practice. In September, top priority was given to practise for the Wing formation flypasts at several R.A.F. stations which were holding annual Battle of Britain Open Days.

During October Pilot II George was posted to 33 Squadron, Butterworth, flying Tempest F.2s before another lengthy spell on Hornets, ending his service with nearly 1,000 hours on type.

Exercise *Emperor* commenced on the 7th when several Hornets operated in the high-level bomber role, attacking targets in East Anglia and the Midlands. One one day, attacks were being made on naval vessels when Flt.Lt. Gilchrist's Hornet struck a ship's mast. *Emperor* accounted for twenty-three sorties and all target, mainly bomber airfields, were located.

In December, low-level navigation exercises were flown to both France and Germany without incident apart from Flg.Off. Dick's Hornet, which suffered a bird strike and was forced to make a landing at a B.A.F.O. base.

1951

On 8 January, an accident occurred when Flt.Lt. Gilchrist in PX308 had completed a high level cine exercise and commenced a GCA let down. Although warned of his low position on the glide path, the approach was continued with some reference made over the radio to a presence of petrol fumes inside the cockpit. Unfortunately, the Hornet struck a light pole situated one mile from end of the runway, crashed and burst into flames on impact, Flt.Lt. Gilchrist suffering injuries. During the month No.41 Squadron commenced re-equipping with Meteor F.4s, converting on squadron via the T.7

Hornets known with 41 Squadron:

Hornet F.1:

PX232 EB-X;	PX242 EB-X;	PX244 EB-T;
PX252 EB-H, -Z;	PX277 EB-W;	PX278 EB- ;
PX282 EB- .		

Hornet F.3:

PX289 EB-W;	PX294 EB-E;	PX298 EB-V;
PX300 EB-Y, -Z;	PX302 EB-D;	PX307 EB-X;
PX308 EB-B;	PX311 EB-C;	PX314 EB-C, -F;
PX330 EB-X, -Y;	PX350 EB-Z;	PX357 EB-X;
PX363 EB-B, -Y;	PX366 EB-A, -Z;	PX395 EB-W, -X;
PX397 EB-V.		

Commanding Officers:

Sqn.Ldr. W. Hoy DFC, Sqn.Ldr. H.H. Moon, Sqn.Ldr. J. Wallace DSO, DFC.

Squadron Pilots:

Officers:

Flg.Off. A.M. Andrew, Plt.Off. W.H.A. Dick, Flt.Lt. J.M. Gilchrist, Flg. Off. F.K. Hindle, Flt.Lt. R.A. Harvey, Flg.Off R.L. Maslen, Flt.Lt. T. Robinson, Flg.Off. W.A. Schofield.

N.C.O.s:

Pilot II E.V. George, Pilot II F. Dowson, Pilot II Jones, Pilot II W. Watson, Pilot I K. Williams, Pilot I Wright.

Pilot I Moxon's Hornet after flying into trees while intruding over Stradishall, October 1950

Hornet F.3s PX298 EB-V and PX311 EB-C of No.41 Squadron with a Sea Hornet F.20 at Culdrose, December 1948

PX351 and PX344 of No.64 Squadron flown by Pilot I J. Norman and Pilot I J. Hartley

THE LINTON HORNET WING, RAF LINTON-ON-OUSE

No.64 Squadron

1946

No.64 (F) Squadron, commanded by Sqn.Ldr J.T. Shaw DSO DFC, became first to re-equip with Hornet F.Is, exchanging its last Mustang IVs in May 1946. The squadron's first Hornet arrived at Horsham St.Faith on 16 February, flown over from Shawbury by Wg.Cdr. P.M.G.Bond and watched with some interest by pilots and groundcrew. The new fighter was demonstrated at Horsham St.Faith on 20/21 February by Wg.Cdr. Bond and Pat Fillingham, the de Havilland production test pilot. PX283 was air-tested on 8 March after spending a fortnight of maintenance and two more F.Is arrived from Shawbury on the same day.

Despite further deliveries, serviceability remained low and prevented further flying. Three surplus Mustangs were flown to Llandow. A planned sortie on 4 April by four aircraft resulted in one becoming unserviceable with a faulty radiator flap. All Hornets were grounded for a time for essential modifications to wing radiators. Pilots were taken into the hangars for instruction on servicing and daily inspections.

In a bid to improve matters, the station Oxford flew twice to Hatfield to pick up urgently needed spares. On 13-16 May, five aircraft were collected from Shawbury, although Flg.Off. Scott was compelled to land at Kemble with a lose canopy which was quickly rectified by groundcrew.

Flt.Lt. W. Harbison was one of the first pilots to convert to the Hornet; he was formerly with 118 Squadron, flying Spitfire IXs and Mustang IIIs. Posted to 64 Squadron, he flew Mustang IVs. Following a mandatory dual check on the Mosquito T.III, he made his first Hornet solo on 22 May. As Flight Commander, he soon mastered the Mosquito, ultimately becoming responsible for providing dual check flights for pilots lacking experience on twins.

His initial impressions of the Hornet were of its delightful handling and its outstanding visibility from the cockpit, marred only by restrictions due to the close proximity of its two Merlins. He recounts coaxing Hornets to 38,000 feet. In mock combats against Meteor F.IIIs and Vampire F.Is, he considered that the Hornets could more than hold their own. Much to his dismay he was posted to No.263 Squadron "loath to give up flying Hornets".

Within a few months of re-equipping, there were two fatal accidents, the first occurring on 20 March, resulting from low flying. PX283 colliding with trees one mile N.N.E. of Wroxham, Norfolk, Flg. Off. Hardie, a Mosquito instructor, being killed. A second accident involved PX253 which crashed on 7 May, ½ mile N.E. of High Green, Norfolk, just 25 minutes after taking off. The port engine and leading edge detached, giving Plt.Off Baugh no opportunity to bale out. Investigations into the crash revealed the cause as faulty welding on the port engine bearers.

After intensive efforts by the ground staff, two

sections of three aircraft were available for formation flying. On 8 June, ten aircraft were on strength for a flypast over London, led by Flt.Lt. MacKilligan. Flying was severely restricted by a serious shortage of maintenance crews, most of whom were in the process of being posted or due for demobilisation.

Squadron pilots were eager to take advantage of the Hornet's prowess in single-engine, or even "dead stick", aerobatics. One eye witness recalls seeing three Hornets in "Vic" diving over Horsham St. Faith from 10,000 feet, the leader of the formation having both engines feathered and each wingman flying on one apiece, before they climbed up for a loop.

On 8 July, a Group exercise took place in which Hornets acted as targets for Meteor F.IIIs which were controlled by G.C.I. (Ground Controlled Interception) followed by another on the 12th at 12,000 feet, resulting in two interceptions by Meteors. Modification checks were completed in time for the C.O. and Flt.Lt. Harbison to carry out a successful interception of Spitfire LF.XVIs from No.19 Squadron. Hornets were grounded again on the 24th to ensure higher standards of maintenance. This resulted in flying hours being significantly affected despite frantic efforts to render all aircraft airworthy. Flying in August included a successful well-timed flypast by nine aircraft over the American Embassy.

In 1946 Horsham St.Faith became the sole R.A.F. Fighter Command Station to open its doors to the public. No.64 Squadron participated in flying displays, with Hornet flypasts, firstly with one engine feathered followed by a quieter pass by Sqn.Ldr P.M. Gardiner - both engines feathered!

A nucleus of squadron pilots was formed by the arrival of several former World War Two N.C.O. pilots, mainly of Warrant Officer rank. W/O K. Williams arrived at 64 Squadron to discover news of an imminent move to Linton-on-Ouse, being soon whisked Northwards on 7 August aboard the Station Flight Oxford. After an hour's check on the Mosquito T.III, he soloed Hornet "J". Ken had a relatively short stay with 64 Squadron, being soon posted to a Ferry Training Unit, sampling the equally potent Tempest VI. Eventually Ken returned to his "beloved Hornets" during 1948, posted to No. 41(F) Squadron, Church Fenton, flying Hornets until the arrival of Meteor F.4s. The initial flight to Linton-on-Ouse was abandoned due to bad weather which forced the squadron to divert to Manby.

Ten aircraft were scheduled to appear in the Battle of Britain flypast over London. One returned to Linton with electrical problems, another dropped out of formation with a "cooked" Merlin due to a serious glycol leak - and then there were eight! By a coincidence, news was received on 19 September to the effect that the squadron strength for home-based squadrons was to be cut to eight aircraft and ten pilots.

Flying during October consisted mainly of Exercise *Foolem III* which was successfully completed without any interceptions by defending Meteors. On the 4th, three Hornets were flown to Wittering and handed over to 19

Squadron, all pilots being forced to return by rail, a journey that took five hours. Another *Foolem* exercise was carried out in spite of a lack of serviceable aircraft, two Hornets being loaned from 65 Squadron. The Silver section leader failed to get airborne after an engine cut on take-off.

Maintenance crews worked long hours on 9 December in an attempt to provide six aircraft for the next day's exercise although the C.O.'s aircraft returned with an over-revving engine. A subsequent exercise to Cap de Barfleur with five aircraft led by the C.O. was interrupted by bad weather, one aircraft diverting to Topcliffe.

1947

Pilot II Norman joined 64 Squadron in January to find Linton-on-Ouse snowbound in that infamous winter of 1947. A former 6 Squadron pilot, he flew Hurricanes and Spitfires in Cyprus and Palestine. A check-out on T.III TV984 was followed by his first Hornet solo. On the 17th, Flt.Lt. Whitehead was compelled to return from a cross-country exercise after losing his cockpit hood. Four aircraft were detached to a temporary base at Tangmere for a flypast over H.M.S. *Vanguard*, eventually cancelled due to a heavy snowfall which stranded pilots for a week. Industrial clag combined with fog had reduced visibility to such an extent that it became almost impossible to observe opposite sides of the airfield. These conditions persisted until early May, with flying activity somewhat restricted.

Operations in April included Operation *Busride*. Station Commander W/Cdr. H.J. Maguire DSO and squadron pilots were kept active testing their aircraft. G/Capt. G.M. Buxton OBE arrived from West Raynham to air test his personal aircraft. On the 11th, six Hornets set course for Manston, the first leg of a long distance navigation exercise to Fayid. Pilots engaged in this exercise included G/Capt. Buxton, W/Cdr. Maguire, Sqn.Ldr J.T. Shaw DSO DFC, Flt.Lts Woodcock, Whitehead and Miller. The exercise was considered to have been a success, a forerunner of more similar long range navigational exercises.

A Group Exercise was held, Flt.Lts. Woodcock and Whitehead flying down to RAF Coltishall to participate in Operation *Web Foot* in co-operation with four Hornets from 19 Squadron. During deployment, a coastal convoy was pinpointed, top cover provided by two Hornets and attacks made by two pairs of Hornets. Several Meteors made attempts at interception.

Flying practice continued, strenuous attempts being made to convert more pilots to the Hornet, W/O A.M. McKelvie was given periods of dual in the Servicing Flight Mosquito, followed by his first Hornet solo. F/Sgts. A.J.Norman and D. Young also underwent dual in the T.III. Most flying during the month was accounted for by Mosquito dual and air tests. W/Os Hook and McKelvie flew training sorties.

In May, Flt. Lt. Woodcock and Pilot II Hook took

Hornet F.I PX284 at Horsham St. Faith with No.64 Squadron in 1946

part in Operation *Web Foot II* on the 13th in conjunction with Hornets from No.19 Squadron. Both pilots carried out a strike, identifying a ship without being intercepted. C.O. Sqn.Ldr Shaw, with Flt.Lt. Mackilligin as No.2, set off for Operation *Web Foot III*, but Shaw was forced to return early due to engine trouble.

W/O Jim Hartley, a former Spitfire pilot, Desert Air Force, commenced Hornet conversion on 2 May. Following two periods of dual on T.III TV984, his first solo occurred on 7 May. Jim Hartley's first visual encounter of a Hornet was in the Summer of 1946 during his service with 43(F) Squadron, Zeltweg, Austria. A solitary aircraft appeared in the circuit, landing for refuelling and topping up with a quantity of "beverages". After taking off, the unknown Hornet pilot treated the base to an impromptu aerobatic display, clearly impressing several former ex-*Luftwaffe* fighter pilots working in various offices. The Hornet became their main topic of conversation for days afterwards, some pilots really convinced it was a carbon copy of the ill-famed Me 410!

Jim Hartley's impressions of his first Hornet flight were "just another single-engine first solo". After flying Spitfires, Jim Hartley considered the Hornet "as easy and beautiful an aircraft as the Spitfire, seeming a natural progression". Compared with the constant weaving during taxying always associated with Spitfires, forward view from the Hornet was a real bonus.

Towards the end of June, cross-country flights were undertaken, one flight taking in Douglas, Isle of Man, Edinburgh and Flamborough Head before a return to Linton. The squadron were briefed for an exercise with the Fleet. The Squadron Briefing Officer added a final dry comment, "Don't fly too near the ships or you risk being fired at!" During this fleet exercise, 64 Squadron deployed to Coltishall, the average flying time of sorties amounting to 2½ hours.

During July, Sqn.Ldr A.G. Page DSO DFC, a former Battle of Britain pilot, took over command of the squadron. On occasions he led the squadron for the sole purpose of encouraging individual aerobatics; these efforts were viewed from a safe distance. After carrying out a series of barrel rolls and loops, he called on each pilot in turn to repeat his manoeuvres.

In September, 64 Squadron engaged in formation practice for the forthcoming Battle of Britain Flypast over Buckingham Palace. On the day visibility deteriorated to such an extent that flares had to be lit along the route, extending from the Ford plant at Dagenham.

On the 15th, the Station Commander, G/Capt. A.C.P. Carver, accompanied by Flt.Lt. H.Peebles, flew to Gibraltar, ostensibly to make an attempt on the speed record for this particular route, but also to participate in the Battle of Britain display. Weather conditions on the return flight were more favourable, G/Capt. Carver attaining a speed of 435.82 m.p.h. which, subject to confirmation, established a record.

The fourth week witnessed the commencement of Exercise *Bulldog*, Nos. 19, 41, 64 and 65 Squadrons operating from Linton-on-Ouse. Heavy mist occurred on most days, greatly hampering operations. On Monday, the last day of the exercise, Linton itself was subjected to attacks by formations of Harvards and Prentices flying from various flying training schools.

A change-over from the 50-hour to 100-hour cycle of inspections took place during the month.

In October, squadron pilots attended No.3 Fighter Command Instrument Rating Course, using Harvards with instruction by No.41 Squadron. In the fourth week, eight Hornets set off from Linton at 14.10 bound for Manston, arriving at 15.05, prior to flying on a navigational exercise to the Middle East. It was considered prudent for the Hornets to operate in four pairs to avoid any additional strain posed by close formation flying over long distances. Pilots for the pairs were: No.1: Sqn.Ldr Page, C.O. and Flg.Off. Cowood; No.2: W/Cdr. Nel (Boss of Linton Wing) and Plt.Off. Turner; No.3: Flt.Lt. Glaser and W/O Hartley; No.4: W/O McKelvie and W/O Hook.

Some last minute panic ensued on discovering that two pilots had forgotten to bring along their current vaccination "chits". After some frantic telephone calls between Linton and Church Fenton, matters were soon resolved. The first leg was to Istres, with Lyon/Bron chosen as a diversion airfield. After clearing Customs, the C.O.'s aircraft was found to have a compass fault, quickly rectified by ground staff. PX246 developed an oil leak, shrugged off in order to keep to E.T.A. Climbing to 10,000 feet, all Hornets set off as planned. Passing over Beachy Head, this height was maintained throughout the first leg. Considerable cloud cover was encountered en route; Bourges was pinpointed at 09.45, using the pressure pattern navigation method. Arrival at Istres commenced at 10.50 hrs, aircraft finishing up 25 miles west of their destination. The first pair were soon preparing to take-off after a quick turn round. Pair No.3 took off but returned with brake problems on SH-J. W/O McKelvie became concerned with the oil leak, found to be issuing from a collector box.

Pair No.4 took off at 11.40, arriving at Elmas, Sardinia, at 13.15 after meeting extensive cloud cover. Flg. Off. Cowood's Hornet was found to have a split radiator, necessitating a replacement being flown out from England. Following advice from Malta radio, an alternative route was chosen to Bizerte and Sfax to avoid bad weather. After setting course for Bizerte, the North African coast was sighted after fifteen minutes. Reaching Sfax, course was altered, ruling out any possibility of drifting out over the Mediterranean. On landing at Castel Benito, the oil leak on W/O McKelvie's Hornet had worsened, the cause being traced to a fractured bolt in the constant speed unit. W/O Hook volunteered to stay with McKelvie during their enforced stay at Castel Benito.

The problem could only be solved by having a replacement flown out from England. Meantime W/Cdr. Nel, Sqn.Ldr Page and Plt. Off. Turner passed through on their way back to Linton, all visibly suffering from lack of sleep and the effects of intense heat.

Boredom was relieved temporarily, by the arrival of six Lincolns returning from a goodwill visit to Turkey. A signal from Flg. Off. Cowood, still marooned at Elmas, made enquiries about the well-being of the castaways. A visiting Halifax, RT893, was grounded, also suffering from a faulty C.S.U.

On 2 November, W/Os Hook and McKelvie were making desperate attempts to combat the extreme heat and boredom. Sixteen Swedish SAAB B-17s arrived on a delivery flight to the Ethiopian Air Force. On 12 November, a Mosquito from No.29 Squadron arrived with the replacement C.S.U. bolt. After more irritating delays, McKelvie's Hornet was ready to depart, only to develop an R/T fault.

During later ground running, engine temperatures rose to danger level and needed a full hour to cool off. At 2.15 p.m. both Hornets took off for Elmas. Yet further snags arose on reaching Istres; McKelvie's starboard radiator flap stuck open, causing irritating trim problems. The faulty R/T had been caused by accumulated wax deposits, all cleaned off with good results.

To further complicate matters, a cold front was causing concern with a forecast of poor conditions along the Southern coast of England. Leaving Istres, both Hornets climbed to 12,500 feet, passing through scattered snowclouds to arrive at Manston just before noon. Here they were to encounter the attention of an over-zealous Customs official. On returning to Linton, both pilots were immediately sent on leave for two days.

Two Hornets were detached to Stradishall for fighter affiliation with Lancasters of 35 Squadron, accompanied by four Hornets from 19 Squadron. Contact was made with the bombers around mid-day at 5,000 feet. During mock attacks, PX284 collided with TW647, crewed by 115 Squadron.

Two Hornets intercepted B-29s at 12,000 feet without being observed by the bomber crews, although some pilots experienced low boost pressures.

During December, there was little flying apart from several periods devoted to formation flying and aerobatics. Three aircraft required engine changes. On the 22nd, PX274 crashed after striking high ground near Bacup, Lancs, while descending through cloud.

1948

In January, Flt.Lt. Peebles and P.II Hartley were engaged on bomber interception exercises, operating alongside Hornets of the Church Fenton Wing against Lincolns and Lancasters of Bomber Command. This exercise was considered a success, attacks being made from the three-quarter rear position, closing to 200 yards. Gunsights had been fitted to some aircraft; others were grounded for a fortnight due to lack of spares.

Next month the accent was on cine-camera exercises, formation flying, instrument flying and single-engine procedure. Lone Hornets roamed around the country on cross-country flights, a typical route being a round flight to Margate via the Isle of Wight.

On 7 March, all pilots were hard at work on annual A.P.C. at Acklington on air-to-air cine-camera exercises until the end of the month. Live ammunition was also fired. In April air-to-air live firing continued for a week, followed by bomber co-operation with Lincolns and Lancasters. W/O Hartley went aloft in Lincoln KC-G, acting as an observer. The final part of month was also devoted to air-to-air firing. A batch of new F.3s arrived, including PX344, PX393 and PX296. Surplus F.1s were

British-based Hornet F.3s

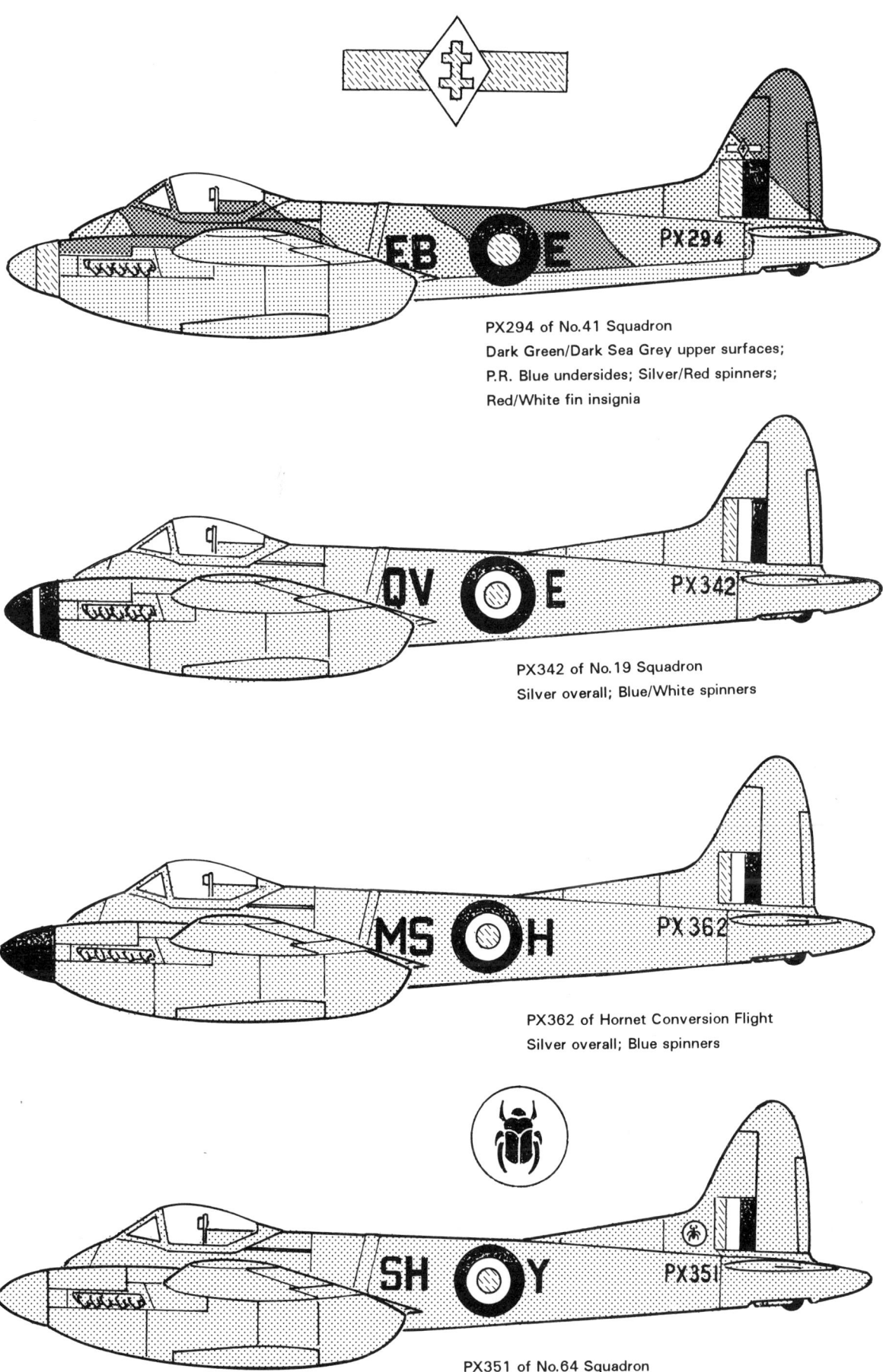

PX294 of No.41 Squadron
Dark Green/Dark Sea Grey upper surfaces;
P.R. Blue undersides; Silver/Red spinners;
Red/White fin insignia

PX342 of No.19 Squadron
Silver overall; Blue/White spinners

PX362 of Hornet Conversion Flight
Silver overall; Blue spinners

PX351 of No.64 Squadron
Silver overall; squadron badge on white disc

No.65 Squadron's P.IIs Hook and Sherborn return from a Battle of Britain display

Hornet F.3 PX362 YT-L of No.65 Squadron (via R.C. Sturtivant)

PX393 SH-W of No.64 Squadron

ferried to Shawbury.

Some problems arose with the Mk.IV Gyro Gunsight due to its low position on the instrument panel. There was feverish activity inside the hangars to provide aircraft for the proposed visit to Sweden.

Sqn.Ldr Roberts AFC took over command of the squadron. Exercise *Dawn* commenced on 13 May when Hornets made two separate attacks on Royal Navy destroyers in the North Sea. *Dawn* was the largest combined exercise since 1939, involving new techniques in the art of shadowing opposing naval forces. Lincolns of Bomber Command, escorted by Hornets of 12 Group, carried out attacks on the Fleet off the Northern and Eastern coasts of Scotland. Attacks were also carried out on naval forces off the Norwegian coast.

Some pilots commenced 12 Group Instrument Rating Course, operated by 41 Squadron at Church Fenton with Oxfords used as instrument flying trainers. Sqn.Ldr Hoy was C.O. and Chief flying Instructor. Pilot I Hartley and other pilots succeeded in gaining their Green Card instrument ratings.

F.3 PX345 was added to squadron strength. An F.1, QV-W of 19 Squadron, was given a short air test after maintenance checks.

On the 11th, the squadron flew out over the North Sea to provide an escort for a formation of Swedish Air Force Mustangs on a goodwill visit. The Swedish pilots were also escorted on the 14th during their return flight. Major Blair, a U.S.A.F. exchange pilot, arrived on the squadron, and was soon airborne for a short ten-minute local flight in Oxford PG943. Major Blair was given an

instrument flying check in Mosquito T.3 VT609 by Pilot II Norman whilst en route to West Raynham. On the 24th, the squadron commenced what were to be regular interceptions and mock attacks on U.S.A.F. B-29s which were operating at 30,000 feet.

Air Marshal Sir Basil Embrey, newly-appointed A.O.C. Fighter Command, lost little time in deciding that high-level interception and low-level intruder roles were incompatible. All training was to be concentrated on dawn to dusk low-level (minimum height fifty feet) cross-country flying over the U.K. and the Continent. It was generally agreed that the Hornet's manoeuvrability at altitude was somewhat sluggish, together with its slow overtaking speed when intercepting B-29s.

On 25 July, PX396, flown by Flt.Lt. Peebles commenced a single-engine approach after losing throttle control on the starboard engine. The landing was made 700 feet down the runway at high speed and without flaps fully lowered. Following a high speed touch down, the Hornet left the airfield, overturning after entering a cornfield. The week of the 16th-23rd found the squadron engaged in air-sea firing off Bridlington, followed on the 20th and 21st by air-to-sea firing at the Paston gunnery range. Exercises were held with the R.O.C., involving two sorties.

In September, top priority was given to Exercise *Dagger* when the squadron joined forces with 65 Squadron, taking part as the "enemy". The base was shared with Spitfire XIVs and XVIs of Nos. 609 and 612 Squadrons, Royal Auxiliary Air Force, representing part of the defence system.

Dagger commenced early on the 3rd, lasting until the 5th with Hornets operated in a loose "Finger Four" formation at 100/150 feet, as Low Level Day Intruders. After flying out to the Continent, they returned to make attacks on Finningley which was defended by Spitfires of the R. Aux. A.F. During these exercises, Hornets were painted with orange distemper bands around the rear fuselages and fins for identification purposes. At the end of the exercise, the squadron had flown a total of fifty- five hours, most flights lasting three hours and involved lengthy sea crossings. During intruding over "enemy" airfields, many jet aircraft were classed as written off on the ground. Hornets were now considered ideally suited for a day intruder role. Despite periods of poor visibility, all sorties were carried out. Personnel at Linton-on-Ouse put in some very hard work, achieving good results during the exercise. *Dagger* was the first full-scale R.A.F. exercise held since the war and chiefly involved Bomber, Fighter and Reserve Commands. Linton itself was subjected to two low-level attacks by Hornets, when due to their high speed no adequate warning had been received. By the time the alarm had been given, all the Hornets were out of sight.

At de-briefing, pilots voiced their initial impressions as follows: Control and Reporting systems were over-congested and the principles of close control were subordinated by a panic use of as many fighters as possible against large-scale "enemy" raids.

Except on rare occasions when standing patrols succeeded in intercepting intruding Hornets, most defending pilots found the sudden arrival of intruders came without any prior warning.

On the 15th the squadron was busy with practice for the annual Battle of Britain Flypast which took place on the 18th. On the last day of month, practice interceptions were made on Lincolns of Bomber Command.

In October, routine B-29 interceptions continued over several weeks, the squadron making contact with the incoming B-29s at 30,000 feet, whose air gunners found the nimble Hornets difficult to track compared with Meteors. On the 24th, 64 Squadron was engaged on Operation *Hedgehog*, accounting for three-hour flights. When not engaged in B-29 interceptions, pilots were often flown as passengers in the Superfortresses to observe results first hand.

On 3 November, the squadron flew up to Dyce for exercises with Spitfire XIVs of No.612 (County of Aberdeen) Squadron, Royal Auxiliary Air Force. Soon after arriving at Dyce, 64 Squadron flew in formation over Aberdeen, prior to co-operation exercises using cine-cameras during practice interceptions and mock combats. On the 6th another formation flypast was made over Aberdeen before departing from Dyce on the 7th for a low-level cross-country flight to Turnhouse. Soon after returning to Linton, 64 Squadron pilots received many boxes of kippers, courtesy of 612 Squadron, in addition to other mementos given during their stay at Dyce.

Pilot III C.N.C. Mitchell joined 64 Squadron in December, having completed No.13 Hornet Conversion Course at 226 O.C.U. Bentwaters during the previous month. Waiting for a serviceable Hornet, he completed a course on the Meteor F.3. His conversion to the Hornet entailed almost fifteen hours of instruction on Oxfords and five on Harvards. Hornet F.1, PX238, was used for a first solo. On 4 December he flew F.3 PX385 to 30,000 feet on a sector reconnaissance lasting two hours.

All aircraft were airborne on 3 December for B-29 interceptions, a particularly large target of twenty-eight bombers. Between 10 and 17 December, the squadron made some B-29 interceptions; P.III Mitchell's Hornet developing hydraulic trouble. During Operation *Sunrise*, P.II Norman acted as a reserve pilot for this exercise with the Fleet Air Arm. Visiting R.A.F. pilots were quite impressed by the relative severity of carrier-type landings, all carried out with precision by 801 Squadron Sea Hornet pilots.

1949

On 6 January, fighter affiliation exercises were carried out with Lancasters, Pilot II Mitchell being forced to return early due to a suspect port engine. In the afternoon, Pilot II Hartley air tested PX216, the first PR.2 prototype, after maintenance checks. PX216 was the personal mount of W/Cdr."Tiny" T. Nel, Boss of the Linton Hornet Wing.

Individual aircraft were active on high and low level cross-country flights lasting several hours. Monthly flying totals averaged twenty hours.

In the second week of February, the squadron was fully occupied with air-to-ground firing and formation practice. Resident Oxford NM296 was in regular use as a trainer for refresher instrument flying training. On the 18th, the squadron was engaged in "Ack-Ack" co-operation with the Army. During the 24th, B-29s were intercepted, with Hornets flying on two-hour sorties. Pilot II Mitchell and his wingman set off on the 28th for a cross-country flight at 2,000 feet covering a route to Linton-Bangor-Barnstaple-Penzance-Norwich-Linton.

During March 6th, 12th and 13th, Operation *Forth/Clyde* involved the squadron in sorties to Bishopbriggs and Abbotsinch when P.II Hartley with his No.2 flew under the Forth Bridge, taking cine-film in the process. On his return he faced a cool reception, explaining in his defence that briefing had clearly stipulated not flying above fifty feet.

Meanwhile some pilots attended No.7 Instrument Flying Course at Tangmere which lasted from 7th-17th March. Oxfords were in use for instrument flying instruction and included LB530, LW988, LX737, PF943 and RR340.

A.P.C. at Acklington commenced on 27 April and lasted until 13 May, involving air-to-air and air-to-ground firing plus some exercises with the R.O.C. The average

Cadets of Flygvapnet, the Royal Swedish Air Force, manhandle PX355 SH-Z at Uppsala in May 1948 while loaned to 65 Squadron for a goodwill visit

time of firing sorties amounted to thirty minutes, with some live firing directed at towed gliders or drogues. After taking-off from Acklington, Pilot II Hartley with P.IV Martin-Jones as Number Two, headed toward some towed gliders (at £400 per copy), three being quickly despatched by Hartley, without Martin-Jones having fired one round. During air-to-ground firing it was possible for pilots to achieve high marks, due to firing short bursts and exercising some degree of patience by extra firing passes. In common with other fighters of that period, the Hornet's cockpit became polluted by cordite fumes during live firing with odours seeping into pilots' clothing.

Exercise *Foil* commenced on Saturday 25 June and was to continue until the last day of month. The squadron carried out no fewer than forty low level strikes against airfields, radar stations and pinpoints on bombing ranges. Hornets were operated in pairs and flown to within forty miles of the Dutch coast before turning around to head toward targets underneath radar cover. Five Hornets were eventually judged as lost, these running into standing air patrols, although no aircraft were actually intercepted before reaching their targets. 64 Squadron's tally included ten aircraft destroyed and thirteen damaged, apart from numerous hits on buildings, radar sites, control towers and suspected casualties among ground personnel.

Objectives for the squadron on the first days of Operation *Foil* included Neatishead, Liverpool, West Malling and Swingate Radar. Average flying time for each sortie amounted to about two hours. During the middle phase, attacks were carried out on Coltishall and Horsham St.Faith, where a section of Hornets bounced U.S.A.F. F-80 Shooting Stars in the process of taking-off without being intercepted. During the final three days, low-level attacks were continued on targets which included Sandwich and the Isle of Wight. On the final day, 64 Squadron flew a further eighteen sorties against airfields and other targets, their score increasing by a further seven aircraft destroyed plus eight damaged, again for no loss. This brought the exercise to a satisfactory conclusion, final tally amounting to seventeen aircraft destroyed plus twenty-one judged as seriously damaged. Among the objectives for the final phase were Rufford and Hopton. At West Malling, 64 Squadron Hornets found resident Meteors as "sitting ducks"! A total of 64 sorties were flown amounting to almost 150 hours.

Foil had included aircraft from Bomber, Fighter, Flying Training and Reserve Commands. Meteors of 56 Squadron, Thorney Island, were assigned to 12 Group, Fighter Command. Other units which participated were US and Dutch Air Force units, A.A. Command and the R.O.C. On 30 June, No.56 Squadron departed for

Thorney Island, Hornets of 19 and 41 Squadrons returning to Church Fenton on the 3rd, following their temporary deployment at Linton-on-Ouse.

After the recent hectic activity, 64 Squadron pilots were to be fully occupied with practice for the A.O.C.'s flypast.

On 8 August, P.II Hartley was briefed for a Continental cross-country flight and selected leader to an unknown visitor who was his Number Two. Setting off at fifty feet, course was set for the Humber Estuary. After crossing the coast they met a blanket of sea mist, Hartley becoming uncomfortably aware of ships' masts passing close beneath his wings and glancing out sideways he discovered that his unknown companion had wisely pulled up. Easing up to 150 feet above the mist layer, Hartley spotted his Number Two flying a few feet in front. After mist had cleared, formation was rejoined in loose line abreast as stipulated at 50 feet. Complete radio silence was maintained throughout the flight, standard procedure during intruder missions. After nearly four hours, a rather tired and sweaty P.II emerged from his cockpit to discover the identity of his mystery companion. It was none other than W/Cdr. Bob Braham (Triple DSO & DFC), former war-time Mosquito night fighter ace. The Wing Commander soon congratulated his leader, informing the C.O. how much he had enjoyed the trip, especially since he was now flying a desk at the Air Ministry.

The squadron made flypasts over Birmingham and RAF Padgate on the 22nd and 30th.

In September a flypast was made over Marham. Rehearsals on the 17th for the Battle of Britain display included a low-level aerobatic display by Pilot II Mitchell, who participated in the glider attack and flypast. Setting off in "Finger Four" formation, 64 Squadron Hornets were active on the 25th and 26th when they took part in Exercise *Bulldog*, attacking targets at Trimley Heath, Knettishall, Coningsby, Hemswell, Wartling, Wittering, Marham, Manby, Horsham St.Faith and Sopley. These sorties accounted for individual flights ranging between two to three-and-a- half hours.

Sorties were made throughout October for air-to-ground and air-to-sea firing. No.64 Squadron flew a "Balbo" over to Acklington on 15 November, venue for the regular A.P.C. which commenced on the 21st, continuing until December 14th. The squadron achieved an average of two firing sorties each day, with the first week taken up exclusively with air-to-air firing. Air-to-ground was to take preference towards the end of camp. The squadron flew back to Linton-on-Ouse - "Balbo" style.

1950

The 12th of January proved to be a tragic day for the squadron. Four Hornets were returning from a practice formation intruder sortie, landing in consecutive pairs. Number 3, PX351, flown by P.IV Hampton, a newly converted pilot, turned to port in an attempt to line up

with the runway. Power was reduced when the aircraft stalled, dropping a port wing before cart-wheeling and disintegrating. A further possible cause of the accident was attributed to the Hornet's starboard wing being uplifted by the leader's prop wash.

Hornets set off on the 24th for a Continental cross-country to the famous Mohne Dam. The arrival at Linton of Meteor T.7 coded SH-P was clearly an ominous sign that the Hornet's days at Linton were coming to an end. Pilot II Norman made his final Hornet flight, setting off on a Continental cross-country exercise to the Friesian Islands-Münster-Rotterdam-Southwold-Linton. On the 27th air-to-ground firing was carried out whilst on a day's detachment at the College of Air Warfare at Manby.

Exercise *12 Bore* started on 21 March, Hornets operating at 20,000 feet. Another deployment was made to APS Acklington on the 28th for air-to-air and air-to-ground firing, lasting until 16 April. During the third week of April several practice attacks were made on two airfields, preceded by low-level cross-country flights over the designated low flying area. This practice was a prelude to Exercise *Stardust* when 64 Squadron Hornets raided several airfields situated in "alien" South-East England. Exercise *Stardust* commenced on the 30th and despite poor weather, attacks were carried out on Thorney Island and Odiham. On 1 May, bad weather on 30 April led to the exercise being extended by a further day. *Stardust* was specifically designed to test the control and reporting systems of No.11 Group. The squadron flew a total of 173 sorties during May which accounted for 188 flying hours.

Sqn.Ldr Roberts AFC left the squadron, his place being taken by Sqn.Ldr Thompson, posted up from Brize Norton. W/Cdr. Braham arrived from West Raynham to fly with the squadron and as a consequence, the squadron balance sheet for the pilots' fining system became richer by two shillings.

Accent was now placed on formation flying practice for the forthcoming display at Farnborough. It was an accepted fact that 64 Squadron was considered best in the Wing, having been allotted dual roles of providing six aircraft for a mass flypast by the Hornet Wing.

In addition, 64 Squadron provided six Hornets for co-operation with 66 Squadron for a mock low-level intruder attack and interception over the airfield. Practice for this event occupied the greater part of flying activity.

Great credit was due to ground personnel who occasionally provided 100% serviceability under difficult conditions. No further flying was carried out until the last week of the month. The whole squadron stood down to enjoy some well-earned leave.

An A.P.C. was held at Sylt and several low-level cross-country flights carried out. During A.P.C. one Hornet of a pair was incorrectly refuelled, both landing at Wunstorf in Germany. Following formalities of a Customs check at Lakenheath, both returned to Linton eight hours later.

R.O.C. exercise *Normidex*, planned to cover two

Hornet F.3 PX396 SH-O of No.64 Squadron (R.C.Sturtivant)

week-ends, turned out to be a disappointment due to bad weather, causing cancellation or part completion of most sorties.

Another write-off occurred on 2 June following a twenty-five minute air test for PX392. Flown by P.III Verrico, the Hornet was returning to Linton after a port engine failure. The approach was made without flaps and in attempting to counter an overshoot by raising the undercarriage, the Hornet was extensively damaged and duly placed on the scrap dump. The rather shaken pilot received a recommended "Rocket" from the head of the accident investigation team.

Formation night flying was carried out at the beginning of the month, much to the bewilderment of several squadron pilots. Practice "Mayday" calls introduced during flights had resulted in varying degrees of response from ground stations. On the 4th a small flying display was laid on for the benefit of the R.O.C.

Hornets were deployed again to Sylt from 10th to 31st August for armament practice, divided into four groups: air-to-air, air-to-ground, low-level bombing and firing R.P.s. As things turned out, the weather provided an almost 100% flying factor, allowing operational air-to-ground firing plus live firing against drogues towed by Tempest TT.5s, in contrast to the usual Martinets. This was to be a month devoted entirely to armament practice, assisted by a well-planned programme and exceptional serviceability.

During the detachment to Sylt, it was discovered that the number of tyre changes had considerably increased due to a high rate of landings on the rough surfaces of runways and to taxiing on pitted perimeter tracks.

Highest daily scores for R.P. firing went to Sqn.Ldr Thompson, bombing to P.III Burgham, Flt. Lts. Wylie, Gossland and Crow.; to Flt.Lt Gossland for air-to-air and air-to-ground: to Flt.Lt Crow for air-to-air.

Operations: A series of experiments were carried out during September in which speed and accuracy were the keynote, including the completion of low-level cross-country flights, with all participating aircraft required to rendezvous at a given destination. Following rendezvous, 64 Squadron flew back to Linton in formation. Some diversions were also introduced in the form of races and full combat manoeuvres, providing squadron pilots with valuable experience of low-level attacks and interceptions.

Towards the middle of the month, a series of day/night and night/day cross-country flights were practised with the object of familiarising pilots in flying round the clock.

Battle of Britain Displays included set piece displays plus individual aerobatic performances by several squadron pilots, all serving to maintain very high standards of flying and airmanship. All displays followed intensive rehearsals until a satisfactory standard was achieved.

Individual competition was intense during "Treasure Hunts", carried out in various low level areas situated in Scotland and East Anglia. Results of speed, accuracy and map reading exercises proved extremely beneficial, although they involved undoubted difficulties in accurate pin-pointing at minimum height, maximum speed and spot point navigation. The usual monthly quota of instrument flying included G.C.A.s and QGHs. A series of height and tracking exercises were made for purposes of calibration of radar equipment at Sector H.Q.

A sector exercise on the 26th was brought to a satisfactory conclusion when after landing it was discovered no Hornets had been intercepted, despite a change of role to high and medium level bombing, all within range of coastal radar stations. Complete radio silence was strictly observed once aircraft became airborne.

Captain Dietrich of the U.S.A.F. arrived on the squadron, taking up duties on A Flight and was Squadron Ground Training Officer. From September 1st, all N.C.O. aircrew relinquished their previous "Pilot" rank category and became Sergeants.

In October, a two-flight system had been recently introduced and the squadron soon received the opportunity to prove its practicability, results indicating a marked success. This system was to be employed during Exercise *Emperor*, held between the 7th and 15th, when all pilots experienced two-flight operation. Prior to the commencement of *Emperor*, a number of smaller exercises were held, including intruding over B.A.F.O. bases and simulated medium level bombing attacks around East Anglia. A total of 162 sorties were flown, totalling 281 hours.

Exercise *Emperor* necessitated "Maximum Effort" intruder operations over targets in Southern England, eventually adjudged to have been a complete success. Several accidents were to occur during *Emperor* including an incident on the 10th, following a long flight at low level. A section of Hornets had commenced an attack on Odiham airfield when Sgt.Plt Verrico, flying PX358, allowed his port propeller to contact a steep grass bank after mis-judging his pull-out from a shallow dive. He made a forced landing in a nearby field, his aircraft sustaining extensive damage. This became Verrico's second Hornet write-off within a year; the "top brass" were far from amused.

Two new pilots arrived on the squadron on 5 October. Sgt. D.R. Edmunds and Sgt. P.W. Grant had previously completed a Hornet Conversion Course at Linton. Four Hornets were operated from Horsham St. Faith for a sector exercise. A simulated night/dawn attack was also attempted but only four of six aircraft eventually landed back at Linton.

At the end of November, facilities at Theddlethorpe Range were used for essential air-to-ground and R.P. firing practice. Most pilots achieved one successful shoot using cannon and R.P.s. Due to distance involved, cannon and R.P.s were loaded and fired off independently during each sortie. Weather during the month proved to be rather poor due to seasonal fog and extremes of meteorological conditions.

An important announcement was made on 18 December with reference to the squadron relinquishing its cherished role as low-level long range intruders from that date. Re-equipment with Meteor F.8s would enable the squadron to perform an entirely different role of high level interceptor defence fighters.

In the first half of the month 64 Squadron were engaged in regular low level flying and ground attacks. The latter part of month was interrupted only by the Christmas break, sorties being concentrated on height climbs and high level interceptions. A sector exercise took place on 8 January 1951, involving Hornets, Vampires and Meteors, followed by a flypast on the 12th for some recruit training wings.

Hornets known to have equipped No.64 Squadron: Serial Nos./Codes

Hornet F.1:

PX225 SH-D;	PX236 SH-T;	PX238 SH-C;
PX241 SH-N;	PX244 SH-P;	PX246 SH-S;
PX247 SH-Q;	PX248 SH-R;	PX250 SH-H;
PX251 SH-M;	PX253 SH- ;	PX274 SH-G;
PX276 SH-P;	PX277 SH-O;	PX279 SH-A;
PX280 SH- ;	PX283 SH- ;	PX284 SH-B;
PX285 SH-E;	PX287 SH- .	

Hornet F.3:

PX294 SH-F;	PX295 SH- ;	PX296 SH-N;
PX298 SH- ;	PX303 SH-T;	PX332 SH- ;
PX334 SH-P;	PX340 SH-W;	PX341 SH-S;
PX344 SH-P;	PX345 SH-V;	PX346 SH-M;
PX351 SH-Y,-M;	PX353 SH-K;	PX358 SH-Y;
PX364 SH-U;	PX369 SH-B;	PX385 SH-Z;
PX391 SH-R;	PX392 SH-X;	PX393 SH-O, -W;
PX396 SH-O.		

No.64 Squadron Pilots:

Commanding Officers: Sqn.Ldr J.T. Shaw, DSO, DFC (1947); Sqn.Ldr A.G. Page DSO, DFC (1947-8); Sqn.Ldr Roberts, AFC (1948-50); Sqn.Ldr Thompson, (1950-51)

Officers;

Flg.Off. Brett, Flt.Lt. Burge, Flg.Off. Cowood, Flt.Lt. Glaser, Flt.Lt. Greenfield, Flt.Lt. Harbison, Flg.Off. Loveland, Flt.Lt. Mackingham, Flg.Off. Thompson, Plt.Off. Turner, Flt.Lt. Whitehead, Flt.Lt. Woodcock,

N.C.O.s

Pilot III Burgham, W/O Dougan, Sgt. D.R. Edmunds, Pilot II Feasby, Sgt. P.W, Grant, P.IV. Hampton, W/O (later P.II) J. Hartley, Flt.Sgt. Herring, W/O Hook, P.IV Martin-Jones, Pilot III Mitchell, W/O (later P.II) J.Norman, W/O Turner, P.III Verrico, W/O Watson, W/O. Williams.

Flt Lt G.M. Smith in PX394, YT-G of No.65 Squadron

No.65 (East India) Squadron

1946

The squadron was based, initially, at Horsham St.Faith and began trading in their Spitfire Mk.XVIEs for new Hornet F.Is in June 1946, the first aircraft arriving on the 17th, followed by a second on the 20th . Commanding Officer, Sqn.Ldr Charlton ("Wag") Haw DFC, DFM, Order of Lenin, was a former 504 Squadron Battle of Britain Hurricane pilot. After spending some time in Russia with No.81 Squadron, he later flew Spitfire IXs to the end of 1944, when he flew Mustang IIIs on long-range escort missions to Berlin.

The Hornet's cockpit was not unfamiliar to the C.O. as among other RAF pilots he visited Hatfield in 1943 as a guest of de Havilland, inspecting the Hornet mock-up. During 1946/7 Sqn.Ldr Haw flew PX252, which was decorated in 65 Squadron pre-war style red chevron markings on both upper wings and fuselage sides. These attractive markings were eventually removed in favour of squadron code "YT" on the orders of Fighter Command.

Despite the arrival of Hornets, 65 Squadron retained several Spitfires on strength due to the poor delivery rate. The first F.1 to arrive was PX225 on 26 February, further deliveries were made over a protracted period stretching from June to the end of September. These were PX240, PX252, PX226, PX232, PX282 and finally PX242 on 29 September.

Periods of unserviceability kept most Hornets grounded. One irritating problem concerned suspect radio equipment which caused a fair amount of head-scratching among ground staff. Leaks were causing short circuits in the sets so ground staff resorting to a final desperate remedy of turning offending sets upside down and much to everyone's amazement this measure actually worked! Problems were encountered with cockpit canopies, causing yet further delays in aircraft serviceability. It was not unknown for canopies to detach in flight, causing injury and some structural damage.

Sqn.Ldr Haw was not too impressed by the Hornet's relatively large turning circle, especially when compared with the Spitfire, making a practice of comparing turning radii in talks to his pilots.

On 10 December, four Hornets, led by Sqn.Ldr Haw, set off for an exercise to Cap de Barfleur. The C.O. and W/O Evered were forced to turn back with faulty radiator shutters. The remaining pair joined up with four Hornets from 64 Squadron. After reaching Barfleur, course was altered to make an attack on Thorney Island from 7,000 feet to assist G.C.I. radar stations.

1947

Severe winter conditions in 1947 curtailed flying at Linton and were to include long periods of poor horizontal visibility caused by smog.

February 1st: Despite the prevailing bad weather 65 Squadron was scheduled to provide part of an escort for King George VI aboard H.M.S. *Vanguard* on his departure from Portsmouth bound for South Africa. Returning to their base at Linton-on-Ouse, Hornets were landed between valleys of heaped-up snow, previously cleared off the runways by teams of German Prisoners of War. Sqn.Ldr Haw did all he could to keep his pilots occupied during the prolonged spell of wintry weather, including organised sport and wildfowl shooting expeditions.

W/O Dowson (ex-176 Squadron Beaufighters and Mosquitoes in S.E.A.C.) commenced his Hornet conversion on 28 May with dual flying in Mosquito T.III TV984, soloing PX226 on the same day. W/O Dowson's stay with 65 Squadron proved to be short-lived, his previous experience on Beaufighter night fighters making him prime candidate for instructional duties with the newly formed No.41 Instrument Training Squadron at Church Fenton. After a period of formation flying, QGH homings, low-level rendezvous and aerobatics, he reluctantly headed for Church Fenton.

Further serviceability problems arose due to shortages affecting gun sights which were only fitted for annual practice firing at APC Acklington, then removed in readiness for fitting to the next Hornets arriving for A.P.C. Several pairs of aircraft from 65 Squadron flew to Fayid on the Suez Canal for the regular long range navigation exercise.

This did not pass without incident. The C.O., in PX252, had both throttles jam in low power setting during final approach to El Adem. Flt.Lt. Guest's aircraft needed a complete radiator change, replacement parts being flown to Castel Benito by an Anson of No.12 Group. Flt.Lt. Aitken only got as far as Istres due to a burnt-out generator, a replacement being flown out by an aircraft from 64 Squadron.

During June, drastic measures were made in order to provide sufficient airworthy aircraft when some degree of cannibalising took place, several Hornets becoming "Christmas Trees". Flying was severely curtailed due to recurring throttle seizures, Rolls-Royce engineers making on-site modifications to throttle intakes. Four aircraft became available for detachment to Coltishall, two taking part in Exercise *Webfoot* in co-operation with the Home Fleet. Two Hornets maintained a standing patrol, being vectored on to attacking Lincolns.

All aircraft were grounded in July due mainly to the discovery of misalignment on engine bearer brackets. Vibration in flight had caused engine bearer bolts to shear. During August, four out of eight aircraft were grounded, all awaiting adjustments to engine bearer brackets. Only two of the remaining four were considered as airworthy.

One day in August, Sqn.Ldr Haw was about to wave away his chocks when a member of the ground crew discovered that his pitot head cover was still in place and without waiting for steps an airman wrenched off the fabric cover. On becoming airborne, Haw became aware that his airspeed indicator had stuck at 85 m.p.h. and promptly made a quick circuit. The vigorous tug had succeeded in bending the pitot head downwards at thirty degrees, fortunately not involving a new pilot on his first Hornet solo.

Serviceability improved in September, which allowed the resumption of full flying training, including aerobatics. During the beginning of the month, 65 Squadron Hornets made an appearance at Squire's Gate for the Blackpool Air Display. Flt.Lt. Whitehead caused some commotion by flying at zero feet along the sea front, most of the spectators deciding to lie flat until the Hornet had passed over. Flg.Off. Menzies performed individual aerobatics, including a roll with both engines feathered.

A high state of serviceability was achieved in October when four aircraft provided bomber escort to Lancasters and Lincolns. The defence put up against approaching Meteor F.IIIs was surprisingly effective. Operations in November included an exercise by a single Hornet, whose pilot remained at readiness inside the cockpit with engines previously warmed-up. Time to unstick from receiving the Scramble order was one minute.

1948

Pilot II J. Sherburn joined the squadron on 23 January and was shortly to achieve some distinction in the art of aerobatic flying. On 11 February, he set off to Antwerp with his number two for a Continental cross-country exercise. Another N.C.O. pilot, P.II Farmer, joined the squadron on the 27th, after completing No.9 Course at 226 O.C.U. at Bentwaters, where he converted to the Hornet via Airspeed Oxfords. His first solo in XL-D/ PX238 followed five hours of dual on Oxfords. The course flying syllabus for Hornet conversion consisted of single-engine flying, feathering/unfeathering, low-flying, aerobatics, height climbs to 25,000 feet and practice homings.

Operations in January were limited by bad weather. Two aircraft, led by the C.O., completed a successful bomber affiliation exercise. The average daily serviceability in February amounted to four aircraft. Fitters installed GM-2 gunsights in preparation for Armament Practice Camp.

On 22 March, Mosquito T.3 VT609 ferried P.II Farmer to Acklington for annual firing at APC Acklington, although at the time his total experience on Hornets amounted to less than 12 hours. PX362 was collected from 37 M.U. Burtonwood on 15 April and flown directly to Acklington for use at A.P.C. At the end of A.P.C., P.II Sherburn achieved "Above Average" assessments in Sighting Theory, Armament Theory and

PX337 YT-E of No.65 Squadron

Armament Practice.

Several trips were made to M.U.s to pick up the first F.3s. It was decided not to use all aircraft for A.P.C., the majority being kept at Linton in preparation for the visit to Sweden. In order to bring the squadron up to full strength, Hornets were borrowed back from Nos.19 and 64 Squadrons.

No.65 Squadron was engaged in Operation *Dawn* on 13 May, carrying out low-level attacks on Royal Navy destroyers in the North Sea and also providing Hornets for bomber escort, in co-operation with 64 Squadron for a joint Linton Hornet Wing exercise.

Another newcomer, P.II Bob Stubbs, joined the squadron on the 18th, having recently graduated from the Hornet Conversion Course at 226 O.C.U., progressing to Hornets via twin experience on Oxfords. One wonders whether Mosquito T.3s were in short supply at this time. Due to the trickle of deliveries, 65 Squadron was forced to operate a mixed fleet of F.1s and F.3s.

No.65 Squadron pilots set off for a goodwill visit to Sweden, as guests of the Swedish Air Force and although officially a 65 Squadron show, due to current shortages Hornets had to be borrowed from 64 Squadron. Before taking off for Sweden, Sqn.Ldr Haw's Hornet decided to develop technical problems, becoming unserviceable. Quickly commandeering a reserve aircraft, he set off only to find that his undercarriage would not fully retract and he was also unable to throttle back to cruising r.p.m. After carrying out a few "circuits and bumps", the Hornet's troubles eventually cleared. Sqn.Ldr Haw rapidly caught up with the main formation.

Meanwhile, unforeseen engine snags had arisen in the supporting York, forcing the Captain to return to Lyneham. He had to orbit the base for some time to reduce his fuel load. The York carried the deputy A.O.C., G/Capt. F.L. White, C.O. of RAF Linton-on-Ouse and ground staff, plus some assorted spares.

The Hornet formation was led by W/Cdr. W.A. Nel, DSO, DFC who ordered the pilots to adopt an open formation with 150-200 feet. Oxygen was used throughout the flight from take-off to the cruising altitude of 10,000 feet. Navigation was accomplished by a new pressure pattern technique, pre-planned by Sqn.Ldr S. Munns, 12 Group Navigation Officer. Engines were set for cruise at +4 lb boost/2,400 r.p.m. with half-hourly increase to +12 lb/2,850 r.p.m. Wing Commander Nel's Hornet was equipped with a new G4F compass, other Hornets retaining their Magnasyns with E2s as back up.

On approaching Stockholm they discovered a small track error of only two miles. The formation was tightened up before making a flypast over Stockholm. The squadron finally arriving at Uppsala after flying for over three hours. 65 Squadron flew to Gothenburg on the 28th before departing for Linton on the 31st. The Swedish social arrangements were well planned, as one former pilot recalled "very little time for flying". Meantime the C.O. was forced to spend some time on the West coast due to an engine failure on take-off, returning to Linton at 20,000 feet in atrocious weather. The radio became unserviceable en route although by using careful dead reckoning a descent was made through a cloud break over Scarborough.

U.S.A.F. exchange pilot, Capt. Rhodarner, arrived on the squadron in June, soon receiving one hour's instrument flying in VT609, the Station Flight Mosquito. On the 4th, 65 Squadron made head-on attacks during interceptions of U.S.A.F. B-29s flying at 30,000 feet. The squadron also made an interception of an approaching formation of Swedish Air Force Mustangs on the 11th whilst they were en route for a goodwill visit.

Re-equipment with new F.3s had commenced. F.3 PX339 was collected on the 17th from 10 M.U. Hullavington. Surplus F.1s were now ferried away, Hornet F.1 PX226 being flown to the M.U. at

Burtonwood on 22 June. PX240 also departed on the 24th, bound for 27 M.U. at Shawbury. A small number of F.1s were delivered to 19 Squadron. No.65 now had its full complement of F.3s.

On July 20th and 21st, air-to-sea firing took place over the Paston firing range. A formation flew to Duxford on the 24th prior to flying next day when they were engaged in exercises with the R.O.C., two sorties being flown totalling four hours. On the 30th, the squadron performed a flypast over Catterick, this following a busy morning when pilots were engaged on battle climbs.

P.II Farmer was flown to Andover in Oxford NM296 on 3 August to collect W/Cdr. Nel's personal Hornet PR.2 WA-T/N for delivery to Linton. On the 9th, a formation practice was carried out in preparation for the A.O.C.'s inspection, due on the 10th when the squadron was scrambled for a formation flypast which included a pass on one engine. On the 13th, pilots made height climbs in "Line Astern" formation to 26,000 feet.

Exercise *Dagger* commenced on 3 September when 65 Squadron Hornets became part of an attacking force known as "Southland", making low-level attacks on airfields at Horsham St.Faith, West Malling, Church Fenton and Bentwaters. *Dagger* continued on the 5th with further low-level intruding over West Raynham. P.II Farmer and his section made an effective low-level attack on Middle Wallop airfield.

In all cases the defending force (known as "Northland") were taken completely by surprise, the marauding Hornets operating at "nought feet" over their bases. Camera footage from the Hornet's cameras indicated beyond doubt that almost half of defending jet fighters would have been destroyed or damaged before taking-off.

A message was received from C.-in-C. Bomber Command complimenting the Linton Hornet Wing on their great success in the exercise, the first large-scale R.A.F. exercise since 1945. During *Dagger*, it became standard procedure for sections of four Hornets to fly eastwards before returning across the North Sea at low level to escape radar detection. Hornets were flown in loose "Finger Four" formation, cruising at around 320 m.p.h. until sighting their objective, when full throttle was applied.

On 15 September, the squadron made its contribution to the Battle of Britain Flypast. The Battle of Britain Air Display was held on the 18th when several pilots flew flights of up to three hours for flypasts over Cranwell, West Malling, Thorney Island, Middle Wallop, Odiham, and Ouston before making a final pass over Linton. In total some fifteen minutes were devoted to single-engine flying. The display at Linton included a smooth aerobatic display by Flg.Off. Menzies, who concluded his show with a flypast with both engines feathered, followed by a slow roll.

During the 28th and 29th, P.IIs Hook and Stubbs, flying PX339 and PX352, intercepted formations of U.S.A.F. B-29s at 23,000 feet. A Lincoln was inter-

cepted on the 30th flying at 17,000 ft.

During October, on the 5th, 8th, 12th, 18th, 19th, 21st, 22nd and 28th, the squadron was to make numerous B-29 interceptions, all contacts duly recorded on cine-camera. Exercise *Hedgehog* commenced on the 24th with the R.O.C., followed on the 26th by the strafing of army convoys. Between 27 September and 15 October, several pilots attended a course at Instrument Training Squadron, Tangmere, which was equipped with Oxfords. P.II Sherburn flew F.3 PX339 on a flight endurance test, managing to keep the Hornet in the air for a creditable five hours, fifteen minutes.

A long distance navigation exercise was made on 7 November when 65 Squadron departed for Manston, leaving for Luqa on the 9th. The route taken was Manston-Luqa, Luqa-Fayid, total flying time amounting to around ten hours. During the exercise Sqn.Ldr Haw was compelled to make no fewer than six single-engine landings, the trouble being traced to seized throttle butterflies caused by undue expansion and unusually high outside temperatures. These problems continued to plague Merlins for some time, dissimilar materials being considered to be the root cause of jammed throttles. During the flight from Fayid to El Adem, Hornets were flown low over the desert regions, most pilots reporting the presence of wartime debris which was still recognisable, including many damaged vehicles. Further problems occurred with the existing radio installation on the C.O.'s aircraft, which led to an unscheduled let-down over the Dover area.

Soon after returning to Linton, 65's pilots were actively engaged in a display of formation flying for the benefit of the R.O.C.

On the 22nd, P.II Farmer attended No.3 Instrument Training Course at Tangmere, flying Oxfords for sixteen hours on instruments.

Several B-29 interceptions were carried out during December.

The 16th was a far from uneventful day for Pilot II Stubbs in PX340 who was making a controlled descent in extremely poor visibility with the cloud base "on the deck". Concentrating on his instruments, he was advised by the ground controller to look ahead for the runway, only to observe the rapidly growing outline of hangars looming ahead directly in his path.

1949

In January, P.II Stubbs in PX352 made a height climb to 30,000 feet followed by a spell of aerobatics and single engine flying. On the 24th, four Hornets flown by Sqn.Ldr W.A. Toyne, with Flt.Lt. Don Wylie and P.IIs Bob Stubbs and Fred Farmer, set off for the regular navigation exercise to the Middle East, destination Fayid via Luqa and El Adem. P.II Farmer failed to reach Fayid after a coolant pump failure. Flt.Lt. Wylie was forced to shut down one Merlin, also due to a faulty coolant pump. On the return flight, a stop was made at Istres, all four aircraft arriving back at Linton on the 30th after being

No.65 Squadron in May 1947 poses before PX252. In the photograph are Sqn.Ldr Haw, Flt.Lts Aiken and Guest, Flg Offs Russum, Wilson, Menzies and Kees, WOs Dowson, Clarke and Evered

fog-bound for two days at Manston.

Two "rogue" aircraft were put up for disposal. The new replacements were given acceptance checks, although seat modifications kept them inside the hangars.

Oxford NM296 was used on 11 February for periods of refresher training on G.C.A. approaches. Air-to-ground firing was carried out on the Skipsea range. On the 21st, Pilot II Farmer was forced to make a single-engine landing after encountering problems with his starboard Merlin. These occurred at 30,000 feet during a high-level cross-country flight, requiring a forty-five minute return flight on one engine.

Flying targets were exceeded during February despite a series of petty faults. This achievement reflected the hard work put in by maintenance crews who often worked late at night in an endeavour to provide serviceable aircraft.

More drama lay in store on the 25th for P.II Stubbs in PX340 who was engaged on a cine-camera exercise. He was soon destined to encounter a series of engine problems which forced him to feather his starboard engine due to a fire. Shortly afterwards, the remaining engine also caught fire, necessitating an immediate shut-down. Using his excess speed to gain precious altitude to 4,000 feet, he skillfully executed a wheels-down, "dead stick" landing at Linton-on-Ouse.

On 2 March, 64 & 65 Squadrons flew together for a Wing formation flight. Yet another saga for P.II Stubbs on the 6th when flying during the initial phase of the *Forth/Clyde* exercise. Flying in PX356 at very low level as Number Two to Wing Boss, W/Cdr. Nel, his port propeller struck the waters of the Tay. Within seconds, severe engine vibration caused Stubbs to execute an immediate belly-landing in which he suffered a fractured spine as a result of a high-speed touch-down. The Hornet disintegrated in the spectacular crash resulting in the following newspaper report: "'After the cockpit section had stopped bouncing the pilot climbed out".

Due to a tight formation at extremely low level, the Wing Commander had left his Number Two with insufficient space for manoeuvre. PX356 had arrived only hours previously from 10 M.U. as a replacement for a rogue aircraft.

The "Rogue" displayed alarming characteristics at low speeds between 160-220 knots. Geoffrey de Havilland arrived at Linton-on-Ouse by train to test the errant Hornet. On landing, he soon agreed that it was indeed worthy of further investigation by D.H. at Hatfield. On being asked how the Hornet was to be despatched he replied "By air of course"! Common sense prevailed and the rogue Hornet was dismantled for despatch by road.

The *Forth/Clyde* exercise on the 12th and 13th was a full-scale effort, when Hornets were intercepted on several occasions by Spitfires and Meteors. The exercise also involved 65 Squadron in a search for a ship equipped with radar. Reconnaissances were made to Cupar, Dunfermline, Tantallon Radar Station and intruding over Turnhouse aerodrome. The exercise was continued with a low-level attack on Leuchars and an armed reconnaissance to Glasgow. On the 15th, "Scrambles" were made to 30,000 feet. Night flying was commenced on the 22nd and a new training programme for low-level intruding was introduced.

In April the squadron was scrambled to provide a fighter escort for the Secretary of State for Air. On the 20th, Captain Moffatt, U.S.A.F., in PX394 had just completed a low-level cross-country flight. On landing he made his customary wheeler when suddenly the nose tipped up and the Hornet overturned, sustaining Cat.5 damage. The accident was attributed to over-harsh use of the brakes. The U.S. Captain was unused to tailwheel aircraft, having overturned PX361, which badly bent both propellers, only seven days previously as a result of energetic use of the brakes to correct a swing.

On the 22nd, PX216 was flown to Newton by P.II Farmer, who returned in F.3 PX304.

The squadron attended A.P.S. at Acklington between 25 April and 19 May for live firing at towed gliders and target drogues. Sorties were limited by aircraft becoming unserviceable with cracking and loose gun bay bulkheads. On 11 May, PX353 suffered total engine failure during take-off from Acklington. The 27th was occupied with further B-29 interceptions.

Exercise *Midsummer* was held on 21 June when elements of the Home Fleet were exercising in the North Sea on passage to and from the Norwegian coast. Units of the Fleet approached the English coast sufficiently near to allow a series of limited scale exercises to be carried out by aircraft of 12 Group, Fighter Command, who provided sixteen Meteor F.4s of Eastern Sector and a similar number of Hornet F.3s of Yorkshire Sector.

H.M.S. *Implacable* reinforced her C.A.P. after re-arming all her returning strike aircraft, anticipating an attack by land-based aircraft. Attacks on the carrier were made by Meteors and Hornets, the Hornets operating in the anti-shipping role.

Sqn Ldr C. Haw, CO of 65 Squadron

In common with other Hornet squadrons, 65 Squadron received notification from Command via 12 Group that henceforth the squadron's operational role was to be changed from daylight intruder/medium level fighter to that of daylight low-level intruder.

Exercise *Foil* commenced on the 25th as a large-scale test of British defences. No.65 Squadron was "loaned" to 1 Group, Bomber Command, together with three other Hornet squadrons of the Yorkshire sector as a daylight intruder force. Attacks by Hornets were mainly concentrated on fighter airfields and radar installations. Prior to the commencement of this exercise, flying practice had to be curtailed due to a need to conserve flying hours and a lack of aircraft. Essential gun beam modifications also affected all aircraft. On 13 June, three new F.3s, PX305, PX328 and PX355, were collected from Hullavington, bringing the squadron strength up to eight aircraft.

Essential repairs were made to the main runway (04/22) at Linton-on-Ouse, involving re-surfacing of tarmac joints. The work was completed on 24 June, just in time for *Foil*. Fortunately, the weather proved to be fine and warm.

Sorties were made under realistic wartime conditions, requiring landfall to be made on or near the Dutch coast, prior to setting course for targets. Meanwhile Linton became congested, having no fewer than four Hornet squadrons based on the airfield for exercises. No.65 Squadron's targets for *Foil* included low-level attacks on Langtops, Liverpool and Finningley. High altitude attacks were made over London on the 30th. P.IIs, Farmer, Sherburn and Stubbs, flying PX352, PX328 and PX346, were part of section of F.3s which climbed eastwards towards Belgium, preparatory to launching a mock attack on the capital at 20,000 feet from the Channel. Prevailing weather conditions dictated a good look-out owing to the close proximity of aircraft from other squadrons engaged in the attack. These pilots were not aware of any interceptions during the run-in to the target.

Foil accounted for some thirty-nine sorties by the squadron, totalling ninety-seven hours. On 2 July, low-level incursions made over the Fens with further attacks on Martlesham Heath and Idlicote Hill. Low-level attacks were made on the 3rd against Bawdsey and Sandwich Radar Stations.

Flt.Lt. G. Smith took over command of the squadron.

Between August 4th to 8th, the squadron was engaged in formation aerobatics. Continental cross-country navigation exercises were flown on three days and 65 Squadron made a flypast over Birmingham on the 22nd. Two aircraft, accompanied by two from 64 Squadron, carried out an attack on Odiham as a test of the early warning system in the south-east.

Between September 8th and 10th, formation practice was carried out for the Battle of Britain Flypast on the traditional 15th. On Open Day on the 17th, P.II Sherburn in PX355 executed low-level aerobatics with displays at

Hornet F.I PX232 of 65 Squadron at Linton-on-Ouse in late 1946

Linton and Dishforth. Four Hornets from the squadron carried out displays and dummy attacks at base and Dishforth.

September 21st to 23rd was a warming-up period for Exercise *Bulldog* with no operations demanded on these days. *Bulldog* itself commenced on the 24th, lasting until the 26th. Planned morning exercises were delayed by fog until 10.30, although numerous dawn sorties were requested and prepared. All sorties consisted of low-level intruding against airfields and radar installations, with many successes being recorded against aircraft on the ground. There were few interceptions by defending fighters, despite twenty-one sorties being flown. Flying hours totalled approximately forty-five hours.

On the 15th, Sector Commander, G/Capt. A.C.P. Carver in PX305 left Bovingdon bound for Gibraltar to participate in the Battle of Britain display there. Encountering bad weather en route, a stop was made at Madrid for refuelling. Weather conditions were more favourable on the return journey on the 19th, Carver succeeding in establishing a point-to-point speed record of 435.6 m.p.h.

Flying practice for October was largely confined to cine-camera exercises in preparation for Armament Practice Camp at 65's regular venue of Acklington. Practice controlled descents, formation flying, single-engine flying and low-level cross-countries were followed by night flying during the nights of the 18th and 24th.

There was limited flying from 1st until 14th November when the squadron deployed to Acklington, only to encounter poor weather conditions. Despite indifferent weather, eighty sorties were flown, accounting for 46.30 flying hours. A Hornet flown by G/Capt. Lees spent some eighteen hours flying during a Middle East detachment.

The squadron's stay at Acklington was extended until 14 December with more success than the previous three weeks. Weather conditions became more reasonable, good air-to-air scores being recorded. Regrettably there were a few bad scores, although P.I Cempel, P.I Green, P.II Sherburn and Flg.Off Hutton turned in good results in air-to-air firing. P.II Sherburn won the squadron kitty for best air-to-air and air-to-ground combined average. Overall, 65 Squadron's position in the Hornet Wing could only be classed as average, second in air-to-air and third in air-to-ground results. On 14 December, the C.O. led the squadron back to Linton where bad visibility, plus some Meteors in the circuit, combined to spoil a good flypast over the airfield.

P.I Cempel's Hornet suffered torque link failure on touching down, sustaining Category C damage. Weather conditions were poor during the remainder of the month, Linton closing down for eleven days, seven of which were to allow essential repairs to the main runway which had been unserviceable throughout the month. The C.O. decided that before re-commencing flying, all aircraft needed a good clean, pilots joining ground staff in this operation.

1950

Exercise *New Year* began on 12 January with an attack on Langtoft. On 9 February, P.II Woods in PX398 carried out a height climb, finishing off the exercise with a controlled descent through cloud. Local visibility had deteriorated and Woods returning to Linton with his port engine feathered after hydraulic pump failure. After using the emergency hand pump to lower the undercarriage, only one green light lit up. Distracted by a chain of events, P.II Woods neglected to lower the flaps until the last moment. At higher than normal speed, his Hornet overshot, hit a bank of earth and overturned. The 21st was the start of Exercise *Pancake*.

Three other emergency landings occurred in February, P.II Shepherd making two single-engine landings while P.I Green made another in the Mosquito due to failure of the unfeathering circuit.

On 5 March, exercises were carried out with R.Aux.A.F. aircraft, with Hornets adopting the role of medium-level bombers. Five aircraft flew to Horsham St.Faith on the 20th, acting for Eastern Sector as an intruder force for "Crossland" in a one-day war against "Stapletonia", the Yorkshire Sector. All sorties were completed with some success, although a standing patrol of Meteors made several interceptions.

Exercise *12 Bore* was held on 21 April and included some local low-level intruding over Church Fenton and Linton. On the 27th, 65 Squadron flew in formation to Acklington A.P.S. for gunnery practice, returning to Linton in formation on 13 April.

Exercise *Stardust* commenced on the 30th with poor weather experienced on the first day, which necessitated an extra day being added. Three new pilots were posted to the squadron, priority being given to their flying in preparation for a forthcoming exercise.

During *Stardust*, the squadron made eight low-level attacks, all but one considered a success, and these were continued on 1 May with attacks at high level.

Flg.Off. Hutton and P. II Sherburn won the Meteor v Hornet synchronised aerobatic competition in May. Despite being scheduled for inclusion in the R.A.F. Display at Farnborough, the event was cancelled due to lack of time.

PX339 YT-A of No.65 Squadron at Cranwell, 18.9.48

On the 9th, P.II Sherburn became outright winner in the finals for R.A.F. Display aerobatic demonstration, held at Tangmere. On the 23rd, he flew PX305 down to Cottesmore for an aerobatic display. Both Hornet squadrons were airborne on the 27th for a Wing formation. On June 11th, P.II Sherburn flew PX353 to Newton for an aerobatic display. The squadron flew in formation on the 24th to West Malling, followed next day by another combined Wing formation.

The squadron deployed to West Malling on 4 July, using the airfield as a base for their appearances at the Royal Air Force Display at Farnborough.

Between 10 August and 1 September, the squadron flew to A.P.C. at Sylt for air-to-ground and air-to-air firing and low-level bombing. On the 12th and 13th, aircraft were active with flying sequences for the Battle of Britain display. PX348 was ferried on the 19th from 10 M.U. Hullavington to Linton.

Over-riding all other flying in October, Exercise *Emperor* was scheduled to last from the 7th to the 15th. A need to conserve hours led to a drastic curtailment of flying in the early part of the month. During *Emperor*, 65 Squadron carried out its normal role of low-level intruding. However as this particular exercise itself had not been specifically designed for such operations, many odd sorties were also undertaken. The squadron performed reasonably well, making many successful ground attacks on targets, including Leeming airfield, radar installations and similar targets. The sortie rate averaged nine per day, totalling 150 hours in seven days, largely achieved through the intensive efforts of squadron ground crews working very long hours with great enthusiasm. The 15th was the final day of *Emperor*, after which flying practically ceased owing to most aircraft being due for, or undergoing, minor inspections. A grand total of 225 hours 30 mins of flying was carried out, believed to be the highest since 65 Squadron equipped with Hornets.

On the 7th, P.II Sherburn had a change of mount, flying Spitfire F.22 PK351 for a period of aerobatics.

On November 17th, Sgt.Pilot Sherburn flew PX349 down to a temporary base at Waterbeach, taking-off later for a flight to H.Q. Fighter Command for an aerobatic display especially for H.R.H. Princess Elizabeth. On the 18th a telegram was received from C.-in-C. Fighter Command congratulating Sgt.Pilot Sherburn on a "Smooth and impressive show which had contributed materially to the visit"' After 1,000 hours flying Meteors and Canberras, Flg.Off. Sherburn was seconded to R.A.E. as a test pilot, flying most first-line types. Eventually he accepted a post with Short Bros. & Harland as a production test pilot, test-flying Skyvans, Belfasts and Beechcraft.

January 1951 witnessed the arrival of the first Meteors, the following being delivered during the month: Meteor T.7 VT637; Meteor F.4s VT109, VT174, VT217, VT258, VT308, VT326, WA963, WE920, WE921 and WE922. Conversion to Meteors commenced during the first week, Hornet flying being mainly due to

Hornet F.3 PX353 at Uppsala, Sweden, on a goodwill visit in May 1948

some necessary air tests before ferrying to M.U.s. On 9 February PX328 was flown to 27 M.U. Shawbury; PX365 and PX360 were given air tests on the 13th and 20th March.

During April, despite re-equipping with Meteors, several Hornets still remained inside No.5 hangar where strenuous efforts were being made to render them airworthy for ferrying away, including PX337, PX301 and former Linton Conversion Flight Hornet, PX292.

Hornets with 65 Squadron. Serial Numbers/Codes where known:

Hornet F.1

PX225 YT-D;	PX226 YT-S;	PX231 YT-P;
PX232 YT-R,	PX240 YT-L;	PX242 YT-G;
PX252 YT-HH;	PX278 YT- ;	PX280 YT-A;
PX282 YT-B.		

Hornet F.3:

PX298 YT-H;	PX301 YT- ;	PX304 YT-A;
PX305 YT-B;	PX328 YT-K;	PX330 YT- ;
PX335 YT-H;	PX337 YT-E,	PX339 YT-A;
PX340 YT-B;	PX346 YT-E, -F;	PX349 YT-C;
PX352 YT-J, -C;	PX353 YT-D, -K;	PX355 YT-G;
PX356 YT- ;	PX361 YT-A;	PX362 YT-L, -E;
PX388 YT-H;	PX394 YT-G;	PX398 YT-H.

Squadron Pilots 1946-51;

Commanding Officers:
Sqn.Ldr C. Haw DFC DSO; Sqn.Ldr Toyne; Flt.Lt. G. Smith.

Officers: Flt.Lt. Aitken, Flt.Lt. Beldin, Flt.Lt. Coussins, Flt.Lt. Guest, Flt.Lt. Jay, Flg.Off. Kees, Flg.Off. Menzies, Flt.Lt. Smith, Flt.Lt. Wylie, Flg.Off. Wilson. Capt.R.J. Moffatt, U.S.A.F..

N.C.O.s: Pilot I Cempel, W/O Clarke, W/O Dowson, W/O Evered (All 1947)
Pilot II Auty, Pilot II Farmer, Pilot II Fewtrell, Pilot I Green, Pilot II Hook, Pilot II Norman, Pilot II Sherburn. Pilot II Stubbs, Pilot II Williams, Pilot II Woods.

PX232 YT-R at Fayid, Egypt, in May 1947 (D.A.Wyldes)

Far East Air Force Hornet F.3s

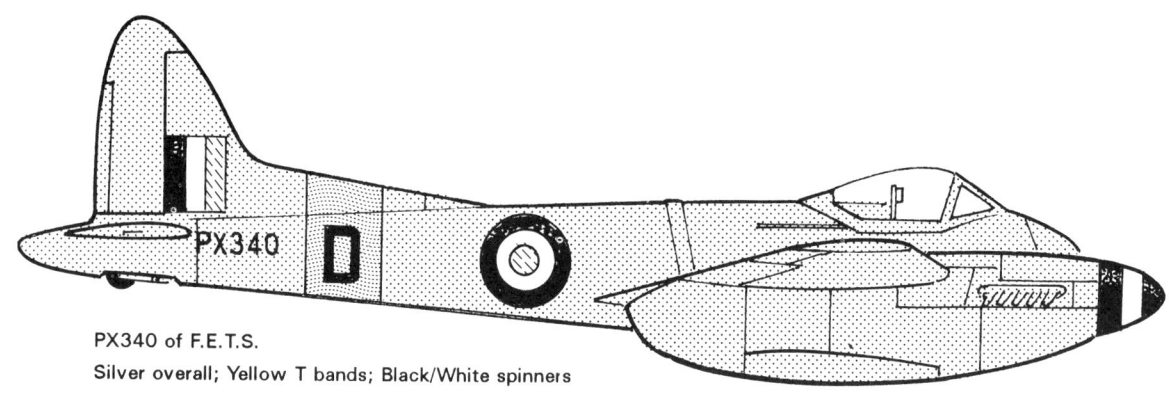

PX340 of F.E.T.S.

Silver overall; Yellow T bands; Black/White spinners

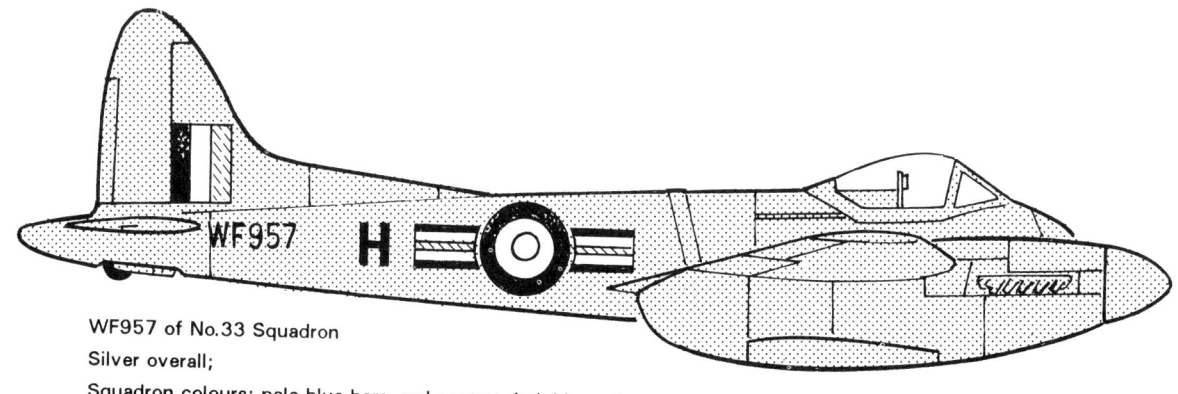

WF957 of No.33 Squadron

Silver overall;

Squadron colours: pale blue bars, red centre; dark blue edges

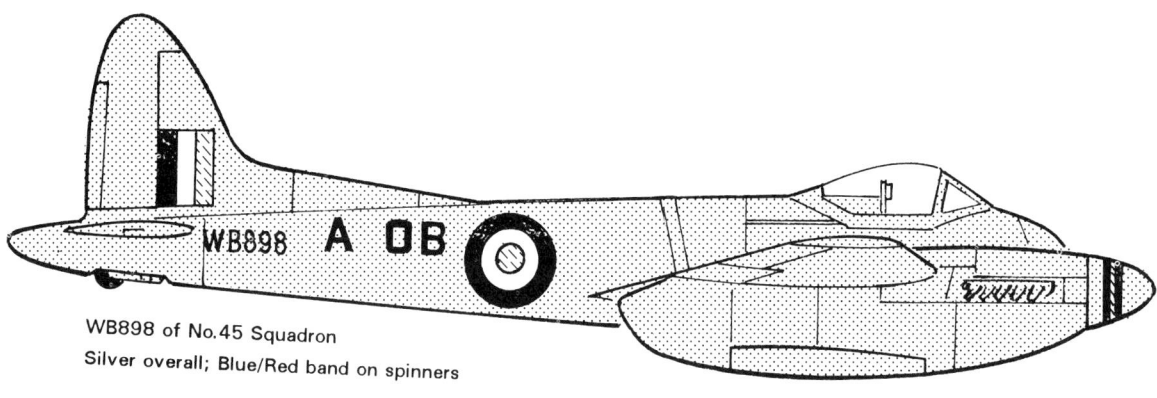

WB898 of No.45 Squadron

Silver overall; Blue/Red band on spinners

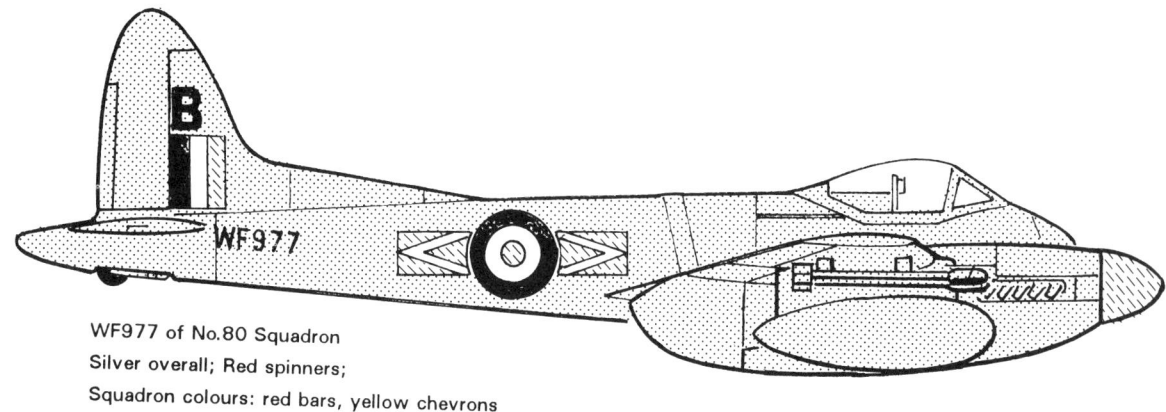

WF977 of No.80 Squadron

Silver overall; Red spinners;

Squadron colours: red bars, yellow chevrons

Hornet F.3 WB874 of No.33 Squadron in the wet at Butterworth

Far East Air Force

No.33 Squadron

1951

The squadron discarded its Tempest F.2s at Tengah during April 1951, most being absorbed into the Royal Indian Air Force. Sqn.Ldr. C.C.F. Cooper was Commanding Officer, with Flt.Lt. Hoskins as Flight Commander.

The few Hornets that had arrived were soon to be employed in the anti-terrorist role, using all the fire power then available, i.e. bombs and cannon fire. Following later clearance for R.P. firing, squadron armourers made a practice of riding out "shotgun", grasping the canopy before disembarking at the take-off point in order to make the projectiles "live"'.

Sgt. Derek Taylor arrived at Tengah in May, following twin conversion at 203 A.F.S. Swinderby, where he flew fifty hours dual and solo in Mosquitoes and thirteen hours in Hornets at the Linton-on-Ouse Conversion Unit.

Weapons training was carried out with the squadron at Tengah before he was assessed "combat ready". Eventually he was to carry out almost daily air strikes against the Communist terrorists.

Meanwhile, the U.K. Hornet squadrons were now in the process of re-equipping with Meteors so it was decided to transfer all Hornet conversion training to F.E.T.S Seletar. As a consequence, Derek Taylor became one of the last pilots to transition to the Hornet via the Linton Conversion Unit.

In addition to routine training, particular emphasis was placed on squadron pilots attaining a high standard of proficiency in close tactical formation flying over the jungle areas.

WB870 was destroyed in a fatal accident on 10 August 1951 when the pilot lost control during aerobatics, crashing into a house near Bedok and killing the three occupants. It later transpired that the pilot had been authorised to practice single-engine flying. After a period of aerobatics flown below regulation height, the Hornet was seen approaching from the sea at high speed before entering a tight turn at low altitude. The investigation team concluded that the accident was due to inexperience on type.

During October, Hornets were detached, operating from Tengah and actively engaged in air strikes against targets situated in Gemas, Rompin, Mersing, Rawang and Jasin areas. Requisite air-to-ground gunnery practice was carried out using the range facilities at Ghina Rock.

In November/December, air strikes were continued against a variety of suspected C.T. (Communist Terrorist) hideouts in areas at Endau, Bidor, Tampin, Muar, Ipoh and Rompin. In between these air strikes, time was allowed for low-flying exercises, height climbs and battle climbs with the inevitable tail chases.

1952

During January 1952, 33 Squadron relocated to

Butterworth, Penang Province, and apart from occasional deployments was destined to remain there until its eventual amalgamation in 1954. Target practice facilities were provided by a range at Song Song.

Air strikes during the six months ahead included sorties against targets in Kuantan, Tapah, Bentong, Jeniang, Ipoh, Fraser's Hill, Triang, Bongsu, Kangsar and Kulim areas and those south of Kulim and west of the Rasa and Kulim areas. As the campaign continued, the frequency of air strikes was to be increased.

On 4 June, an air search was mounted for missing Auster AOP.6 VF602 of No.656 Squadron. A formation flypast was carried out on the 23rd for the benefit of visiting V.I.P.s. WB881 was badly damaged on the 25th after swinging off the runway on touching down, having entered a drainage ditch.

Air strikes were stepped up in July with sorties over the Bongsu, Rasa, Bidor and Fraser's Hill areas and Belum Valley. On the 28th, a single air strike was mounted against targets in the Tronoh area, followed by three separate attacks on the 29th over the Kampar Hill area, each sortie lasting an hour. The scale of activity can be compared to actions by the 2nd Tactical Air Force after the Normandy landings in World War II, although lacking any trace of accurate flak.

Seven strikes were carried out over the Kampar Hill area over a four-day period from 28th July. Three further sorties were flown over the same target on the 30th and 31st August. Relentless strikes continued, with strafing attacks over the Raub, Gap Road, Bongsu and Rawang areas. Average flying time of these sorties was in the region of two to three hours.

Strikes during September and October were continued with the Kuala Krau, Kulim, Paka, Rasa, Manong, Relau, Sungei Lembing, Tansong and Kulim areas receiving the usual consignment of R.P.s and cannon fire.

Pilots received their annual instrument rating checks in Mosquito T.3 RR311, which usually lasted an hour. The relentless air strikes continued with little respite for pilots and ground crews, seven occurring between the 2nd and 28th. Targets were situated in the Kuala Krau, Kulim, Paka, Rasa, Manong and Relau areas. Practice flights were also made using R.P.s in thirty and sixty degree dives. In November and December the regular air strikes, were interspersed between some occasional night cross-country navigation exercises. The air strikes were carried out over the Relau, Cheras, Ulu Langat, Telor Datok, Tapah Road, Chukai and Tapah Road areas.

On 11 December, tactical exercises, air tests and low flying filled a period left by the temporary lull in offensive operations. Strikes were eventually resumed on the 23rd. There was to be no let-up on Christmas Day, when Hornets made two strikes over the Sungei Labir area. The year's strike operations were concluded by an attack on the Kampar area.

1953

The New Year saw a further lull in offensive operations. They were resumed on the 20th until the 23rd, with strikes over the Kuala Kubu and Tanjong Malim areas. Hornets flew three-hour patrols over the Cameron Highlands, which were situated some seventy miles north of the Malayan capital, Kuala Lumpur.

On the 26th, WB871 lost an engine cowling during aerobatics which caused the undercarriage to jam. The Hornet was subsequently abandoned over the open sea. On the same day, WF879 came to grief when power was lost during take-off from Butterworth, forcing the pilot to raise the undercarriage to prevent the aircraft from overshooting the runway.

During February, occasional high altitude flights were made using a Hornet F.4 which took mosaic photographs for intelligence purposes. Further strikes were directed against targets in the Kubu Bharu and Telok Datok areas.

March was generally a quieter month for the squadron, apart from an air strike on the 3rd against pre-selected targets in the Leng Gong area. The main flying activity was formed by target identification practice, formation tail chases, cloud flying and height climbs. On the 11th, PX338 made a belly-landing at Butterworth when the undercarriage failed to lower.

Operations were re-commenced on 1 April by an air strike mounted against targets in the Sungei Siput area. Several hours were flown for formation practice. Photographic reconnaissance flights were flown over Jeniang. Air strikes were made over the Cameron Highlands and Broga area. This action required 33 Squadron Hornets to make a day's detachment to Kuala Lumpur.

A subsequent combined operation with seven Lincolns of No.1 Sqn, Royal Australian Air Force, was abandoned due to bad weather over the target area, bombs being jettisoned on alternative targets. The combined operation had also included nine Hornets from 45 Squadron plus a further twelve from 33 Squadron. A following repeat operation was also unsuccessful, most bombs falling well away from the suspected terrorist camp. This type of attack was quickly abandoned, Hornets reverting to strafing attacks.

In May, several hours were spent honing up skills in aerobatics, tail chases and low flying practice. WB872 became another casualty on the 14th when after making a dummy attack, it was seen to roll over and dive into the ground near Kroh. On the 18th, escort duties were carried out in support of helicopter incursions into the jungle. During the 23rd and 24th, air strikes were carried out at Sungei Siput, all aircraft later making landings at Tengah. After attacks over Kluang on the next day, they returned to Butterworth.

On 2 June, the squadron participated in the Queen's

WB874 of No.33 Squadron starting up for a strike from Butterworth

Coronation Flypast in conjunction with Hornets of 45 Squadron with a combined formation flight over Kuala Lumpur.

On 1 September, Sqn.Ldr. N.P.W. Hancock DFC, a former Battle of Britain pilot, took over command of the squadron to become O.C. Flying and Senior Squadron Leader at Butterworth. His first flight in F.4, PX346, did not pass without incident. The starboard propeller reduction gear housing developed a serious oil leak, forcing an engine shut-down and single-engine landing at Butterworth. The third week of September witnessed an increase in offensive activity with four separate air strikes against targets in Bongsu plus a single sortie over the Changun area.

During October, air strikes continued with attacks on targets in the Bongsu, Leng Gong and Besair areas. In common with many Hornet pilots, Sgt.Pilot Wallace reached a three-figure total of air strikes when he reached his century.

In November, air operations were stepped up, no fewer than twenty-two strikes being flown over the notorious and well-cratered Bongsu area. It was common practice to mount three strikes each day, the Hornets returning for re-arming within twenty minutes. The squadron armourers and ground crews were to be kept extremely busy!

Pairs of Hornets had been allocated specific areas every twenty minutes during daylight hours. Bongsu itself was an area of jungle measuring an area ten miles long

and three miles wide, surrounded by rubber plantations and within sight of Butterworth. At the time it was believed to contain two separate elements of the "Malayan People's Liberation Army". Between 19 and 25 November, no less than 236 air strikes were mounted against C.T. targets.

Following a temporary cessation of operations, a certain amount of jungle defoliation had become evident and despite thorough combing by army units, no visible evidence of a terrorist presence was discovered.

In December, attention was focussed on areas in Sungei Siput, Kuala and Kubu Baru. Two planned strikes over Chemor had to be aborted.

1954

New targets were selected in January; these included areas in Korbu, Raub, Bentong and Dabong. Due to the greater distances being flown, most flights were of two hour's duration.

Hornet F.4s were employed in a P.R. role, taking reconnaissance photographs of suspected targets, including those situated in the Gurun area. WB885 was written off in a fatal accident on 3 February when power was lost on both engines during a take-off from Butterworth. After overshooting the runway, the Hornet overturned.

Helicopters were escorted over the jungle in addition to two separate strikes over the Cameron Highlands and

Sungei Siput area. The constant activity against the C.T.s soon resulted in pilots reaching three-figure totals for air strikes; Sgt.Pilot Wallace was to achieve 137 before leaving the squadron.

On 29 June, WB872, flown by Flt.Lt. Williams, lost a starboard radiator panel during a pull-out from a steep dive attack and was force-landed in a padi field. Attempts were made to recover the aircraft but the ground proved too soft to bear the weight of lifting equipment. This led to the Hornet being dismantled for scrap. Vital components were removed before selling the aircraft at a local auction for the princely sum of $125 (Malay) - worth £13.17.9d.

June/July proved to be a bad period, with three Hornets being written off in accidents. First to go was F.4 WF972 on 28 June when its canopy shattered, forcing the pilot to make an emergency landing.

Runway re-surfacing at Butterworth commenced during July. A section of Hornets was detached from the 13th to the 23rd to the civil airfield at Alor Star, which was situated near the Thai border.

WB898 crashed on the 15th during A.P.C. after striking the sea in a diving turn whilst attacking a target being towed by a barge. PX302 became a further loss when it suffered a sudden loss of power on one engine during a pairs take-off and collided with WF971.

Ominous signs of structural deterioration occurred during July 1954 when PX306, flown by Flg/Off. Froud, was diving to attack C.T.s near Ipoh. The plywood skin on his starboard wing started to separate. This alarming experience caused Froud "some premature grey hairs". PX306 became one of the first Hornets to exhibit main spar separation and resulted in the Hornet's immediate scrapping. As a direct result, some speed restrictions were imposed. Some reports have indicated 290 knots and a reduction of dive angle to thirty degrees.

Similar problems with glued joints led to the sudden withdrawal of all F.E.A.F. Mosquitoes which had previously filled the vital role of maintaining squadron proficiency in instrument flying. They were replaced by Vampire T.11s, all squadron pilots being progressively converted.

During August, several air interceptions were made on U.S.A.F. B-29s which were operating from Clark Field, Philippines.

On 28 and 29 October, Hornets pounded away at terrorist camps, assembly areas and suspected hideouts in the Sungei Siput area, North of Ipoh. During these attacks some 60 tons of bombs, 500 rockets and thousands of cannon shells were unleashed on the targets. Concentrated attacks were made in support of Operation *Shark* with additional firepower provided by guns of the Royal Artillery.

WB873 made a wheels-up landing at Butterworth when the fuselage was damaged beyond repair after the target towing hook was forced upwards, causing severe damage to the main fuselage structure.

On 24 November, the squadron reached a new milestone having flown 4,000 air strikes.

Strikes between 1st and 3rd December included attacks by four Hornets on C.T. positions in Bukit Mertajam and Bukit Seraya hill areas, Central Province. They were continued for three hours and witnessed by local villagers. This attack was the first full-scale operation since August when the area was subjected to mortar and shell fire. Targets at Bukit Mertajam were situated close to Butterworth, with squadron ground crews having a grandstand view. During the engagement, Flying Officer Froud recalls making six firing passes inside ten minutes!

A comparative late-comer, Plt.Off. P.R. Sheppard, joined the squadron after completing No.19 Operational Conversion Course at Butterworth during December 1954 and January 1955. This was to be the final Hornet entry. Prior to commencing his Hornet conversion Plt. Off. Sheppard had served with the Ferry Training Unit, flying both Mosquito T.3 and Vampire FB.5. Possessing considerable Mosquito experience, his subsequent check-out on T.3 RR314 was a mere formality. His first Hornet solo in PX342 included a height climb to 25,000 feet, aerobatics and low flying.

Offensive flying during the month involved target identification over the Chemor area. Time was allotted to close and battle formation, dogfights and single-engine flying. On 25 February, PX368 was ferried to Seletar for inspection.

On March 14th, 16th and 17th, air strikes were continued over the Klian Inton and Kroh areas. On 17 March, the C.O., Sqn.Ldr. N.P.W. Hancock, took off in F.4 PX346 for the squadron's 5,000th air strike. His target was a suspected jungle camp to the north of base near Kroh.

On the 18th, F.3 WB879 was ferried to Seletar for storage and consequent scrapping. On the 24th, several sorties were made with R.P.s and low-level bombing. As a change of routine, between the 25th and 30th, three cross-country exercises were flown at low level.

On 31 March 1955, Sqn.Ldr. Hancock handed over command of 33 Sqn. This was to be his fourth and last command. Since taking over command he had flown some 275 hours on Hornets.

No.27 A.P.C. was held at Butterworth from 1st to 21st April with no Hornets being in evidence. Training flights were made using Vampire T.11s and FB.9s. Height climbs to 40,000 feet were accomplished in the FB.9s. Plt.Off. Sheppard completed the A.P.C. to join 33 Squadron which had only recently amalgamated with 45 Squadron.

On 2 April, tragedy struck 45 Squadron when PX350 and PX362 collided during a low-level flypast at Butterworth when the lower aircraft made a break and struck the tail section of his companion. The Hornet's tailplane, fin and rudder were completely severed from the fuselage. Both pilots were on their way to meet their wives who were about to disembark at Singapore docks.

May became a depressing month for 45/33's pilots, now tasked with a thankless job of ferrying their Hornets to Seletar for breaking up.

PX302 after colliding with WF971 on take-off at Butterworth, 29 July 1954

Hornets with No.33 Squadron

Squadron code letter: 5R (Replaced later by motif)

PX289 5R-Y, -T;	PX293 5R-V*;	PX298 G;
PX302 G;	PX305 5R-P, A;	PX306 J;
PX311 5R-Q;	PX328 5R-X;	PX335 A;
PX338 5R-H;	PX340*;	PX342 W,
PX346 5R-Y;	PX348 G,	PX352 ;
PX365 5R-P*;	PX384 5R-F, E;	PX386 R;
WB870 M;	WB871 5R-P;	WB872 5R-S;
WB873 5R-X;	WB874 5R-W,	WB875 5R-R;
WB876 5R-O;	WB877 5R-B;	WB878 5R-D, D;
WB881 E;	WB883 J;	WB885 5R-S;
WB886 F;	WB889 5R-A;	WF957 5R-H.

*F.3s converted to F.4s.

Hornet F.4:

WF970 5R-E, 5R-O, J;		WF971 5R-J;
WF972 5R-T;	WF973 5R-O;	WF975 5R-C;
WF979 Q.		

Mosquito T.3: RR308, RR312, RR319 Z, TV956 L

Commanding Officers:
Sqn.Ldr C.C.F. Cooper, Sqn. Ldr N.P.W. Hancock DFC.

Known Squadron Pilots:

Officers:

Flg.Off Ashworth, Flt.Lt N.G. Alderdice, Flt.Lt W.N. Baggaley, Flg.Off Brand, Flg.Off Bezzant, Plt.Off Caris, Flg.Off Close, Flg.Off Davis, Flg.Off Dawson, Flg.Off Duck, Flt.Lt J. Evans, Flg.Off J.Froud, Flt.Lt Hoskins (Flight Commander), Flg.Off Lumsden, Flg.Off E. Mellor, Flt.Lt R. Parsons, Flg.Off R.D. Austin-Smith, Plt.Off Sheppard, Flg.Off Thompson, Flg.Off Walker, Flg.Off Walsh, Flt.Lt Williams, Flt.Lt Wilson, Flt.Lt Young

N.C.O. Pilots:

Sgt. R. Bickerton, Sgt. R. Binfield, F/Sgt. W.R. Boyce, Sgt. Cheesergh, Sgt. P. Forrow, Sgt. George, Sgt. J. Hargreaves, Sgt. T. Kirk, Sgt. T. Saunders, Sgt. D. Taylor, Sgt. W. Wade, Flt.Sgt. K. Williams, Flt.Sgt. George, Sgt. Wallace, F/Sgt. Zmitrowitz.

PX298 5R-G being armed with four R.P.s and two 500-lb bombs

Hornets of No.45 Squadron on the flight line being loaded with R.P.s and 500-lb bombs

No.45 Squadron

Based at Tengah, 45 Squadron commenced conversion from Brigands to Hornets in February 1952. First to arrive was WB898 which landed at Tengah on 25 January. The last Brigand was cheerfully handed over to No.84 Squadron during the following month. With deliveries at a trickle, full squadron strength was not attained until the latter part of the year.

No.45 Squadron was commanded by Sqn.Ldr I.S. Stockwell, DFC, who was to continued his leadership until 15 December 1953. The C.O. flew on the squadron's first air strike on 11 June against insurgent targets near Triang, an area long suspected of being a Terrorist Camp. A second air strike was mounted on the same day against targets in the Fraser's Hill area. The camps themselves were situated in dense jungle and became extremely difficult to detect and attack from the air.

Great reliance was placed on relating ground intelligence to aerial photographic maps, plus detailed and accurate map reading by squadron pilots. On some occasions Auster spotter aircraft assisted by dropping smoke markers to indicate target locations. Attacks by Hornets usually involved discharging their R.P.s and bombs from steep dives.

Additional tasks for the squadron consisted of providing escorts for visiting V.I.P.s and various convoys bound for Malaya. Air escorts were also provided for Army support aircraft and helicopters which were engaged in air drops into the jungle to re-supply Commonwealth ground forces or for any casualty evacuations.

Strafing attacks were carried out on each side of the road to Fraser's Hill, ahead of buses which were conveying pupils to and from the Fraser's Hill School during term time.

Operations were resumed against the C.T.s with dive bombing over those areas which had been previously marked by low flying Auster AOPs flown by Army Officers. The marked area was then subjected to a barrage of R.P.s plus final strafing attacks using cannon ammunition.

Flying hours for squadron pilots during June were rationed due to the continuing shortage of aircraft. Despite lacking R.P. offensive capacity, 45 Squadron maintained attacks against the C.T.s using conventional bombs and cannon fire. Although it was difficult to observe results from the air, the campaign was continued to prevent a large build-up of C.T. forces.

On 5 June, the C.O. led 45 Squadron for the Queen's Birthday flypast over Padang, Singapore. Throughout 1952, it became routine practice for the squadron to deploy to Kuala Lumpur for operations.

Three Hornets of No.45 Squadron armed with R.P.s on the runway at Butterworth (via Bruce Robertson)

Despite a high accident rate, No.84 Squadron persevered with Brigands and acted as a back-up squadron. On 28 August, WB912 of B Flight failed to recover from a dive during a strafing attack on C.T.s and became the squadron's first Hornet accident.

After practice for the September Battle of Britain Flypast, nine Hornets were on strength for leading a formation over Singapore on the 15th.

Other less well known tasks for the squadron included exercises with naval ships en route to Korean waters.

Operations over the Malayan jungle were continued in co-operation with R.A.A.F. Lincolns, Sunderlands, Brigands of 84 Squadron and Vampires. Attacks were made to coincide with ground action by the Army, who were directly responsible for close air support.

Bill Morrison, former Flight Commander B Flight, recalls several incidents whilst carrying out air strikes over the Malayan jungle. During one air strike, he suffered a hang-up with one 500-lb bomb which stubbornly clung to the Hornet's bomb rack despite the aircraft being subjected to high g manoeuvres. The offending bomb eventually detached on touch-down at Tengah, fortunately without detonating. Some days later Flt.Lt. Morrison was in the process of turning on to the runway, only to hear his Number Two inform him that one of the 500-pounders had just fallen off on to the runway!

In addition to maintaining air strikes, occasional patrols were mounted over a vital water pipeline from Reservoir Hill, a large freshwater lake situated several miles from Tengah. Since this pipe served the island of Singapore, it was always considered a likely target for the terrorists.

On 2 June 1953, 45 Squadron, in conjunction with Hornets of 33 Squadron, carried out flypasts over Singapore and Malayan towns to commemorate the Coronation of Queen Elizabeth II. In addition, a further escort was provided for an aircraft conveying H.R.H the Duchess of Kent and her son, H.R.H. the Duke of Kent during the final stage of their flight to Singapore.

Fighter affiliation exercises were carried out with U.S.A.F. Superfortresses. Interception exercises were flown against carrier-borne Royal Navy Sea Furies en route from Korean waters via Singapore on return to the U.K.

Several unofficial skirmishes occurred, Hornets taking on Vampires of 60 Squadron in mock combats when the FB.9's tighter turning circle caused a few problems. Previous encounters with F.A.A. Sea Furies were fairly inconclusive, although Bill Morrison clearly remembers the inevitable post-dogfight "booze ups".

Sqn.Ldr. I.S. Stockwell handed over command of 45 Squadron on December 1953, having flown a total of seventy-six air strikes. He was eventually to retire an as Air Commodore. Sqn.Ldr. Stockwell considered that the

Hornet proved to be a reliable aircraft, its structure standing up extremely well to almost constant steep diving attacks and R.P. firing techniques, involving frequent high "G" loads on sorties. The airframe stood up well in humid conditions in the Far East, although extreme vigilance was needed by ground crews to detect any early signs of deterioration in the wooden structure and corrosion of light alloy components.

Flg.Off. Wilson joined the squadron during late November 1954, having passed through F.E.T.S. His recollections include reference to the aging process which had begun to affect several Hornets, including some ex-U.K.-based aircraft in the earlier PX serial range. Tropical humidity and infestation from termites were taking their toll.

Following the amalgamation with 33 Squadron, further deterioration was discovered in some airframes and resulted in a decision to scrap the entire Hornet fleet in May 1955. He further recalls ferrying PX342 on 16 May to Seletar for scrapping - "very carefully"!

On 31 March, Nos. 45 and 33 Squadrons were amalgamated, although the suggestion for a mix of squadron codes (one on each side of the fuselage) was not adopted. The amalgamation proved to be short-lived.

F.3s WB879, WF959, PX310, PX340, PX342, PX386 and PX391 soldiered on until May when scrapping began in earnest. Reluctantly discarding their Hornets, pilots returned to Butterworth after collecting Vampire FB.9s at Changi (including WR204 on 20 May). Some Meteor T.7s and Vampire T.11s were taken on charge for jet conversion.

No.45 Squadron's association with de Havilland was to continue when they re-equipped with Venom FB.1s at Butterworth during October 1955.

Hornets with 45 Sqn.

Hornet F.3:

PX298 OB- ;	PX310 OB-M;	PX312 OB- ;
PX312 OB- ;	PX332 OB- ;	PX342 OB- ;
PX350 OB-S;	PX352 OB-R;	PX353 OB- ;
PX354 OB-S;	PX357 OB- ;	PX362 OB- ;
PX367 OB- ;	PX369 OB- ;	PX389 OB- ;
WB875 OB-N;	WB876 OB-O, E;	WB877 OB- ;
WB879 OB-T;	WB883 OB- ;	WB898 OB-A;
WB908 OB-L;	WB911 OB-B;	WB912 OB-C;
WF954 OB-Q;	WF956 OB-N;	WF959 OB-K;
WF961 OB-D;	WF966 OB-N;	WF967 OB-H.

Hornet F.4:

WF973;	WF975 N

Pilots known to have served with 45 Squadron

Commanding Officers:
Sqn.Ldr I.S. Stockwell, Sqn.Ldr V. Jacobs.

Officers:
Flt.Lts W. Brittain DFC AFC, Breslain, Connors, P. Cornish, Greenwood, D. Helps, D. Muth DFC, W. Morrison AFC, Russell, R. Whitham. Flg.Offs: J. Alderton, Armstrong, J. Bowler, Cooper, R. Cordey, Fraser, Hempstead, N. Holmes, Kirkpatrick, B. Lacey, C. Lake, O'Brien, Pattison, E. Peters, Phillips, Sullivan, Wilson, Plt.Off Sheppard.

N.C.O.s:
F/Sgt. M. Clark, Craighill, F/Sgt. N. Grove, Sgt. Millington, Sgt. M. Retallack, Sgt. Holden-Rushworth, F/Sgt. Reeder, Sgt. G. Turley, Sgt. J. Vigar.

Hornets with 45/33 Squadron.

F.3: PX293, PX310, PX335, PX340, PX342, PX348, PX384, PX386, PX391, WB879, WF957, WF959
F.4: WF970.

PX347 OB-H of No.45 Squadron at Seletar, 1955 (via R.C. Sturtivant)

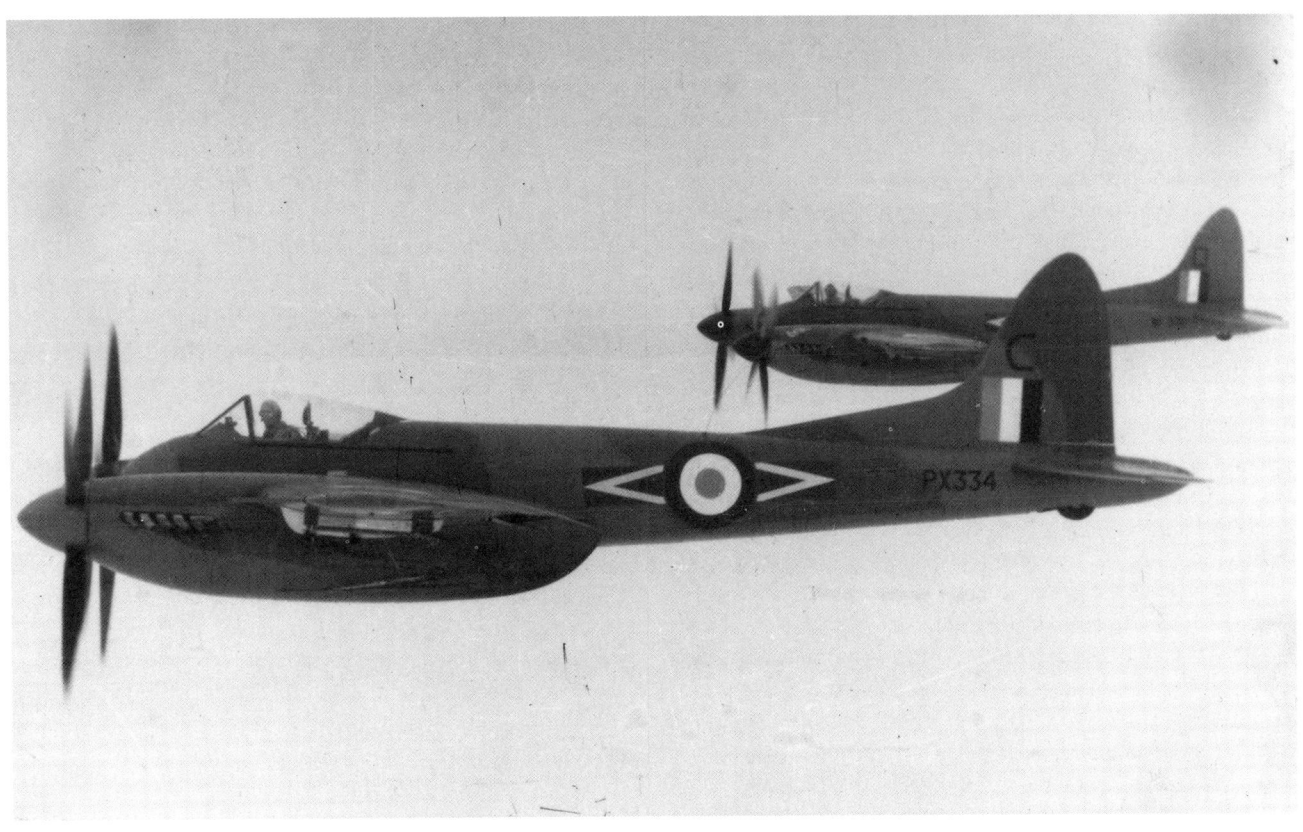

Hornet F.3s of No.80 Squadron (via Air Comm. W.H. Clayton)

No.80 Squadron, Kai Tak, Hong Kong

The squadron re-equipped with Hornets at Kai Tak during December 1951, replacing Spitfire F.24s. being under the command of Sqn.Ldr. J.M.V. Carpenter DFC, a former Battle of Britain pilot. Flight Commanders for A and B Flights were Flt.Lt. H.S. Horth AFC and Flt.Lt. E.L. Heath.

No.80 Squadron co-operated with Vampire FB.5s and FB.9s of No.28 Squadron at Sek Kong, New Territories, in an air defence role for the colony.

Kai Tak was situated in a corner of the hills around Kowloon where take-offs and landings demanded high levels of concentration, all approaches being curved. As a consequence there was no night flying or in marginal weather conditions. It was also considered extremely dangerous to attempt single-engine approaches, all asymmetric exercises being made at a safe height. Any real instances of engine failure resulted in a mad dash by pilots to view the proceedings. F/O Croydon's first single-engine emergency landing was not without drama when the Hornet used the whole length of Runway Thirteen. Reaching the sea wall, he turned left across a road and over the parade ground and eventually stopped outside the Aircraft Servicing Flight. Since Kai Tak was a regular stop-over for civil, U.S.N and U.S.A.F. aircraft, the crew room was nearly always deserted, most pilots preferring to be outside awaiting regular landing incidents.

No.80 Squadron operated a mixed fleet, some aircraft still retaining the original all-silver finish, in contrast with camouflaged Hornets.

By March 1953, however, all aircraft were adorned with the new maroon rectangle with gold diagonal bars which had been approved by Wg.Cdr. J. Kettlewell, O.C. Flying. All letter codes were transferred to the fin and most aircraft lettered with the pilots' names, A Flight having red spinners and B Flight blue spinners. The C.O's Hornet was alone in having white spinners.

A firing range at Port Shelter was conveniently situated only five miles from Kai Tak and provided facilities for gunnery/bombing exercises. R.P.s with concrete heads, twenty-five-pound practice bombs and occasionally, live 250- and 500-lb bombs were dropped at frequent intervals. Due to its close proximity to Kai Tak, several sorties could be flown during a single morning. All air-to-air firing was carried out over the sea. A Beaufighter TT.10, SR912 of the Station Flight, was used for towing target drogues.

During April 1953, six Hornets were being deployed for a goodwill visit to Clark A.F.B. in the Philippines when WB897 developed hydraulic failure. After being made serviceable, it was flown back to Kai Tak on 28 April by Sgt.Plt Chamberlain who had been flown over in the Beaufighter. On 8 September, the Hornets were engaged in a co-operation exercise with H.M.S. *Concord* then sailing off the Chinese coast. On the following day, an air defence exercise took place over the Hong Kong area.

Newcomer Flg.Off. G. Frost, had passed through a Mosquito conversion course at 204 A.F.S. at Bassingbourn and after further training at F.E.T.S he was posted to 80 Squadron, serving until April 1955. He relates one experience which concerned two pilots who were making a customary farewell beat-up of the firing range hut. Both were blissfully unaware of their simultaneous approaches and missed colliding by inches.

In order to carry out any night flying, it became a necessary routine for pilots to be attached to 33 and 45 Squadrons at Butterworth and Tengah on an exchange basis. Apart from the necessity of providing continuation training, these detachments also allowed 80 Squadron pilots an opportunity to fly operational sorties against C.T.s.

When acting as duty squadron, it became a regular routine for a pair of Hornets to fly twice daily reconnaissance flights around the colony and the surrounding sea. On one occasion Flt.Sgt. Kearn, together with his No.2 Flg.Off. Phillips, discovered a Royal Navy launch under fire from a Chinese gunboat. The sudden appearance of two Hornets caused the Chinese captain to abandon his attack. By now, however, the launch had sustained some damage plus several casualties, although it managed to reach harbour.

On 17 January 1954, Flg.Off. Phillips and Flg.Off. Frost were briefed for an unarmed reconnaissance to investigate suspicious contacts in the Pearl River estuary. Owing to starting problems with Frost's Hornet WB906, his Number Two had commenced his take-off, unaware that Phillips' Hornet was catching up. After raising his undercarriage, Frost caught his slipstream and forced back on to the runway, damaging both propellers. He quickly jettisoned his canopy before an inevitable splash in Hong Kong harbour. The Hornet floated long enough for his rescue from these notoriously polluted waters. A launch sent out to attend a visiting Sunderland promptly diverted to haul Frost out of the murky waters. The visitor aboard the Sunderland was the C.-in-C. Far East, who was kept waiting until the rescue was over.

12 April 1954 witnessed the demise of WF974 when it sustained structural damage during an inadvertent spin which occurred during practice single-engine flying at high altitude. During the descent both engines were splayed out due to severe lateral loads, with wing skins suffering damage. No repairs were attempted and Flg.Off Bill Croydon, the pilot, later to retire as an Air Commodore, recollects that on recovering from the spin, "both engines had partially come off the mountings. The Merlins seemed as if they were bedded on springs when the Hornet met any turbulence".

As with most emergencies, a fair-sized audience had gathered to witness the landing. With only a cursory examination, 974 was classed as Cat.5, spare parts only!

On 26 May, F/O Croydon in F.4 WF978 set off on an armed reconnaissance only to suffer a bird strike and be forced to return early. Cockpit environment in tropical conditions could and did become extremely hot and stuffy, Flg.Off Croydon almost falling asleep at the controls whilst flying at 200 feet when on patrol off the Chinese coast.

Tragedy struck the squadron on 26 August during a flypast by four aircraft over the troopship *Empire Halladale*, which was departing for the U.K. At the conclusion of their flypast, each Hornet made a separate flypast. Ply.Off Howard commenced an upward roll, lost control and crashed.

A Naval co-operation tactical exercise was carried out during September with the Essex Regiment, which consisted of armed reconnaissances and practice interceptions. On the 28th, an air strike was mounted on H.M.S. *Warrior* when the Hornets were intercepted by Sea Furies. Although the Fireflies were considered as "easy meat", the Hornets met their match with the Sea Furies. After making his attack, Flg.Off Croydon was "scooting off" at near wave-top level only to notice with astonishment a Sea Fury appear from below. The pilot of the Sea Fury had succeeded in making his interception without detection and looked upwards as he climbed away.

During October, the squadron made a practice interception and later escorted a Hastings which was carrying the C.-in-C.

Continual practice was made in preparation for the Air Display which was due to be held at Kai Tak on the 16th.

In November, the squadron was fully occupied with R.P. firing, armed reconnaissances plus regular meteorological flights. During December, flying activity was mainly devoted to air firing at drogues which were towed by Meteor T.7 WG976.

1955

Between January 7th and 9th, Exercise *Leeward* involved the squadron in co-operation exercises with 28 Squadron at Sek Kong, with 80 Squadron Hornets making high and low level attacks. On 4 March, the squadron flew an air/sea rescue mission following reports that an incoming U.S.A.F. C-47, AF 6632, was approaching the island on one engine. During the month several armed reconnaissances and practice interceptions were flown over Mount Davis and Ping Shan.

No.80 Squadron's role was basically ground attack/reconnaissance, in addition to its air defence and air/sea rescue duties. Together with its sister squadron at Sek Kong, 80 Squadron Hornets took turns at intercepting unidentified aircraft flying within fifty miles of Hong Kong waters. Low-level armed reconnaissance flights were carried out over colonial waters, keeping a sharp eye on the Chinese military posts on surrounding islands. Originally, these patrols were flown with Hornets unarmed until the infamous interception and bombardment of a Royal Navy launch. During armed patrols all aircraft carried 600 rounds of 20 mm cannon ammunition.

Drop tanks now being developed were capable of containing Lindholme Air Sea Rescue gear, this following the shooting-down off Hainan of a Cathay Pacific Airways DC-4 by Chinese MiG-15s, when the squadron conducted an intensive search.

Servicing Hornets was entrusted to the Hong Kong Engineering Company, who were found capable of superb overhauls. Several aircraft had only recently emerged from major servicing when orders were received to scrap the entire Hornet fleet. Virtually brand-new Merlins were systematically sledge-hammered into almost worthless scrap; fuselages were simply sawn up.

At about this time a certain R.A.F. Corporal decided to capitalise on the imminent scrapping, masquerading as a Wing Commander. He proceeded to entertain local scrap merchants with drinks provided on the patio of the airmens' mess. Soon he had accepted the highest tenders, receiving 18,000 Hong Kong Dollars with a further equal sum payable on delivery. This spectacular deal was discovered when the second cheque arrived on the genuine Equipment Officer's desk. By now the richer Corporal was on board a troopship bound for the U.K., soon to be whisked back to Hong Kong to face Court Martial, receiving nine months of detention in Stanley Military Prison.

No.80 Squadron was officially disbanded on 1 May 1955, although several Hornets were given air tests and some pilots were engaged on Army Co-operation duties with No.27 Heavy Anti-Aircraft Battery, using Harvards which included Mk.IIB FX488. No.80 Squadron was eventually re-formed at Laarbruch, West Germany.

Hornets with No.80 Squadron

Squadron code letters W2 (Replaced by motif)

F.3:

PX292 H;	PX294 H, M;	PX297 V;
PX334 C;	PX334 C*;	PX343 C;
PX345 G;	PX355 F, G;	PX357 G;
PX366 E;	PX368;	PX390 R;
WB880 C;	WB882 R;	WB888 A, L;
WB897 X;	WB899 T;	WB903 A;
WB904 Z;	WB905;	WB906 F;
WB907 D;	WB909 N, H, F, L;	
WF958 M;	WF962 A.	

*F.3 converted to F.4

F.4:

WF969 D;	WF974 M;	WF976 P, Q;
WF977 B;	WF978 Q.	

Mosquito T.3: RR270, RR282, VT620.

Commanding Officers:
Sqn.Ldr J.M.V. Carpenter DFC & Bar.
Sqn.Ldr Cullen. (from January 1954)

Squadron Pilots:

Officers:
Flg.Off Bathe, Flg.Off Bowden, Flg.Off Chapman, Flg.Off Croydon, Flg.Off Doggrell, Flg.Off Eckell, Flg.Off Hill, Flt.Lt Heath, Flt.Lt Horth, Plt.Off Howard, Flt.Lt Humphreys, Flt.Lt Hutton, Flg.Off L'Estrange, Flg.Off Morgan, Flg.Off Murgatroyd, Flg.Off Phillips, Flg.Off Sceats, Flg.Off Skinner, Flg.Off Stappard, Flt.Lt Steff-Langston, Flg.Off Vowles, Flg.Off Whitson.

N.C.O.s:
Sgt.Pilot Chamberlain, Sgt.Pilot Clarksom, Sgt.Pilot Heard, Sgt.Pilot Shannon, Sgt.Pilot Janisewski.

Hornet F.4 WF977 of No.80 Squadron with squadron colours en route to Clark Field, April 1953
(80 Squadron archives)

Hornet F.3 WB885 of the F.E.T.S. flown by Plt Off Stappard, February 1952

Far East Training Squadron, Seletar and Butterworth

Hornet Conversion Flight

This unit was responsible for converting newly arrived or inexperienced pilots, some of whom had gained their wings at training schools in the U.K. or Southern Rhodesia. After completing advanced training on Mosquitoes at Advanced Flying Schools, potential Hornet pilots were required to complete a conversion course which included a further five hours on Mosquito T.3s. Resident T.3s included RR312, RR314, RR319, TV976, VA882, VA888, VP349 and VP354.

The Hornet conversion course syllabus amounted to forty-five flying hours, with regular checks on the T.3 including basic familiarisation, general handling, aerobatics, night flying, navigation exercises and asymmetric flying.

Bombing and gunnery practice occurred during a week's camp held at Butterworth, with dive-bombing at forty-five degrees using R.P.s and bombs over a nearby range off the North-West coast, north of Penang.

The first course commenced training during August 1951. Sgt.Pilot Wallace was a typical pupil, having been recently trained in Southern Rhodesia. Prior to commencing his Hornet conversion at F.E.T.S., Sgt. Wallace had flown several hours on Oxfords. The first

Hornet solo in WB884 took place after two dual trips in the T.3 totalling nearly two hours. At the time, No.1 course also catered for small intakes who were converting to the Brigands then in service with No.45 Squadron.

On completing his course at F.E.T.S., Sgt. Wallace was flown to Butterworth in a T.3, attending No.27 A.P.C. The course syllabus for armament practice included the carrying of four 60-lb. R.P.s or eight 11-lb practice bombs in addition to 20 mm cannon ammunition. Munitions were discharged at targets in sixty-degree dives. All the practice bombs were carried on light series carriers which were capable of being fitted to standard R.A.F. bomb hooks. The electrical system had been re-aligned to allow practice bombs to be released individually or in sequence. After completing the armament course, Wallace flew WB884 back to Seletar before being posted to 33 Squadron, then based at Tengah.

Flg.Off. Allen was a much later pupil and about to complete his Hornet conversion only to receive news of a posting to a Meteor squadron. He described the Meteor as a heavy lorry compared with the Hornet.

Air-to-air firing was also included in the course syllabus, with resident Beaufighter TT.10s being used for towing sleeve/drogue targets. On occasions, some pilots achieved considerable accuracy with R.P.s, recording strikes between two and ten yards from the centre of range targets.

One of the F.E.T.S Hornets (WB901 of Station Flight) was stripped of all armament, suitably ballasted and fitted out for meteorological flights, complete with barometer and wet/dry bulb thermometers. The routine daily Met. Flight began at 09.00 hrs with a climb to about 30,000 feet with only internal fuel carried in the inner tanks.

The final phase of the F.E.T.S course usually included a long flight to Labuan Island, off North Borneo, with lunch at Labuan before returning to Seletar during the late afternoon. Inevitably, the unpredictable weather plus aircraft serviceability often resulted in delayed departures, some pilots being stranded for a week.

F/O Bill Croydon graduated from F.E.T.S and was duly posted to 80 Squadron at Kai Tak, flying to Hong Kong aboard Sunderland GR.5 VB888 for the first leg to Cat-Lai, Saigon. The Sunderland was given a short air test before departing for a lengthy eight-hour flight. Bill Croydon eventually arrived at Kai Tak.

Hornets used by F.E.T.S:

PX292, PX295, PX309, PX313, PX340 (F.4 Conv.), PX345, PX368, PX391, WB873, WB879, WB880, WB884, WB885, WB888, WB889, WB901, WB905, WB910, WF960.

F.E.T.S Hornets were painted with standard yellow training bands, aft of the fuselage roundels; letter codes were carried by some aircraft.

Mosquito T.3; RR312, RR314, RR319, TV976, VA888, VP349, VP354

Vampire T.11; WZ587, WZ610 (Used for demonstrating R.P. firing)

Harvard IIB of Station Flight, FX476.

Commanding Officer:
Sqn.Ldr. Hitchcock.

Staff Instructors:
Flt.Lt. Sutton (Flight Commander), Flt.Lt. P. Thompson, Fg.Off. Paton.

F.E.T.S.'s base at Seletar (D.A. Hornton)

PX360 at Sharjah in transit to F.E.A.F. (Roy Mercer)

PX292 outside F.E.T.S. hangar on arrival at Seletar

No.1 Overseas Ferry Unit/Ferry Training Unit. Pershore, Chivenor, Benson and Abingdon

Before despatch to F.E.T.S., Hornets were subjected to shake-down trials totalling about five flying hours to discover and eliminate any defects. No.1 Ferry Training Unit possessed some Mosquito T.3s and two hack Hornet F.3s, PX296 and PX329, which provided the ferry pilots with type experience,

Hornets were ferried out complete with long range tanks, flying for four-and-a-half hours over distances up to 1,700 miles. Navigational equipment consisted of a radio compass and maps. The routes flown included legs: Abingdon - Luqa - Fayid - Bahrein - Mauripur - Dum Dum - Rangoon/Mingaladon - Seletar; Benson - Istres - El Adem - Mafraq - Shaibah - Bahrein - Mauripur - Palam - Dum Dum - Mingaladon - Butterworth - Seletar; Benson - Istres - Tunis - Idris - El Adem - Fayid - Habbaniya - Shaibah - Bahrein - Mauripur - Bombay - Dum Dum - Mingaladon - Butterworth - Seletar. Other airfields were used on occasions. PX360 is known to have staged through Sharjah on its delivery flight. The journey took between six and fourteen days, depending on weather conditions. It was not uncommon for ferry pilots to encounter bad weather or technical defects. Whilst ferrying PX313, Sqn.Ldr. Rose had a close shave due to a jammed radiator shutter. The Merlin was shut down to prevent overheating and feathered accordingly. Meanwhile the other engine started to overheat due to the high ambient temperatures between Bahrein and Karachi. Sqn.Ldr. Rose "managed to arrive at Sharjah before the Merlin became molten metal"! Inhospitable terrain on certain legs of the journey demanded the carrying of appropriately worded "Chits" in case of a forced landing within Bedouin territory. It became customary for Hornets to be ferried out in flights of four aircraft in order to ease navigation.

On arriving at Singapore, pilots often returned to the U.K. in style, courtesy of B.O.A.C.

After being air tested, WB871 (flown by A.V.M. Bonham-Carter) set off on a delivery flight to Kai Tak, Hong Kong, accompanied by another Hornet. On arrival at Calcutta, the aircraft became unserviceable. After sending the other pilot to Singapore in a B.O.A.C. Constellation, the A.V.M. pressed on to Clark Field.

By now the top brass were fully aware of the approaching V.I.P. being the new Air Officer Commanding at Hong Kong, and sending a "four-ship" formation of Lockheed Shooting Stars to provide an escort. Several different accounts exist which confirm at least part of the following account. On nearing Clark Field at low level, the A.V.M. evaded his escorts, treated the reception committee to a noisy beat up and shut down one engine. In a gentle dive he swept over Clark Field at nearly 350 m.p.h. As a finale, he flew fly past with both propellers feathered! On being greeted by the Base Commander, A.V.M. Bonham-Carter took off his flying helmet in order to attach his hearing aid.

Not all ferry flights were to be free of incidents. On 3 December 1951, three Hornets set off from Seletar on delivery to 80 Squadron at Kai Tak. On nearing the Philippines they encountered severe tropical storms. During the bad weather let-down, Flt.Lt. Peebles in WB887 lost contact with Clark Field. On breaking cloud he became aware of the close proximity of high ground and quickly warned the other pilots. After making an unsuccessful attempt to make radio contact with the ground controllers, he climbed to 5,000 feet and baled out. Plt.Off. Heard in WB902 was not so fortunate, failing to hear neither the order to remain above 4,000 feet nor the emergency message from the formation leader to pull up. Heard's Hornet struck high ground at San Baitalome. The cause of this tragedy was attributed to unsatisfactory two-way radio, torrential rain, extreme turbulence plus inadequate G.C.A. and S.C.I. equipment at Clark Field.

Most Hornets were ferried to Hong Kong by 80 Squadron pilots due to their being familiar with Kai Tak airfield. Hornets were flown in formation and accompanied by a far distant Valetta which was used as a communications link. The Valetta also carried ground crews. Drop tanks were carried which contained 100 gallons apiece, although a critical decision was absolutely necessary on reaching the point of no return between Clark Field and Kai Tak. Drop tanks of 200-gallon capacity would have given the Hornet a 2,000-mile range.

Hornet F.3 PX362 MS-H of the Hornet Conversion Flight, Linton-on-Ouse

Royal Air Force Training and Support Units

No.226 OCU Bentwaters

This unit provided conversion training for pilots emerging from Flying Training Schools or converting from other types.

Hornet F.1s:
PX231, (later 6612M); PX238 XL-D;
PX281 XL-E; *PX252 BB-T, later XL-T

* Destroyed in a fatal accident on 8 January 1949 when P.II Bayton allowed his speed to fall below critical limit during a single-engine overshoot. PX231, PX238 and PX281 also suffered varying degrees of damage during service at Bentwaters.

*   *   *   *   *   *   *   *

Central Fighter Establishment, West Raynham

Hornet F.1s:
PX224, PX275 GO-F.

Hornet F.3s:
PX336, PX348.

No.1 Overseas Ferry Unit, Pershore, Chivenor and Benson

Hornet F.3s: PX296, PX329. Hack aircraft used for training.

*   *   *   *   *   *   *   *

Photographic Reconnaissance Development Unit, Benson

Hornet PR.2: Prototype PX216 6C-R

*   *   *   *   *   *   *   *

Empire Central Flying School, Hullavington

Hornet F.1: PX225

*   *   *   *   *   *   *   *

RAF Henlow

Hornet F.1: 6696M, ex-PX238, as ground instructional airframe.

PX362 MS-H of the Hornet Conversion Flight (via P. Jarrett)

PX238 XL-D of No. 226 Operational Conversion Unit

Hornet F.I PX275 GO-F of Central Fighter Establishment (R.C.Sturtivant)

RAF Halton Apprentice School

Hornet F.1: 6149M, ex-PX210, as ground instructional airframe.

* * * * * * * *

Central Gunnery School, RAF Leconfield

Hornet F.1: 6658M, ex-PX277, as ground instructional airframe

* * * * * * * *

Royal Air Force Flying College, Manby

Hornet F.3: PX309

* * * * * * * *

Royal Aircraft Establishment, Farnborough

Hornet PR.2: VA964, VA965, VA966.

* * * * * * * *

No.12 Group Headquarters Communication Flight

Hornet F.3: PX304. (This aircraft suffered "Rogue" characteristics, in particular with severe aileron vibration above 250 m.p.h.)

Horsham St.Faith Station Flight

Hornet F.I: PX237

* * * * * * * *

Linton-on-Ouse, Station Flight / Hornet Conversion Flight

Hornet F.3:

PX292 MS-K;	PX299 MS-C,-G;	PX354 MS-A;
PX362 MS-H;	PX365 MS- ;	PX384 MS- ;
PX395 MS- .		

Mosquito T.3: TW117

Hornets F.3s were used principally for conversion courses for pilots destined for service with Hornet squadrons pupils arriving from Mosquito T.3 courses at 203 A.F.S., Swinderby. Most progressed to the T.3 via Harvards. The average course included a customary check in the Flight's Mosquito T.3, followed by an unforgettable Hornet solo. The intensive course included a further eleven hours of training with mandatory periods of single-engine flying, aerobatics, formation practice and I/F let-downs completed the course, lasting about a month. Essential weapons training was eventually conducted on squadron or A.P.C., on arrival at an operational squadron either in the U.K. or with Far East Air Force.

Sea Hornets

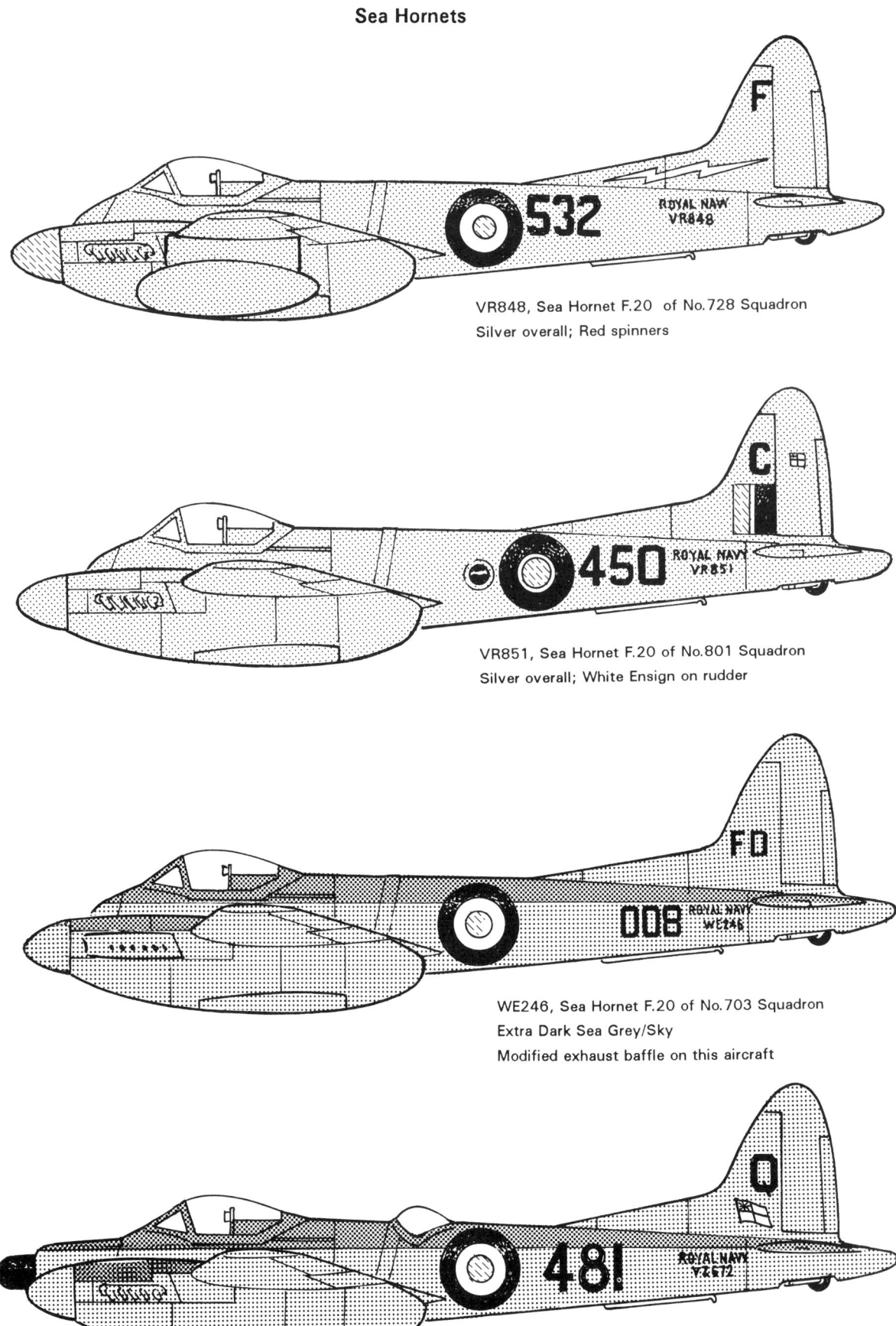

VR848, Sea Hornet F.20 of No.728 Squadron
Silver overall; Red spinners

VR851, Sea Hornet F.20 of No.801 Squadron
Silver overall; White Ensign on rudder

WE246, Sea Hornet F.20 of No.703 Squadron
Extra Dark Sea Grey/Sky
Modified exhaust baffle on this aircraft

VZ672, Sea Hornet NF.21 of No.809 Squadron
Extra Dark Sea Green/Sky
White Ensign on fin

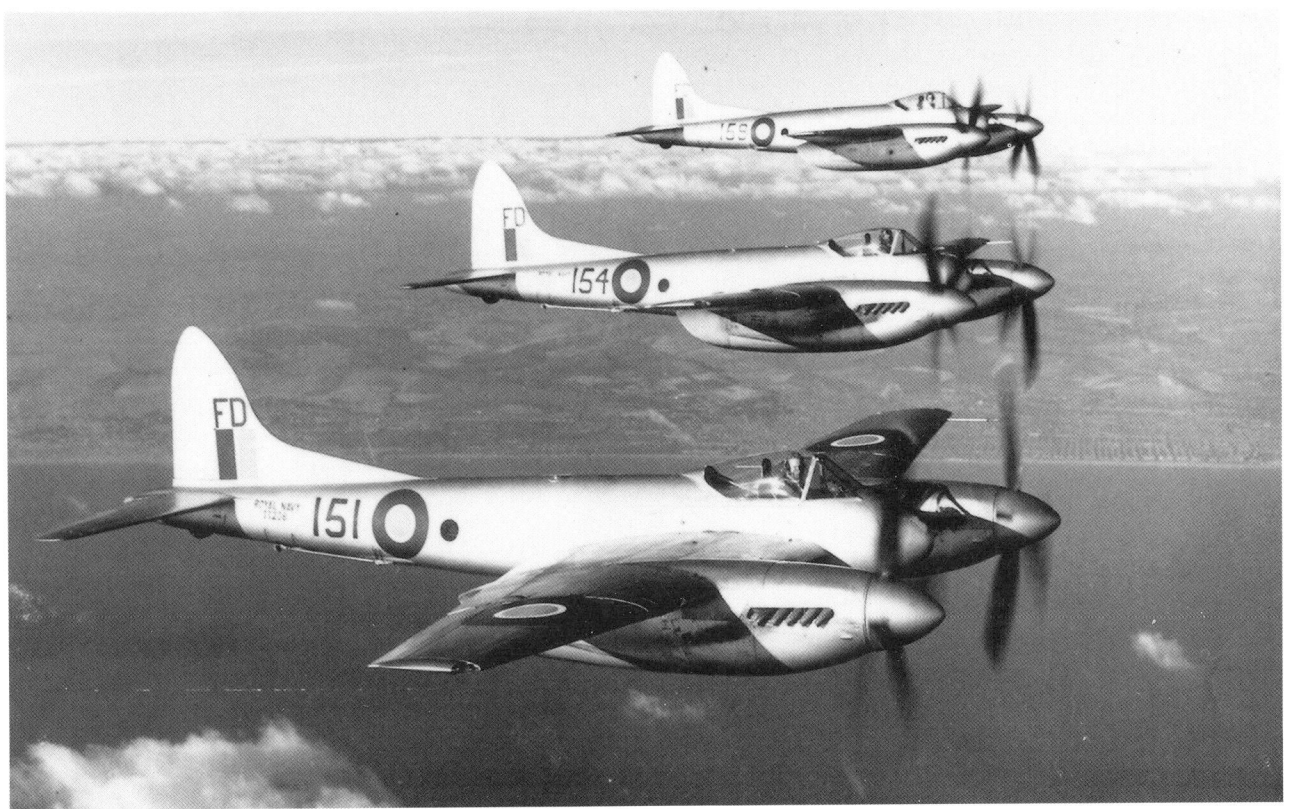

Sea Hornet F.20s of No.801 Squadron flying from Ford (via R.S. Sturtivant)

Sea Hornet Squadrons

No.801 Squadron.

No.801 Squadron, commanded by Lt.Cdr. D.B. Law, was officially reformed at Ford on 1 July 1947, becoming the first and only front-line squadron to be equipped with the F.20 variant. The C.O. had formerly commanded the Fighter Combat Section of School of Naval Air Warfare, R.A.F. West Raynham, where he passed on his combat expertise. Prior to his appointment he underwent a jet conversion course in April 1946 at No.1335 Conversion Unit at R.A.F. Molesworth, flying Meteor IIIs XL-F, W, F and M, although several more years were to elapse before F.A.A squadrons finally equipped with jets. His twin conversion to Sea Hornet took place with 762 Squadron at Ford, using the Mosquito T.III for dual and FB.VI for solo flying.

Preparations for the introduction of the Sea Hornet F.20 into service were commenced earlier at R.N.A.S. Culham, with work-up trials starting at Ford in early 1947. Lt.Cdr. Law began the process of hand-picking pilots for the squadron, all of whom had been previously assessed "Above Average" for flying ability.

One accident occurred at Ford following the failure of a port undercarriage torque link due to a heavy landing. A second hard contact with the runway finally caused the torque link to fracture and resulted in the port undercarriage turning through ninety degrees. The final contact resulted in sudden harsh deceleration and, following a swing, the gear collapsed.

No.801 Squadron embarked for a short period on H.M.S. *Implacable* during 19th to 23rd November for deck landing trials.

1948

The squadron relocated to Culdrose on 8 January 1948, before flying out to *Implacable* again on 5 March.

Six aircraft, TT196, TT200, TT201, TT203, TT204 and TT205, were on squadron strength for a move to Arbroath on 30 April for trials and an intensive work-up.

On 3 May 1948, Lt.Cdr. D.H. Richards, former C.O. of 809 Squadron, took over command of 801 Squadron, and Lt. S.B. Oliver joined 801 Squadron at Arbroath in the middle of May. His second flight in VR855 was detailed for aerobatics only to be abandoned after ten minutes due to excessively high oil temperature on his starboard engine.

"Ollie" Oliver was later Chief Test Pilot, Hunting Group, engaged in test and demonstration flying on the Jet Provost, among other Percival/Hunting/British Aircraft Corporation types. Before flying Sea Hornets, Lt. Oliver had sampled various marks of Sea Mosquito, including the "Ugly Duckling" TT.39, whose single-engine safety speed was an alarming 220 knots! Compared with Sea Hornets, undercarriage retraction times were found to be significantly longer on the Mosquito and when wheels were lowered, they produced considerably more drag.

Deck take-offs were made using 25 lb boost, with firm instructions on the procedure following engine failure. Single-engine landings were considered as hazardous due to the 155-knot critical speed. Official rules were to either abandon aircraft or ditch, should landing ashore prove to be impossible.

On 6 May Lt. Leahy in VR847 had the misfortune to have a port undercarriage collapse on landing at Arbroath. Between the 20th and 25th May, No.801 Squadron pilots were engaged in formation drill, tactical reconnaissance and formation aerobatics. During the following two days, 801's Sea Hornets were aloft for a "Cab Rank", directed by forward air controllers.

Flying activity in June consisted mainly of aerobatic flying and the odd dogfights with Sea Furies. On the 3rd, priority was given to carrier drill in addition to formation aerobatics. On the 17th, Lt. Oliver departed for Hendon in Expeditor KP117, complete with five extra passengers for the purpose of getting married.

In July, 801 Squadron was engaged on a variety of duties including beacon homing, Navexes and wind-finding, with air strikes on targets in Kirkcudbright and tactical reconnaissance with the Territorial Army, attacking troops and tanks at Barry in South Wales.

On the 13th, 801 Squadron deployed to Yeovilton in formation, climbing to 21,000 feet through cloud, using oxygen for most of the flight.

Shortly after arriving at Yeovilton, two sorties were flown on the 14th involving tactical reconnaissances to Stockton Wood for attacks on tanks, anti-aircraft guns and transport. A further strike was carried out on Hayling Island in direct support of the Army. Another strike followed next day in close support of an army beach-head. On the 16th, 801 Squadron returned to Arbroath in squadron formation which was held whilst climbing and descending through cloud.

Live air-to-ground firing was carried out on the 19th at the Tentsmuir Ranges when 801 Squadron was on temporary detachment at Leuchars. Despite the amount of activity, time was allowed for a spot landing competition using Tiger Moth BB812.

On 16 August, the squadron set off again for Yeovilton in squadron formation, using oxygen for a climb to 29,500 feet and avoiding storm clouds en route. After reaching Yeovilton, they were airborne again providing top cover for an attack on Portland Harbour. On completing the exercise, the squadron landed at St. Merryn for refuelling, returning to Arbroath at 20,000 feet.

On the 17th, Lt. Oliver set off in VR840 using full oxygen for a climb to service ceiling, reaching 35,200 feet. Two days later, the squadron departed for Culham in flight formation at 10,000 feet. Lt. Oliver returned to

Arbroath in leisurely style in the Station Flight Dominie NF879. Slow flying practice on the 23rd and 24th was followed by a A.D.D.L.s.

In September, 801 Squadron rehearsed for the Battle of Britain Flypast. On the 22nd, the squadron made a formation take-off before setting off for a cloud flight to Culdrose. Next day, a squadron formation flight was made to St. Merryn, Yeovilton and Portland.

During Exercise *One Step* on the 24th, 801 Squadron providing an escort for Lancasters flying at 16,000 feet. This was followed by a low-level strike against the Home Fleet when Lt. Oliver was "shot down". After completing its role in *One Step*, the squadron returned to Arbroath on the 25th in the traditional squadron formation.

On 7 October, the squadron set off on a formation flight to Lee-on-Solent on detachment for Operation *Shop Window*, a two-day exercise. Low level attacks were made on H.M.S. *Illustrious* and splash targets were strafed before a return to Arbroath. In mid-month, A.D.D.L.s were carried out at Milltown using American batting signals. Lt. Oliver recorded thirteen landings in fifty minutes, with a further thirteen in 45 minutes on the following day. A formation flight on the 20th took the squadron to Culdrose on temporary detachment. Lts. Petrie and Leahy, in VR853 and VR855, carried out deck-landing trials on H.M.S. *Implacable*.

During their detachment in November at Culdrose, pilots were active with formation flying, fighter evasion, low-level formation cross-countries, aerobatics and single-engine flying exercises. On the 13th, 801 Squadron carried out a fighter sweep which was finished with an attack on H.M.S. *Warspite*, aground in Prussia Cove, Cornwall, while being towed to the breaker's yard. A Group tactical exercise on the 19th involved the provision of fighter cover and a sweep over Bardsey and The Smalls.

During December, a series of A.D.D.L.s were carried out which averaged fifteen landings each day.

Exercise *Sunrise* commenced on the 10th with a combined scramble of Sea Hornets and Hornets of the R.A.F. for a fighter sweep which proved to be abortive. On the 15th, a formation flight made at 20,000 feet to Eglinton using oxygen. Lt. Martin was forced to return to Culdrose after an engine fire. On the 18th the squadron participated in a Group formation exercise with fourteen aircraft.

1949

On 7 January 1949, Lt. Oliver in VR854 was forced to divert to Yeovilton whilst flying in poor weather to Culdrose. He had the misfortune to contend with total radio failure which he aptly described as a "Saga". Three days later, he experienced yet another radio failure whilst engaged on a tactical reconnaissance.

No.801 Squadron carried out A.D.D.L.s in preparation for making deck landings on H.M.S. *Implacable*. On the 20th, top cover was provided for a School of Naval Air Warfare air strike on St Merryn.

Sea Hornet F.20 VR838 suffers an undercarriage collapse at Ford in 1947

The squadron made a rendezvous with H.M.S. *Implacable* on the 24th, with dummy runs on the carrier which were followed by a radar exercise.

On 27 January, No.801 flew in formation to *Implacable*, although the Sea Hornets were unable to embark until the next day which was a special one for the few who were making their first deck landings.

February 2nd and 3rd: 801 Squadron was safely aboard H.M.S. *Implacable* and was soon carrying out tactical reconnaissances over Scapa Flow, Peterhead and the Western Isles. A squadron formation landing was made at Lossiemouth before a departure to Arbroath, after which they returned to *Implacable* for a pre-landing beat up.

After completion of trials and training, 801 Squadron F.20s were soon brought up to full strength to twelve aircraft to form an integral part of No.1 C.A.G. Also aboard *Implacable* at the time were Blackburn Firebrand TF.5s of No.813 Squadron.

Now fully at home with their Sea Hornets, 801 Squadron pilots carried out feathered engine and formation flying, strafed towed targets, indulged in "tail chases" and flew tactical reconnaissances for the Royal Marines. On the 14th, close escort was provided for Firebrands of 813 Squadron during a search and strike mission against a Royal Navy frigate north of Cape Wrath. Several pilots flew ashore on a round trip, calling in at Lossiemouth and Donibristle, with a landing at Culham for refuelling before returning aboard *Implacable*.

Lt. K. Lee-White joined the squadron on the 22nd, serving as Air Weapons Officer for No.1 C.A.G., having previously commanded No.813 Squadron's Firebrand TF.5s. After completing a twin conversion course on Oxfords and Mosquitoes with No.762 Squadron at Culdrose, initial Sea Hornet familiarisation was carried out at the first available opportunity - at Gibraltar. Further periods of consolidation on the Sea Hornet were taken at Lee-on-Solent and Lossiemouth. Lee-White considered that "the Sea Hornet proved a delight to fly when compared with the lumbering Mossie".

During March 14th to 16th, drop tank trials were commenced, followed by attacks on H.M.S. *Theseus* and several C.A.P.s. On the 25th the squadron disembarked to Lee-on-Solent.

On 4 April, a demonstration attack was made on the training cruiser H.M.S. *Devonshire* and between the 23rd and 29th, the squadron practised low flying, single-engine landings and day and night A.D.D.L.s. Lt. Lee-White logged no less than 25 A.D.D.L.s in one day. Air-to-air firing was directed at towed drogues. On the 29th, 801 Squadron linked up with Firebrands for a torpedo search mission and a later flypast.

On 3 May, the Group embarked on *Implacable* and several days later engaged in exercises with Vampire F.20s from Culdrose. They included a surprise attack during take-off. During the 7th, a C.A.P. was flown from *Implacable* with Lt. Oliver claiming hits on a Sunderland. Several formation flights were made in addition to aerobatics.

Numerous A.D.D.L.s were made on the satellite airfield at Milltown near Lossiemouth, where gale force conditions caused later postponements. Hoverfly KL111 was used to ferry Lt. Oliver to Lossiemouth. On the last day of the month, practice interceptions were attempted at 15,000-25,000 feet, though without result.

On 1 June, an air strike was made by 17 C.A.G. on the Home Fleet, followed by a mass flypast. A C.A.P. was also flown against Mosquito PR.34s which were operating from Leuchars, although they proved difficult to intercept due to their high operating speed at extreme altitude.

Later C.A.P.s were mounted against patrolling Catalinas of the Royal Norwegian Air Force, with air/ground strikes over Norway.

Exercise *Midsummer* was scheduled to commence on the 21st as part of the Home Fleet's Summer exercises which proved abortive due to eight-eighths cloud at 200-600 feet. On the same day, a C.A.P. against R.A.F. Meteors operating from Horsham St. Faith proved disappointing, with no interceptions recorded. A C.A.P. next day was against Lancasters which were shadowing the carrier. No.801 were diverted to Prestwick and took off at 03.00(!) bound for Lossiemouth at 10,000 feet before refuelling for a return to *Implacable* on the same day.

Anti-submarine patrols on the 23rd were flown through the Western Isles without any sightings. Planned attacks on H.M.S. *Theseus* and *Implacable* for the 29th had to be aborted due to bad weather.

Exercise *Verity*, held on July 4th/5th, was with the French Navy under Western Union auspices. This included a Fleet C.A.P. against Sea Furies and Fireflies from H.M.S. *Theseus*, followed by a further C.A.P. which failed to encounter any opposition. On the 5th, strikes were mounted against H.M.S. *Theseus* and the French carrier *Arromanches*. During a C.A.P. against fleet shadowers, one Dutch Mitchell was claimed as "destroyed".

On the 7th, 801 Squadron flew ashore to Lee-on-Solent, part of a flypast for No.1 C.A.G. which passed over *Implacable*. No.801 Squadron flew to St Merryn on detachment from the 7th to 12th, specifically for R.P. firing on the range. On the final day, Lt. Lee-White flew eight firing sorties, seven with R.P.s.

On the 14th, Lt.Cdr. K. Lee-White MBE took over command of 801 Squadron, and two days later led the squadron formation to 20,000 feet for a deployment to Anthorn. On arrival, the Sea Hornet pilots treated the base to a spirited beat-up. This particular deployment was in preparation for Anthorn's Air Display, held on the same day.

Lt. Oliver in VR853 and Lt.Cdr. Law in VR854 performed individual aerobatics before a full 801 Squadron flypast and stream landing. A late departure for another display at Lee-on-Solent resulted in the squadron meeting heavy thunderstorms whilst en route.

Regular attacks using R.P.s were made on splash targets towed by ships sailing in Bracklesham Bay and on H.M.S. *Devonshire*. On the 20th, a formation flight was made to Arbroath at 20,000 feet and held throughout the climb and descent. During the air display at Arbroath, 801 Squadron shared honours with Firebrands of 813 Squadron for a mock R.P. attack on the airfield. Next day 801 set off in flight formation at 20,000 feet bound for Lee-on-Solent.

Flying activity over the following two days consisted of thirty-degree diving attacks with four R.P.s, flight drill with formation breaks and "Chase-me-Charlie".

In August, 801 Squadron was detached to Lee-on-Solent and carried out a considerable number of A.D.D.L.s and did some night flying with controlled descents. Instrument flying instruction was provided for the squadron using Harvard IIBs KF506, KF550 and KF558.

In September, the squadron flew in a Group formation and made flight attacks on Firebrands and Meteor F.4s. 801 Squadron Sea Hornets claimed many Firebrands. However, the Meteor F.4s succeeded in showing the Sea Hornets a clean pair of heels. On the 5th, the Group embarked again on H.M.S. *Implacable*. Three days later, a C.A.P. was mounted against Sea Furies and Fireflies of 17th C.A.G. operating from St. Merryn.

The C.O. made 801's first catapult take-off from *Implacable* as a preliminary test of newly-installed equipment. This type of take-off was usually employed whilst the carrier was stationary or out of wind, sometimes being used when aircraft were at high all-up weight. Normal take-offs, however, had the advantage of giving a much higher launch rate and were tactically advantageous.

A Fleet C.A.P. was mounted on the 9th when Lt. Oliver claimed a Lancaster, following his first accelerator take-off from *Implacable*. On the 10th, a squadron air strike was carried out against *Implacable*, which was defended by Spitfires of No.502 Squadron, Royal Auxiliary Air Force. Another C.A.P. was flown on the 10th at low level against Barracudas of 815 Squadron from Eglinton; this ended in a theoretical massacre!

On the 16th, following air combat with 813 Squadron Firebrands and after well over two hours flying, 801 Squadron landed at Lossiemouth for refuelling, before returning to *Implacable* in group formation. A formation flight was made in cloud on the 22nd, landing at Lossiemouth before returning to *Implacable* for a low-level C.A.P.. Four days later, 801 Squadron returned again to Lossiemouth for night flying and A.D.D.L.s. A search and rescue exercise on the 29th was followed by a lively combat with two Fireflies, when Lt. Oliver in VR853 suffered a starboard engine failure and made a single-engine landing at Lossiemouth.

A Fleet C.A.P. on 5 October met murky conditions, although a week later a patrol off Stavanger resulted in numerous tangles with Catalinas and Vampires of the Royal Norwegian Air Force.

Sea Hornets and Firebrands of the 1st Carrier Air Group aboard H.M.S. Implacable

In November, Lt.Cdr. D.B. Law took over command of No.1 C.A.G. following his return from 806 Squadron's successful North American tour, soon converting to Firebrands and the massive Wyvern. On the 4th, No.801 provided cover for Firebrands during a strike against *Implacable* which was defended by Vampires.

An exercise on the 7th, code-named *Porcupine*, found 801 Squadron on C.A.P. without any contacts. *Implacable* was sailing in conditions of heavy swell which caused a considerable movement of the flight deck, Lt. Oliver experiencing his first barrier landing. An extra C.A.P. was mounted without result. The heavy seas still persisted which meant a second barrier landing for Lt. Oliver.

Exercise *Porcupine* commenced on the 9th, when 801's Sea Hornets flew C.A.P.s, in the course of which a Sunderland and two Mosquito PR.34s were intercepted, both claimed as destroyed.

Due to the Sea Hornet's relatively high stick force per "G", allied with an unimpressive rate of roll, any opposing Sea Furies could easily lose them during dog-fights simply by reversing turns. Climbing away was a different matter thanks to the Sea Hornet's rocket-like climb.

During December, numerous A.D.D.L.s and carrier circuits were practised with a view to familiarising the pilots with newly-introduced techniques for carrier landings, now identical to those used by the U.S. Navy and quickly standardised throughout N.A.T.O.

When used in a maritime strike role, Sea Hornet pilots experimented with "Fluid Six", a loose tactical formation used when aircraft were loaded with bombs or R.P.s, whereas in a fighter role the standard "Finger Four" pattern was usually adopted.

1950

After air testing the Sea Hornets embarked aboard *Implacable* on 24 January 1950 and carrying out deck landing practice, the carrier set sail for the Home Fleet's 1950 Spring Cruise. All the deck landing signal equipment had been changed to U.S. Navy standard.

VR860 became a deck casualty on the 29th when its tail struck the round-down and parted from the fuselage, the remainder skidding along the deck, its port wing striking No.1 Barrier Stanchion.

During February, attacks were made on the Fleet, together with regular "drogue shoots"' and navigation exercises. Anti-flak and strike missions were flown against cruisers. VR855 was involved in a spectacular deck prang on the 7th when after a fast approach it bounced, the starboard wing striking two Bofors guns, the F.20 alighting in the deck park.

On 1 March, a search was mounted to locate the Mediterranean Fleet, followed on subsequent days by dawn searches and medium/high level attacks on ships.

Navex duties were now directly associated with recently-introduced techniques in pilot navigation which were developed by 801 Squadron to improve the Sea Hornet's capabilities during long sea flights. As a result, several aircraft operated in the visual search role, covering large areas at high speed. This was achieved by means of parallel track pattern navigation methods and in there were some instances when Sea Hornets flew singly. Most practice sorties occurred within the vicinity of Gibraltar and involved attacks on units of both the Home and Mediterranean Fleets in a combined exercise.

Several C.A.P.s were flown with boosted take-offs, flights averaging around two hour's duration. Before the return voyage to the U.K., 801 Squadron participated in an exercise code-named *Superb* with boosted take-offs before C.A.P.s. On nearing the English Channel, a strike escort was flown against H.M.S. *Devonshire*. No.801 flew off on the 31st to Lee-on-Solent and *Implacable* docked at Portsmouth, enabling the ship's company to disembark for well-earned Easter leave.

Due to all personnel being on leave, flying activity during the first weeks of April was mainly confined to air tests, A.S.R. searches and aerobatics. 801 Squadron deployment continued at Lee-on-Solent from the 24th until May 10th, preparatory to re-embarking aboard *Implacable* on the 11th for deck landing practice.

An air search was mounted over the seas near the Mull of Galloway on 17 May in an attempt to find two missing Sea Hornet pilots, Lts. Bell and Hayter. Sadly, the only traces found were some oil slicks and small pieces of wreckage from TT199 and VR851, both having collided. From the 25th to 30th, the squadron participated in a Western Union exercise which was held in the Bay of Biscay. On the first day, Lt.Cdr. Lee-White's F.20 suffered engine failure while 200 miles out to sea. Conditions at sea and a gusty wind were considered as unsuitable for any attempt to make the first single-engine carrier landing. The C.O. was diverted to Merignac airfield, Bordeaux, where a spare coolant pump was flown in from *Implacable*. It was fitted in time for Lee-White to land aboard as *Implacable* entered Brest harbour.

The first days of June found 801 Squadron engaged in Exercise *Shopwindow*, a Fleet demonstration for V.I.P.s and Press, involving surface ships, submarines and aircraft, with various weapons being fired. Another exercise was entitled "F.O.S.M's Summer War" on behalf of Flag Officer Submarines, which gave his submarines an opportunity to carry out tactical exercises against, or in direct support of, merchant ships and warships. Several aircraft were flown to Bramcote on the 9th to 15th.

On the 12th, Lt. Shepherd was killed when the starboard wing of VR862 folded immediately after becoming airborne from *Implacable*. The F.20 rolled and entered the sea inverted. Suspicions were narrowed down to a possible fault with the hydraulic wing locking bolts,

unproven owing to the non-recovery of wreckage. On the 27th, the squadron was engaged on spotting at Cape Wrath, observing results of main armament bombardments from heavy warships. Unfortunately, Lt. Blenkinsop in VZ713 was killed on the 28th when he failed to pull out of a dive while making mock attacks on a warship for A.A. armament practice. Several C.A.P.s were flown against Lancasters and U.S.A.F. Superfortresses which were operating at 29,000 feet.

An air display at Lossiemouth on July 1st included a contribution to the aerobatics by a flight of four Sea Hornets in conjunction with solo display aircraft filling in gaps between passes with individual aerobatics, usually flown by the Senior Pilot. The flying display normally started with a simultaneous take-off by two Sea Hornets from opposite ends of the runway, carefully judged to lift off immediately opposite the crowd enclosure.

Several hours of intensive practice was a prelude to another display at Lee-on-Solent, held on 26 August. At this time, 801 Squadron pilots were required to obtain Instrument Ratings on twin- engine aircraft. With this in mind, a special Naval unit had been established at Rochester Airport, equipped with Oxfords, including PH143, PH246 and PH288. The course lasted a fortnight and required pilots to complete around fifteen hours of instrument flying instruction before gaining instrument ratings. Lt.Cdr. Lee-White was among the first to graduate, leaving Lt.E.M. Welch DFC AFC, 801 Squadron Senior Pilot, in temporary command during his absence. Lt. Welch in VZ710 was tragically killed before the C.O.'s return when he failed to recover from a loop near ground level. The accident followed a special display at Lee-on-Solent, put on for the benefit of visiting officers and cadets from an Argentine training ship. Despite a detailed investigation of the wreckage, reasons was never established although it was considered possible that a failure of the elevator mass balance could have been a contributory cause.

The Air Group became shore-based in September and October following a decision to replace *Implacable* by bringing forward the refit on *Indomitable*. On 21 September, in company with Firebrands of 813 Squadron, 801 Squadron flew to R.A.F. Celle, West Germany, to participate in Exercise *Broadside I and II*, a joint B.A.O.R./B.A.F.O. major exercise. The Sea Hornets were employed in close support and reconnaissance roles. During deployment, 801 Squadron flew local area familiarisation sorties before engaging in many low-level flights. The exercise was extremely popular with the pilots who enjoyed low-level intruding over large areas of Germany. Sadly Lt.Cdr. Abbot, C.O. of 813 Squadron, suffered engine failure in his Firebrand during a return flight from Celle and ditched in the North Sea. Despite a thorough air/sea search, centred on Manston, no trace of pilot or aircraft was ever found.

After the end of *Broadside*, 801 Squadron returned to Lee-on-Solent on 1 October, just in time for a spell of

No.801 Squadron lined-up at Ford with H.M.S. Indomitable codes on the fins (via R.C. Sturtivant)

further intruding in Exercise *Emperor*. The exercise was started on the 7th and was undertaken to test the Air Defence of Great Britain, 801 Squadron regarding themselves fortunate in being able to join four R.A.F. Hornet squadrons in providing additional low-level capability. In order to remain in close proximity to R.A.F. intruder squadrons, 801 Squadron was based at Topcliffe, where the well-rehearsed, synchronised formation wing-folds during taxying caused some gasps of dismay. The Sea Hornets employed similar tactics to the R.A.F. in flying well out to sea before returning at very low level for surprise attacks on airfields. Defending Meteors only achieved limited successes during several off-shore interceptions; however, these were only isolated instances and most pilots easily evaded the jets. Visibility was persistently poor at low altitude and played a significant part in the low interception rate.

The squadron returned to Lee-on-Solent on the 15th to commence a series of A.D.D.L.s as well as trials in new glide-bombing techniques. During November and December H.M.S. *Indomitable* commenced a Work-Up of the ship's company following her re-commissioning. Although the actual Work-Up for the Air Department began on 29 November, 801 Squadron flew from Lee-on-Solent on several occasions to provide *Indomitable's* flight deck crews with essential practice. Particular emphasis was placed on the working efficiency of flight deck equipment, including the performance of arrestor gear, barriers, catapult and deck lifts. Several R.N. airfields were visited during the month.

Eight pilots, together with the A.G.T., flew aboard *Indomitable* on 24 November and following a settling-in period, commenced an intensive programme of air interception exercises, designed to give Aircraft Direction Teams aboard the carrier valuable practice in D/F (Direction Finding). An Autumn cruise was made down the English Channel for some interception exercises with the R.A.F. It was soon discovered that prevailing Mach Number restrictions, imposed when carrying drop tanks, were seriously reducing the number of successful interceptions. R.A.F. jets were flying at high altitude, resulting in a series of long-drawn-out tail chases. On the 27th, permission was received for 801's Sea Hornets to jettison their drop tanks on encountering high flying Canberras or when in hot pursuit. Net results proved to be encouraging and resulted in many good cine-films of invading Canberras.

Fighter v. fighter combat briefings resulted in a comment in 801 Squadron's Record Book:- "The Sea Hornet is proving, surprisingly enough, a good match for the Meteor in air combat".

A deck landing accident occurred on 6 December when Sub Lt. King in VZ715 crashed on the flight deck when both undercarriage legs were torn away. This officer was killed shortly afterwards when his F.20 dived into the ground while strafing tanks. On 23 December, Lt. Cdr. Lee-White handed over command of the squadron.

All aircraft remaining in original silver finish had been re-doped in correct camouflage colours, i.e. Extra

Sea Hornet F.20 VR837 AO/461 at Eglinton in 1948 (A.E. Hughes)

Dark Sea Grey upper surfaces and Sky undersurfaces.

On 18 January 1951, 801 embarked in H.M.S. *Implacable*, before flying aboard *Indomitable*, soon actively involved in a nine-nation exercise code-named *Castanets*. During these exercises 801's Sea Hornets adopted the dual roles of long range strike and fighter escort duties. Another fatal accident on 5 February involved F.20 WE235, which was seen to dive into the sea from a low altitude whilst in the landing circuit for H.M.S. *Indomitable*.

The Sea Hornet F.20s were eventually replaced by Sea Fury FB.11s in March 1951.

Sea Hornet F.20s with No.801 Squadron:
(July 1947 - April 1951)

Letter Codes: C = *Implacable*, CU = Culdrose, FD = Ford, AO = Arbroath

TT196 150/FD, 450/C;	TT198 456/C;
TT199 460/C;	TT200 151/FD;
TT201 153/FD, 453/C/AO;	TT203 152/FD;
TT204 154/FD, 466/C;	TT205 452/C;
TT206 151/FD;	TT207 156/FD, 467/C;
TT208 155/FD, 462/AO/C, 461/C;	
TT209 157/FD, 451/C, 457/C, 453/C;	
TT211 158/FD, 457/C, 458/AO;	
TT212 159/FD, 459/AO/C;	TT248 459/A;
VR837 161/FD, 461/AO/C;	
VR838 160/FD, 460/C;	VR839 152/FD, 452/C;
VR840 155/FD, 455/C;	VR841
VR843 454/C;	VR845 452/C;

VR847 461;	VR849 462/C;
VR850 456/C;	
VR851 456/AO, 450/C, 459/C;	
VR852 454/C;	
VR853 451/C, 451/AO, 454/C;	
VR854	VR855 456/C;
VR856 464/C;	VR857 457/AO/C;
VR859	VR860 453/C;
VR862 460/C;	VR891 160/FD, 459, 450;
VZ707 459/A, 458/C;	VZ708 456/C;
VZ709 450/C;	VZ710 456/C, 463/C;
VZ711	VZ712
VZ713	VZ714 457/C;
VZ715	WE235

Sea Hornet PR.22 (December 1949 to March 1950)

VZ658 465	VZ659 463	VZ660 464

Commanding Officers:
Lt. Cdr. D.B. Law, Lt. Cdr. D.H. Richards, Lt.Cdr. K. Lee-White MBE.

Squadron pilots:
Lt. J.W. Ayres, Lt. E.G. Beechinor, Lt. D.P. Bell, Lt. A.M. Blenkinsop, Lt. A.B.B. Clarke, Lt. P.S. Cole DSC, Lt. W.A.M. Ferguson DSC, Lt. N.D. Fisher, Lt. J.R. Fraser, Lt. A. Gordon-Johnson, Lt. J.W. Hayter, Lt. A.J. Leahy, Lt. T.F. Lowder, Lt. I.H.F. Martin DSC, Lt. S.B. Oliver, Lt. M.H.J. Petrie, Lt. N.L. Sharrock, Lt. Shepherd, Lt. R.A. Shilcock, Lt. A.H. Smith, Lt. Welch, Lt. F.W. Wilcox, Lt. P.G. Young.

No.806 Squadron's tour of North America in 1948. Left to right: Lt. D. Reynolds, R.N., Lt. J,C, Sloane R.C.N., Lt. F.G. Rice, R.C.N., Lt.Cdr. R. Law, R.N., Lt B. Clarke, R.N., Lt. I. Martin, R.N.

No.806 Squadron

Re-formed on 3 May 1948 as the official Royal Navy Aerobatic Team, 806 Squadron was equipped with three Sea Hornet F.20s and a solitary Sea Vampire. Prior to embarkation for North America, all three F.20s were flown to Hatfield on 14 May for final checks and a repaint. When collected from D.H. on the 17th, pilots were requested by engineers to carry out a special farewell beat-up over the airfield. After taking-off, the Sea Hornets were soon sweeping in at "deck" level, leaving three swathes of flattened grass in the wake from their propellers

As was the custom, all pilots for the tour were hand-picked by Lt.Cdr. D.B. Law, the Commanding Officer. On the 18th, the squadron performed an air display before flying to Belfast on the 20th for embarkation on H.M.C.S. *Magnificent*, setting sail on the 25th for the voyage to Dartmouth, Nova Scotia. Of the three Sea Hornets, VR851 450/C and TT209 457/C were on loan from 801 Squadron.

On arrival, 806 Squadron commenced an intensive work-up period in preparation for the forthcoming display, including local flying and constant aerobatic practice between June 8th to 19th by the Sea Vampire and Sea Hornets. On the 12th, one of the Sea Hornets, flown by Lt. N. Fisher, crashed into Halifax Harbour shortly after taking-off. Lt. A.B.B. Clark, Senior Pilot, recalled taking off immediately after Fisher's aircraft, soon entering cloud and breaking through the layer to find no trace of the aircraft. Lt.Cdr. Law flew to New York on the 20th in the Sea Vampire, becoming the first pilot to land at the new Idlewild Airport, and giving displays on the 22nd and 23rd.

From June 28th to July 19th, all aircraft were flown on daily aerobatic practice. Lt.Cdr. Law gave two displays in the Vampire and Hornet on the 21st over Dartmouth. On the 25th, the Sea Vampire was flown to Portland, Maine, for display practice. 806 Squadron was to participate with some distinction for the opening ceremony of New York's Idlewild (now J.F. Kennedy) Airport. Using the Sea Hornet's magnificent single-engine performance, spectacular aerobatic manoeuvres were performed on week-days between 31st July and August 8th. Individual and co-ordinated precision formation aerobatics were relatively unknown in the

U.S.A. at this time and rival U.S. pilots had nothing similar to offer. Set-piece aerobatics on two engines were followed by single-engine loops and, ultimately, with both feathered, making a vivid impression on the large crowd. Seconds before, an articulate F.A.A commentator had requested silence from spectators, thereby adding to the effectiveness of a deathly-quiet diving approach.

An even more spectacular display item consisted of two F.20s, flown by Lt. I. Martin and Lt.Cdr. Law who made take-offs from opposite ends of the Idlewild runway. During their take-off run, one pilot jokingly called up his opposite number to enquire if he was on the correct side of runway, all knowingly audible to Airport air traffic control, causing some momentary panic.

The 806 Squadron "Flying Circus" enlisted the services of two R.C.N. pilots to fly formation aerobatics in their Sea Furies. To the astonishment of Lt. Clark, the over-enthusiastic Canadians formed a habit of tucking in too close during barrel rolls, seriously affecting the leader's aileron control.

During the U.S. tour, 806 Squadron pilots were wined, dined and accommodated at Floyd Bennett Field, where Lt. Clark needed little persuasion in sampling the Grumman Bearcat, considering it somewhat inferior to the F.A.A's Sea Fury. Toward the close of their tour, a drinking party was proceeding when a high ranking U.S.

Navy officer, by now well and truly "oiled", offered 806 Squadron pilots an opportunity of flying the U.S. Navy's new Grumman Panther. On arrival at Dow Field they were introduced to the Boss who promptly enquired how long they intended to stay for their conversion course. "About a couple of hours" came the cheery reply; 806's pilots never flew the Panther.

Before re-embarking on R.M.S. *Aquitania* for the voyage home, 806 Squadron also performed displays at Dorval, Montreal, Toronto and Ottawa, making appearances over Niagara Falls on September 1st. The Canadian cities were treated to memorable displays during week-days until the 11th before the pilots flew to Dartmouth for embarkation. After reaching the U.K., 806 Squadron went ashore and sadly disbanded on 25 September, eventually reforming at Brawdy during March 1953 with Sea Hawk F.1s.

Pilots for North American Tour:

C.O.: Lt.Cdr. D.B. Law DSC; Senior Pilot, Lt. A.B.B. Clark, Lt. I.H.F. Martin DSC, Lt. N. Fisher. Lt. A.H. Reynolds DSC, Lt(E) A.C.R. Hallett.

R.C.N.
Lt. J.C.Sloan, Lt. F.G. Rice.

TT209 of No.806 Squadron on loan from 801 Squadron for the North American tour (via R.Sturtivant)

Sea Hornet NF.21 VX250 of No.809 Squadron flies off H.M.S. Indomitable

No.809 Squadron

1949

No.809 Squadron was reformed at Culdrose on 20 January 1949, commanded by Lt. Cdr. Armour, and became the first and only first-line F.A.A. squadron to be equipped with the NF.21.

Stage 1 Work-Up

Delays were caused by pre-delivery modifications to the throttle butterfly mechanisms and resulted in the first two aircraft being held back until mid-February. First to arrive was VV438, after ferrying from R.D.U. Culham on 17 February. Meanwhile, the second NF.21 was undergoing a complete engine change, due to the supercharger ingesting a loose bolt.

Further modifications to the undercarriage resulted in more irritating delays. Several abortive trips were made to Culdrose by the Station Flight Anson before VV441 was ready for delivery. To complicate matters, VV438 developed numerous snags, necessitating frantic activity

by ground crews to render it serviceable.

No.809 Squadron pilots were now waiting patiently for an opportunity to undergo type conversion although no official handling notes were currently available. In an attempt to solve the problem, Commander (Air) sought permission from F.O.F.T. to use existing pilot's notes for the single-seat F.20 for check-out purposes. A.& A.E.E stepped in and authorised use of existing F.20 notes, commenting, "A.&A.E.E consider that differences in handling are negligible, therefore no supplementary notes are necessary".

Following arrival of the second aircraft, conversion began in earnest, only to be interrupted when VV441 developed a faulty port fuel tank which was replaced before the end of February. Inclement weather further delayed training when several days elapsed before flying was possible.

Single-engine flying kept the squadron fully occupied up to 3 March, until VV441 required rigging checks after reports of buffeting during single-engine flying.

On 11 March, VV435 and VV439 were ready for

ferrying to Culdrose from Culham, VV439 finally arriving on the 25th, albeit with several faults listed on the snag sheet. After yet more irksome delays, VV432 swelled squadron strength to five NF.21s. Despite periods of unserviceability, 809's pilots were constantly airborne practising "Finger Four" formation flying.

On 1 June, four aircraft, VW949 (a new arrival), VV441, VV438 and VV435, flown by Lt. Cdr. Armour, Lts. Phillips, Berry and Packham, were airborne putting extra polish to "Finger Four" formation drill in preparation for the King's Birthday flypast. The following day saw completion of the "Stage One Work-Up" when six aircraft made a stream take-off.

The squadron record book stated in optimistic mood, "This day will go down in the annals of 809 Squadron history". After forming up, the formation treated Culdrose to an impressive flypast in two "Vics"', a grouping adopted for the King's Birthday flypast.

The eighth aircraft, VW948, arrived from Culham and coincided with a welcome period of squadron serviceability when three aircraft were deployed to R.N.A.S. Bramcote for participation in their air display.

Tragedy struck the squadron on 15 July when VW948 crashed whilst flying in the circuit on the down-wind leg. The crew were on a night training flight when engine trouble resulted in R.P.s being jettisoned out to sea, prior to an attempted forced landing at Culdrose. Meanwhile, Lt. Berry ordered his observer to abandon the aircraft, Aircrewman I St. Vaughan's parachute deployed at the last second before he contacted the ground.

Witnesses saw the Sea Hornet suddenly climb steeply before diving into the ground. Sadly, the pilot was killed. Suspicions were immediately focussed on the elevator controls with all Sea Hornets being grounded from 16 July to 11 August. Subsequent checks revealed errors with tailplane incidence settings. Following thorough pre-flight checks, VV441 was air tested without incident although the radio developed problems and the aircraft was classified unserviceable. A replacement aircraft, VW956, arrived from Culham to maintain squadron strength.

On 14 September, 809 Squadron was deployed to Lee-on-Solent for Carrier Drill and additional periods of formation flying. After some months of intensive training, including A.D.D.L.s, the Sea Hornets flew out to H.M.S. *Vengeance* in May 1950, becoming an integral part of the 15th Carrier Air Group.

Stage 2 work-up included air-to-air camera-gun, gyro gun sight procedures, day and night air-to-ground cannon and rocket firing, ground strafing and night intruder exercises.

Stage 3 consisted of day/night interceptions using G.C.I. direction finding equipment, interceptions against bombers and carrier drill with A.D.D.L.s.

With eight Sea Hornets on strength, 809 Squadron became known as "Snow White and the Seven Dwarfs"

each aircraft's nose being adorned with an appropriate Disney character.

A further squadron of NF.21s (No.792) had been formed to provide training for fresh crews, both squadrons eventually amalgamating to equip a twelve-aircraft squadron.

Following deck landing practice aboard H.M.S. *Illustrious*, 809 Squadron returned to Culdrose after twelve days absence.

1950

Flying activity during the first fortnight of January was mainly concerned with an intensive programme of A.D.D.L.s, Lt. Ducker making sixty-four. It became routine for pilots to carry out up to fifteen during one day. On the 18th and 19th, Lt.Ducker made two abortive attempts to carry out deck landing on *Illustrious*, the first being abandoned due to problems with VV438. A second attempt was aborted due to the carrier operating in zero wind conditions.

On the 20th, a detachment was sent to Eglinton as a base for flying out to *Illustrious* for deck landing practice. On 31 January, the squadron flew to Lee-on-Solent, preparatory to departing next day bound for Hal Far with a night stop at Istres. The NF.21s were fitted with long range tanks for a trial long-range navigational exercise. All aircraft returned to Lee-on-Solent on 7 February before flying down to Culdrose. The squadron spent the remainder of the month practising G.C.I.s, fighter affiliation with Lincolns and low level air interceptions.

On 1 March, a "Warstrike" was mounted on the firing range at Treligga. Practice A.D.D.L.s continued throughout the month, Lt. Ducker in VV963 carrying out six within twenty minutes, half of this time being spent flying on instruments! His monthly total amounted to sixty-four ADDLs with a further eighteen on 27 April, his manual dexterity being taxed to the limit.

No.809 flew over to Stretton on 1 May for rehearsals for a flypast over *Ark Royal* on the 3rd. After returning to Culdrose, the squadron carried out a further series of A.D.D.L.s before flying out to *Vengeance* on 10 May for practice deck landings. Remaining aboard the carrier, No.809 continued deck landings and carried out beat-ups for the benefit of the ship's gunners. Several C.A.P.s were flown, with plenty of trade, Lt. Ducker claiming one Norwegian Mosquito, two Sunderlands and two Firebrands.

On 21 June, the squadron deployed to Arbroath for single-engine practice, including single-engine landings at Leuchars. The squadron flew out to *Vengeance* on 4 July, carrying out C.A.P.s during the Navy's "Summer War". Lt. Ducker in VV435 was forced to divert to Lossiemouth after a filler cap key dropped into the control box, jamming the ailerons. Level flight could barely be maintained despite using asymmetric power.

Sea Hornet NF.21 VW948 of No.809 Squadron (via R.C. Sturtivant)

Ducker warned his observer, Lt.Christley, to prepare for baling out as he struggled to keep the Sea Hornet on an even keel. Fortunately, he succeeded in making a landing at Lossiemouth where ground staff retrieved the missing tank key. After an air test, he set off to rejoin *Vengeance* only to discover the carrier under tow. A second attempts on the same day was to prove successful. During the exercise, No.809 made attacks on targets along the Norwegian coast, including Stavanger and its airfield at Sola. Lt.Cdr. J.H.Richards took over command of the squadron.

Lt. M.W. Henley joined 809 Squadron during October, undergoing type familiarisation with his observer Lt.Reynolds in VX250 on the 25th, followed by a further flight next day. Before joining the squadron, Lt.Henley and his observer had completed a night fighter course at 228 O.C.U. R.A.F. Leeming, where he flew the Mosquito NF.36. Training F.A.A aircrew at Leeming started initially as an experiment. Results proved so promising that all future NF.21 crews were R.A.F.-trained. R.A.F. single-engine flying practice in VZ677 had to be abandoned on the 28th owing to technical problems. On 6 December, 809 Squadron carried out air strikes on the Home Fleet.

1951

In January, most flying duties consisted of almost daily G.C.I. exercises and requisite night flying tests. During the fourth week, strafing attacks were made on ground targets, followed by a night "Navex" and periods on instrument flying. February saw the commencement of intensive work for 7th N.A.G. This Night Air Group consisted of 809 Squadron Sea Hornet NF.21s and 814 Squadron Firefly AS.6s.

Air Group Commander was Lt. Cdr. Armour, previously C.O. of 809 Squadron and both squadrons were based at Culdrose. Some idea of the tempo of round-the-clock flying activity can be gained from the log books of pilots who participated in the preparations before embarking on H.M.S. *Vengeance*. Entries in Lt.Henley's log book indicate five flights during the 13th (day and night) which totalled almost nine hours, over half flown at night. Pilots flew mostly at night; the ratio of night:day flying hours was of the order 2:1. Despite wing folding, the Sea Hornet's overall size caused problems with storage and maintenance in the hangars.

Maintenance crews were kept active with routine component checks, the closely-cowled Merlins causing hours of struggle to remove any faulty pumps, valves, etc.

Numerous attacks were carried out on land and sea targets using R.P.s and a sea search was mounted for R.M.S. *Pretoria Castle*. A.D.D.L.s were commenced on the first day of March, together with search and strike exercises with the Home Fleet. During April, the squadron mounted an air search for a submarine, H.M.S. *Affray*, when aircraft were in the air for almost three hours. Further periods were devoted to A.D.D.L.s and firing R.P.s at land targets which completed a busy month for the pilots.

On May 2nd/3rd, A.D.D.L.s were carried out, prior to flying out to H.M.S. *Vengeance*. On the 10th, VW962 was flown out to *Vengeance* flown by Lt. Henley. On the 16th, the squadron made a strafing attack on Lee-on-Solent.

The Sea Hornet's relatively high landing speed proved too much for the contemporary arrestor gear on H.M.S. *Vengeance*, 809's aircraft returning to Culdrose. The carrier was docked at Devonport for essential repairs to the long-suffering arrestor-equipment. On the 30th, 809 Squadron was airborne for a "Balbo", followed by G.C.I.s flying from *Vengeance*.

In July, Lt. Henley and his Observer, Lt. Reynolds, left the squadron, bound for the U.S.A. on exchange posting, soon getting to grips with the Grumman F7F-3N Tigercat. Based at Marine Corps Base, Cherry Point, he flew the Tigercat for some 400 hours, commenting on the Grumman's greater endurance, superior radar and greater load-carrying capacity - "But for sheer joy of flying the Hornet wins hands down".

Before leaving for his exchange posting, Lt. Henley underwent a jet conversion course on the Meteor T.7 and Sea Vampire F.20. The course included high-speed runs at Mach 0.78, Battle Formation at 30,000 feet, night flying and included a forced landing for good measure. F.20s used included VV139, VV142, VV149 and VV153.

After departing from *Vengeance* in August, 809 Squadron re-located to R.A.F. Coltishall for additional training before flying out to Hal Far.

On October 16th, four NF.21s flew in formation from Gibraltar to Lee-on-Solent, averaging a shade under 330 m.p.h. over a distance of 1,040 miles. A fifth NF.21 flown by Lt. D.M. Rouse improved this figure by some 48 m.p.h.

On 5 December, VW963 crashed during final approach to Gatwick when the starboard engine cut and a forced landing was made between two rows of houses. The squadron flew on an exercise, code-named *Mainbrace*, which involved U.S. capital ships. No.809 Squadron made continuous attacks on main "Blue Force" which was heading northwards through the North Sea. Excellent reporting from 809 Squadron NF.21 crews did not pass unnoticed, considerable praise being received from the top brass and newspaper reporters.

In February 1952, the squadron was attached to H.M.S. *Falcon*, R.N.A.S. Hal Far, Malta, embarking aboard H.M.S. *Vengeance* on the 29th. The squadron flew off to make another visit to Hal Far and participated in Fleet exercises, joining H.M.S. *Indomitable* for a brief period in June.

After becoming unserviceable at Gibraltar, VV439 was hoisted aboard H.M.S. *Glory*, which was returning to the U.K. In June, Sea Hornets VW952 and VW953 were on loan to R.N.A.S. Lossiemouth for static display. On 6 June, 809 Squadron was back aboard H.M.S.

Indomitable making goodwill visits to Eastbourne, Vigo and Le Havre before mooring alongside the liner *America*, fresh from her recent Blue Riband run.

On 7 July, the squadron became shore-based at H.M.S. *Seahawk*, with Culdrose as its main base.

Lt. W.J. Hanks was appointed Senior Observer, whose remarks on the existing Air Intercept Radar are worthy of note. The radar equipment, three-centimetre AN/APS 4, was of American origin, whose pick-up range was never sufficient to carry out really good interceptions. Later AN/APS 21 installations in Sea Venoms were also far behind the times due to the higher operating speeds of opposing aircraft.

Exercises were carried in September with the R.A.F. which required a temporary detachment to Leuchars.

During October, the squadron re-deployed to Leuchars to participate in Exercise *Ardent*, making interceptions of incoming Superfortresses before returning to Culdrose. *Ardent* had indicated that when bomber raids became heavy, radar stations became saturated, forcing the NF.21 crews to use "Broadcast" control. In the absence of "Gee" navigational equipment, any interceptions which entailed entering the bomber stream were found to be extremely hazardous. Low temperatures persisted inside the unpressurised observer compartments, especially noticeable during interceptions at 29,000/30,000 feet. Due to an inadequate heat supply, observers resorted to wearing silk scarves inside their flying helmets in a desperate attempt to keep warm. Most night interceptions occurred during the early hours when returning crews duly thawed out with welcome hot coffee.

On 21 November, 809 Squadron joined other F.A.A squadrons in the Fleet Review Flypast over the Solent. The leading jet fighters left 809 Squadron's slower NF.21s tailing on behind. The lowering cloud base caused problems to the rear-most formation and the C.O. wisely moved his squadron to one side to avoid any possibility of flying into the waves.

In December, the squadron flew day and night, carrying out C.I.s, A.D.D.L.s and dropping flares.

1953

Flying activity for the first fortnight of 1953 centred on day and night flight drill plus A.D.D.L.s, before the squadron embarked on H.M.S. *Eagle* for a Spring Cruise in the Mediterranean. Lt.Cdr. E.M. Frazer became C.O., with Lt. Henley as his Senior Pilot. As Senior Pilot it fell to Lt. Henley to be first on *Eagle*, the C.O. occupying the observer's position, and although he caught No.3 arrester wire, both propellers contacted the barrier. After several similar incidents, all aircraft were landed individually, parked aircraft being turned aft before being struck down.

Once into the cruise, H.M.S. *Eagle* was ordered to commence flying "around the clock", Fireflies and

A Sea Hornet NF.21 makes way for a Dragonfly to land aboard H.M.S. Eagle in Grand Harbour, Valletta. In the background are the remains of the bridge wrecked during the abortive Italian explosive boat attack in July 1941

Sea Hornet NF.21 VV440 of No.809 Squadron with long-range tanks (both photos via R.C. Sturtivant)

Attackers by day, Sea Hornets and Skyraiders by night. N.F.T.s were also flown off the carrier during daylight hours. The intense flying activity soon began to take its toll on the Flight Deck Party, with pilots and observers also feeling the strain. On the 31st, the ship's radar became unserviceable during a G.C.I. by Lt. Henley in VW946. To further complicate matters, maintenance problems were not eased by the cramped conditions below decks. The Squadron Engineering Officer became ill, which meant a rapid transfer to base hospital at Malta.

On 3 February, dawn strikes were carried out on the base at Gibraltar. Aircraft were given N.F.T.s before setting off for night G.C.I. exercises. On the 11th, a strike was made against H.M.S. *Eagle* and during the period 17th to 19th, aircraft were engaged on night Combat Air Patrols.

Flights to Hal Far, Malta, were mostly for ferrying senior officers to and from the island.

On 3 March, an air strike was mounted on "Red Force" when four NF.21s were launched from *Eagle* within an hour of "war" being declared between the Home and Mediterranean Fleets. At the time of launching Sea Hornets, the distance between opposing fleets amounted to about 300 miles. Attacks were made using "Gloworm" (launched by the leading aircraft, VW961 with Lt. Henley) to illuminate the target.

It was originally intended to use more Sea Hornets for the attack; however continuing maintenance problems kept them below decks. Nevertheless, the Home Fleet was caught on the hop, not one warning radar being switched on as it was considered highly unlikely such a strike would be mounted - apart from Commander (Air) of H.M.S. *Theseus*, who was not amused by the naked unpreparedness.

On the 11th, H.M.S. *Eagle* sailed out from Gibraltar harbour to launch her aircraft for a flypast over Marshal Tito's yacht, en route to the British Isles for a State visit. At the end of the flypast, 809 Squadron Sea Hornets formed up in pairs to carry out N.F.T.s. Unfortunately, on re-forming for landing on *Eagle*, two aircraft, VW952 and VZ697, touched wings and crashed; an observer was the sole survivor.

On the 12th, 17th and 24th, flying activity included day C.A.P.s and air strikes, flying at 20,000 feet. On the 25th, the squadron flew ashore to Culdrose for a spell of rest. A flypast on the 27th was arranged for the King of Jordan.

After returning to Culdrose, changes of air and ground crews meant further periods of training, in addition to flying practice required for the Coronation Review.

During one briefing, attended by officers from other F.A.A squadrons, Lt.Henley raised the thorny subject of flight endurance, causing some astonishment by mentioning a glaring disparity between Fireflies and Sea Hornets, which had twice the endurance of Fireflies.

Numerous G.C.I. and G.C.A. exercises were carried out in April. Flypast rehearsals took place over Lee-on-Solent. Further rehearsals were made in May for the flypast at Lee-on-Solent. On the 22nd, 809 Squadron was in a flypast over Taunton. A C.A.P. was mounted for exercise *Annals IV*.

The squadron paid a visit to the de Havilland factory at Christchurch to inspect the first Sea Venoms off the production line. Soon after their return to Culdrose, new crews arrived to bolster strength.

Further rehearsals took place on June 5th and 13th for the Coronation Review. On the 8th, the squadron made a flight of around 1,000 miles along the East and South Coasts, an "Around Britain Whizz" according to Lt. Henley, before returning to Culdrose. The Sea Hornets cruised at 180 knots T.A.S. and were in the air for over five hours. They landed at Culdrose with one hour's fuel remaining in their tanks. Due to a fuel transfer problem, the C.O.'s aircraft was diverted to Culham, both crew members enjoying lunch before returning to base.

The Coronation Review was held on the 15th, 809 Squadron being airborne for over two hours on flypasts over the Solent. Once aboard *Eagle*, the squadron flew around Lossiemouth and Invergordon making interceptions, guided by R.A.F. Ground Controllers. On the 29th, Lt. Henley in VW946 participated in a "Ping Pong" exercise which involved Sea Hornet v Sea Hornet in long range interceptions with controlling by an A.E.W. Skyraider. On this occasion the "Guppy" went unserviceable, thus terminating the exercise.

On 16 July, a strike exercise was abandoned due to bad weather when all aircraft were successfully diverted to Eglinton.

The impending embarkation in *Eagle* in September resulted in intensive flying activity, mainly comprising of A.D.D.L.s and air tests.

809 Squadron was now safely aboard H.M.S. *Eagle* for the Autumn cruise, part of a N.A.T.O. exercise which was somewhat restricted due to near hurricane conditions over the North Sea with *Eagle* wallowing badly in the mountainous seas.

After the weather had abated, some flying was carried out. One NF.21 suffered an engine failure and diverted to Keflavik for a single-engine landing. The landing was made more hazardous by the stubborn refusal of a drop tank to release. On the 14th, an air strike was mounted against H.M.S. *Vanguard* using "Gloworm" flares.

On 7 October, 809 Squadron disembarked for two weeks detachment to R.N.A.S. Lossiemouth, making practice interceptions at 20,000 feet, directed on to their targets by Buchan Radar. On the 20th, 809 Squadron re-embarked aboard H.M.S. *Eagle* for duties in the English Channel which included frequent diversions to R.N.A.S. Ford.

New tactics were tried out for R.P. attacks by

Sea Hornet NF.21 VW961 488/J of No.809 Squadron (via R.C. Sturtivant)

approaching the target at high speed and firing the rocket projectiles in level flight. It was considered at the time that this type of attack would be safer from ships' defences than the standard dive attack.

On 9 December, Lt. Henley in VW943 was recalled from a G.C.I. due to formation of radiation fog, despite clear conditions above the layer. Within seconds of landing the fog obscured the flare path which resulted in a prolonged taxy to the dispersal point. Henley met similar conditions during a flight to Glasgow in December, which caused a diversion to Prestwick.

1954

In January, Lt.Cdr. Henley took over command of 809 Squadron with Lt.Cdr. Frazer appointed as Senior Instructor of the Observer School. Lt.Cdr. A.A. Knight took over as Senior Pilot and the post of Senior Observer was filled by Flt.Lt. Fryer (on exchange posting) who became the first R.A.F. officer to be appointed.

A Sea Hornet flown by Lt. Matthews missed all arrestor wires and engaged the barrier and resulted in a spectacular deck prang, although nobody suffered injury.

No.809 Squadron was again aboard H.M.S. *Eagle* for work-up trials which were commenced in the English Channel, prior to entering the Mediterranean. On arriving at Gibraltar, the Admiral informed the C.O. that he did not require Sea Hornets for the remainder of the cruise. 809 Squadron disembarked to perform a variety of duties and the plans to carry bombs on the NF.21 were

shelved, due to the imminent introduction of Attackers.

The squadron was based at North Front, Gibraltar, remaining there until a return to Culdrose on 28 March. The NF.21s were now virtually redundant as carrier fighters, although they continued to operate from North Front for several weeks. Flights were made to Maison Blanche, near Algiers, and interceptions of aircraft carried out in defence of H.M.S. *Eagle*.

All squadron officers enjoyed a comfortable stay at the Bristol Hotel with the sailors billeted at the local "Toc H" Leave Camp at Rosia Bay, all concerned being well cared for. On the 28th, 809 Squadron flew from North Front bound for Culdrose with a stop at Istres; flying time was under five hours.

An unserviceable NF.21 was lost overboard during passage through the Bay of Biscay. The aircraft had faulty brakes and had been moved for strike down on directions from the squadron engineering officer. In rough seas the NF.21 promptly obeyed the laws of gravity during a roll to starboard and slid across the deck to damage a parked Attacker. On a following roll to port, the loose Sea Hornet dived smoothly over the side. There were a few red faces in the Wardroom that evening, not least the Flight Deck Officer who had been persuaded to move the aircraft from an anchored position!

On 7 April, most sailors and several newly-joined officers were posted to Yeovilton to tackle the new Sea Venom FAW.20. On the same day the C.O. took up VW957 for a final spell of aerobatics and single-engine flying. Over the next few days, VW957 was delivered to

Airwork F.R.U. at St Davids. Three aircraft were flown to A.R.D.U. Culham, and six flown north to A.H.U. Lossiemouth. The remaining three set off for Brawdy, flying all the way at 300 knots with the rear seats occupied by surplus pilots.

Sea Hornet NF.21 Postscript

The re-designed undercarriage of the Sea Hornet was fully capable of withstanding high vertical rates of descent, best described by the experience of Lt. Henley who "dropped in" from about fifty feet during a night landing. *Eagle*'s stern had dropped moments before the crucial point of touch-down, only to rise sharply to meet the Sea Hornet on its descent. Following a routine inspection, it was discovered that there was no damage.

Constant heavy deck landings soon resulted in occasional failure of Radio Compass supports which were later modified. Other technical faults were discovered with the Merlin's ignition harness.

Further comments on the NF.21 by Lt.Cdr. W. Henley, DSO (RN Ret'd), former Senior Pilot and later C.O. No.809 Squadron: "I enjoyed flying the Sea Hornet; it handled very well for a twin-engine fighter. Operationally, I think it would have coped well with the Soviet version of the B-29, although A.I. performance was limited. Due to the lack of space within the Sea Hornet's slim fuselage, it was not possible to install the SCR 720 Radar as fitted to the R.A.F. Mosquito NF.36. Overall, its most important contribution was to maintain carrier night flying, thus ensuring the availability of the necessary nucleus of trained crews familiar with night deck landings."

Despite being relegated to second line units, NF.21s were to soldier on with F.R.U.s at St. Davids and Hurn. No serious attempts were made to preserve an example for posterity, although fuselage hulks were discovered at St. Davids during 1957. One example was reported as "not recovered" from Iceland after a forced landing, instruments and radar equipment having been removed.

Those held by A.H.U. Abbotsinch and Lossiemouth were stored briefly until the eventual mass scrapping when vital parts such as landing gear, canopies, propellers, metal components and engines that could have formed the basis of a future part-replica were simply consigned to scrap. Some late production NF.21s were scrapped despite only having "delivery mileage", barely over 10 hours flying. Almost nil-houred Merlins went to the melting pot without a qualm.

Sea Hornet NF.21s with No.809 Squadron

Serial Numbers and codes where known.
CW = Culdrose; J = *Eagle*; Q = *Indomitable*

VV432/486CW	VV434/487J	VV435/
VV437/484CW	VV438/481CW/Q	VV439/482Q
VV440/486J	VV441/	VW945/
VW946/481J	VW947/482J/A	VW948/488CW/Q
VW949/485CW	VW952/485Q/A	VW953/484J/A
VW954/487J	VW955/493CW/483J	
VW956/488Q	VW957/484Q	VW958/485J
VW959/481A	VW960/483A	VW961/488J
VW962/489Q	VW963/485Q	VW968/481CW
VW969/494CW/482Q	VW970/480/487Q/487A	
VX250/485Q/A	VZ672/481Q/CW	VZ673/482Q
VZ674/483Q	VZ677/488Q,	VZ680/484J/A
VZ682/	VZ684/484/489J	VZ697/489A

Commanding Officers:
Lt.Cdr. J.O. Armour, Lt.Cdr. D.H. Richards, Lt.Cdr. E.M.Frazer, Lt.Cdr. M.W. Henley DSC.

Known Pilots:
Lt. A.P. Berry, Lt. N. N. Ducker, Lt. A.A. Knight, Lt. J.E. Maddocks, Lt. D.C. Matthews, Lt. F.C. Musgrove, Lt. P.L. McDermott, Lt. D.R.O. Price, Lt. D.M. Rouse,

Known Observers:
Lt. W.J. Carter, Lt. F.W. Burgess, Lt. D. Christley, Aircrewman Dodd, Lt.Cdr. J.R. Fraser, Flt.Lt. Fryer (R.A.F.), Aircrewman R. Gilbert, Lt. I. Gilman, Lt. W.J. Hanks (Senior Observer), Lt. W. Holdridge, Lt. P.H. Holt, Lt. Hunt, Aircrewman D Jolliff, Lt. T.G.S. Leece, Lt. Melhuish, Lt. A.G.B. Phillip, Lt. Reynolds, Lt. O.J. Roe, Aircrewman T.E.J. St. Vaughan,

VZ697, 489/A of 809 Squadron lands on H.M.S. Indomitable (via R.C. Sturtivant)

Sea Hornet F.20s of No.728 Squadron, VR856 534/HF, TT194 531/HF and VR848 533/HF (via Bruce Robertson)

Royal Navy Second Line Squadrons and Support Units

No.703 Squadron, S.T.U. Ford

During May 1948, 703 Squadron deployed to Lee-on-Solent, taking over responsibility of Service Trials from 778 Squadron.

Sea Hornets on strength:

PR.22:; VW938 006/FD; VZ655 005/FD; WE247 007/FD; WE246 008/FD.

* * * * * * * * *

No.728 Squadron
Fleet Requirements Unit, Hal Far, Malta
(February 1952 -February 1957)

Sea Hornets were to serve with this unit from February 1952 until as late as February 1957. Duties included training of Air Direction/Interception Officers; Air

Defence Exercises; Interception Exercises, which included co-operation with No.849 Squadron, then equipped with Douglas Skyraider AEW.3s. In addition to regular duties, the Defence of Malta (DXM) became an annual exercise. Radar calibration exercises were carried out with various warships, including H.M.S. *Cumberland, Wrangler, Glasgow, Birmingham, Coventry* and *Newcastle*. On 11th/12th August 1954, strikes were mounted on the U.S. 6th Fleet, Lt. Dallosso in TT186 returning with undercarriage problems and finally being forced to use the emergency hand pump. Other strikes were made on the U.S. carrier *Coral Sea*, using Sturgeons and Sea Hornets. Grumman Panthers were observed on the carrier's decks as surprise attacks were pressed home from very low level. During the annual exercises, the air defence of Malta was provided by locally-based R.A.F. squadrons and Sea Hornets operating from Hal Far and aircraft carriers.

728 Squadron operated a mixed fleet, comprising Sturgeon TT.2s TS475, 478, 480, 481, 485, 486, 492,

493, 495 and 496, Firefly Trainer MB554 and Sea Fury T.20s VZ370 and VZ371. The two latter types provided regular and essential instrument flying practice and annual instrument rating checks. In July 1951, 728's fleet was further expanded by the arrival of Vampire F.20s, the following being in service in 1954-5: VV136, 141, 142, 146, 152 and 153. Meteor T.7s VW446 and WL350, provided asymmetric practice and jet conversion. Squadron pilots were required to be fully proficient on all types in the fleet, which also included several Beech Expeditors, FT994, FT995, and KP110, used for communications. It became routine for pilots to fly several types of aircraft during one day, although Vampire sorties were confined to flights of under one hour, compared with 1½-2 hours flown by Sea Hornets.

On 28 August, R.N.A.S. Hal Far held an air day, one event being a handicap air race between an Attacker (803 Squadron), a Sea Hawk (806 Squadron), a Skyraider (849 Squadron), a Firefly (1841 Squadron R.N.V.R.), a Sea Fury (1831 Squadron R.N.V.R.) and a Sea Hornet from 728 Squadron. Not surprisingly, the jets were severely handicapped, the race being won by a Skyraider hotly pursued across the finishing line by a Sea Hornet.

From 17 September 1954, 728 was on temporary detachment to Ta Kali until 10 August. At one time 728's F./FR.20s were to be temporarily adorned with distinctive yellow/gold spinners and lighting flashes, two examples being VR848 and VR856, examples flown to U.K. on occasions, mostly for air display static parks.

Sea Hornets known on strength:

Sea Hornet F.20/FR.20:
TT186 HF; TT194 531/HF; TT197 531/HF; VR848 532/HF; VR856 534/HF; WE240 HF; WE242 530/HF.

Commanding Officers:

Lt.Cdrs. A.D.Corkhill DSC, B. Bevans DSC.

Pilots/Observers:

Lt.Cdr. N.L. Sharrock, Lt. Cdr. A.H. Pickthall, Lt.Cdr. C.W.G. Drake, Lt. P.R. Dallosso, Lt. J.F.O. Wilcox, Lt. C.R. Mellor, Lt. D.A. Rodaway, Lt. C.H. Roncoroni DSC, Lt. W.H. Hands, Lt. P.W. Bradley, Senior Comm. Observer C.D. Simpson, Comm. Pilot A.R. Warren.

* * * * * * * *

No.736 Squadron, Culdrose
(Within 52nd Training Air Group)
February 1950 - June 1951

F.20: TT191

Sea Hornet PR.22 VZ664 451/CW with No.728 Squadron at Culdrose (A.E. Hughes)

No.738 Squadron, Culdrose
(Within 52nd Training Air Group)
May 1950 - August 1951

Reformed at Culdrose from 736 Squadron as an integral part of N.A.F.S. (Naval Air Fighter School). Main functions were to allow recently-qualified pilots to train in air-to-air and air-to-ground firing, prior to posting to first-line squadrons.

In 1950/51, a formation aerobatic team included Lts. Martin and Leahy who carried out displays at Culdrose, St. Merryn, Dartmouth and Syerston.

Sea Hornets on strength:
F.20: TT191, TT197, TT203, TT210, VR837/454/CW and VR858.

PR.22: VW931, VW932, VW936, VW939 (Crashed 15.5.51 when aircraft spun into sea 3-5 miles SW of Porthleven, Cornwall), VZ664 451/CW, VZ639.

* * * * * * * *

No.739 Squadron
(Photograph Development Unit, Culham)

F.20   VR858 (Aug.1949-July 1950)
PR.22   VW938 (May 1947-July 1950)

* * * * * * * *

No.759 Squadron, Culdrose
(Within 52nd Training Air Group)

Reformed out of 738 Squadron, as No.1 Operational Flying School as a part of N.A.F.S.

F.20: TT191 456/CW, VZ712.
NF.21: VV434
PR.22; VW932, VZ664.

Sea Hornet PR.22 TT198 F of No.703 Squadron during carrier trials from H.M.S. Implacable (John Lawson)

No.771 Squadron, Lee-on-Solent/Ford
(51st Misc. Air Group/Southern Fleet Requirements Unit)

Aircraft on charge: May 1950 - October 1952:
FR.20: VR856
NF.21: VW958

* * * * * * * *

No.778 Squadron, Lee-on-Solent
(Service Trials Unit & Carrier Trials Unit)

Whilst serving with 778 Squadron, Lt. A.B.B. Clark carried out trials with the prototype Sea Hornets PX212 and PX214. Flying some 59 hours, Lt. Clark made 72 deck landings during Intensive Deck Landing Trials held in June 1946. After considerable experience of carrier flying, this officer was impressed by the Sea Hornet's excellent forward visibility for deck landings, compared with the usual long noses of contemporary fleet aircraft. He flew all F.A.A types, ranging from the Blackburn Skua/Roc, finally finishing off a distinguished naval career with the powerful and formidable Scimitar.

F.20 prototypes: PX212, PX214.
F.20: TT198 007/LP, TT210 005/LP
FR.20: VR844 009/LP,
NF.21: VW958 001/LP.

* * * * * * * *

No.787 Squadron
(Naval Air Fighting Development Unit),
R.A.F. West Raynham
March 1947 - 1950.

This unit carried out development trials and assessment of the Sea Hornet NF.21. During trials, it became apparent that a poor oxygen supply existed for the observer's compartment. This shortcoming was confirmed on one occasion, when VV436 with Lt. W.G. Black (pilot) and Lt. Hanks (observer) were returning to West Raynham after visiting Culdrose. Weather conditions at the time were beginning to deteriorate, causing Lt. Black to climb to 27,000 feet, after which altitude crept up slowly. After about three-quarters of an hour, Lt. Hanks lost interest in the proceedings, coming to some 40 miles SW of West Raynham. In the meantime, his pilot had been trying to rouse his half-conscious observer over the intercom

NF.21 VW967 553/LP of No.771 Squadron (N.Pritchard)

without success. Similar oxygen flow problems had been encountered by 809 Squadron at Culdrose, de Havillands soon incorporating the necessary modifications for boosting flow to the rear compartment.

Commanding Officer: Lt.Cdr. Shaw,

Senior Pilot: Lt. Denison,

Pilots:; Lts. Black, Lindsay, Petrie, Sabey and Walden

Sea Hornets on charge:
F.20: TT186
PR.22: VW935
NF.21: VV433, VV436 and VW947

* * * * * * * *

No.792 Squadron, Culdrose
(Night Fighter Training Unit)
May - August 1950

NF.21: VZ672 491/CW (Code range CW/481-CW/494)

* * * * * * * *

No.1833 Squadron, R.N.V.R. Bramcote

Single **PR.22**: VW931, June 1951 - February 1952

* * * * * * * *

Fleet Requirements Unit, Hurn
(Operated by Airwork Ltd.)
Circa February 1953 to October 1955

This unit operated a mixed fleet of Sea Hornet F.20 and NF.21 aircraft:

F.20: TT196, TT212, TT213, VR840, VR843, VR864, VZ711 and WE239.

NF.21: VV430, VV432, VV433, VV435, VV436, VW949, VW950, VW966, VW969, VW979, VZ676, VZ677, VZ682 and VZ691.

* * * * * * * *

Fleet Requirements Unit, St. Davids
(Operated by Airwork Ltd).
From circa July 1952 - October 1955

This unit provided Sea Hornets for twin conversion and fighter targets for the Air Direction School, Kete.

Aircraft on strength (1953-1956):

Sea Hornet NF.21:
1952: VW951, VW964, VW966

1953: VV435, VV439, VW949, VX250/425, VZ692, VZ694, VZ695

1954: VV434, VW951/BY, VW954, VW967, VW968
1956: VW958

Aircraft Codes included BQ/415 - BQ412, later range BY/411-BY429

* * * * * * * *

A.H.U. (Aircraft Holding Unit) Lossiemouth.

Cocooned Sea Hornets were held here under open storage, with periodic checks, including flight tests. Test flying to schedule was carried out by maintenance test pilots, one of whom related an experience encountered during a routine test. During a maximum speed dive, severe wing flutter developed, giving the pilot, Cdr. C.A. Brown, the distinct impression of impending disintegration. After landing the Sea Hornet was found to have incorrectly adjusted aileron gaps.

During later thorough pre-flight checks of Sea Hornets, it was discovered that certain parts of the

Sea Hornet NF.21 cocooned for storage (M.M.Gates)

interior wooden structure had become decomposed. Remaining Sea Hornets were quickly scrapped, some examples having flown less than 20 hours since despatch from the manufacturers.

Aerobatic Team with F.20s, October 1953:

TT186, VR850, WE239, WE240 and WE241.

*   *   *   *   *   *   *   *

R.N.A.S. Brawdy

NF.21, used for radar training:
VW950 418/BQ, VW967 424/BY, VZ692 421/BY

*   *   *   *   *   *   *   *

R.N. E.F.T.S./No.3 F.T.S. Leeming

Hornet F.3:	PX357
Sea Hornet F.20:	TT189
Sea Hornet NF.21:	VV434

*   *   *   *   *   *   *   *

R.N.A.S. Culham, No.2 A.R.D.U.
(Aircraft Receipt & Despatch Unit)

After ferrying from D.H. Hatfield or Chester, various marks of Sea Hornet were given acceptance test flights by resident M.U. test pilots. On most occasions all went well, "Snag Sheets" listing few if any serious technical faults. An odd exception occurred during a routine test for an F.20 which passed without incident until reaching the final stage. Test flights normally included some sundry aerobatics, although for some reason no aerobatics were attempted until the Sea Hornet was on the downwind leg prior to landing. The pilot, Lt.Cdr. Roy Kilburn, slow-rolled the aircraft just before turning on to his final approach. After touching down on three points, he quickly discovered that his control column had jammed in the fully aft position. On examination, it was revealed that an 18-inch length of aluminium tubing had jammed the elevator control quadrant, having been left inside during manufacture. An application of negative "G" during the slow roll had caused the tube to move into this dangerous location.

Another incident concerned VW937, a PR.22 due for test on 13 May 1949. Lt.Cdr. Kilburn raised the undercarriage too soon after unstick, the Sea Hornet promptly sinking back on to the runway. The partly-raised gear was whipped back into the nacelles with a loud thump.

On completion of the brief test flight, it soon became evident that only one leg would lock down and after urgent messages to the control tower, Kilburn wisely elected to make a "dead stick" approach with gear fully retracted, both propellers being fully feathered to avoid serious shock loading. A successful belly-landing was made on the grass area between the main runway and the control tower. Following a smooth arrival, the Sea Hornet came to a halt; "evacuation was rapid" due to possible risk of fire, although apart from superficial damage to the undercarriage doors, repairs were of a minor nature.

On 1 May 1951, Sea Hornet F.20 WE236 was destroyed in a crash near R.A.F. Halton. The aircraft was on a test flight from Culham, apparently breaking up in mid-air and narrowly missing property in a residential area.

*   *   *   *   *   *   *   *

Winterisation Experimental Establishment, Edmonton, Canada.

Sea Hornet F.20 TT193 arrived for cold weather trials which commenced on 13 December 1948. Following completion of trials, the Navy did not consider the costs of shipping the aircraft back were warranted. TT193 was offered for sale with a stipulation that the aircraft was to remain in Canada. The Sea Hornet was eventually purchased at a rather modest outlay by W. Ferterber of Spartan Air Services, the transaction including a sizable quantity of spares, support equipment, spare Merlins, engine cylinder blocks, propellers and sundry parts. It has been suggested that members of the air racing fraternity in the U.S.A. had expressed some interest in acquiring the redundant Sea Hornet, which may account for restrictions imposed at the sale.

TT193, re-registered CF-GUO, was pressed into service for aerial survey and photography duties, operating mainly at 20,000 feet for half-inch to the mile photographic mapping duties. Some flights were made at 35,000 feet, the Sea Hornet's altitude performance being considered slightly inferior to a modified P-38 Lightning, equipped with turbo-superchargers and, not least, with provision for carrying a navigator. Ferterber was, however, very impressed by the Sea Hornet's cockpit, acceleration on take-off compared with being released from a catapult, the initial rate of climb, "when it climbed like a dingbat" - and it was exciting to fly.

During 1951 CF-GUO was sold to Field Photographic Surveys in exchange for yet another P-38. After being sold, CF-GUO crashed when it suffered an engine failure whilst flying near Prince George, B.C. It is rumoured that parts of the wrecked airframe were used for instruction by a local High School.

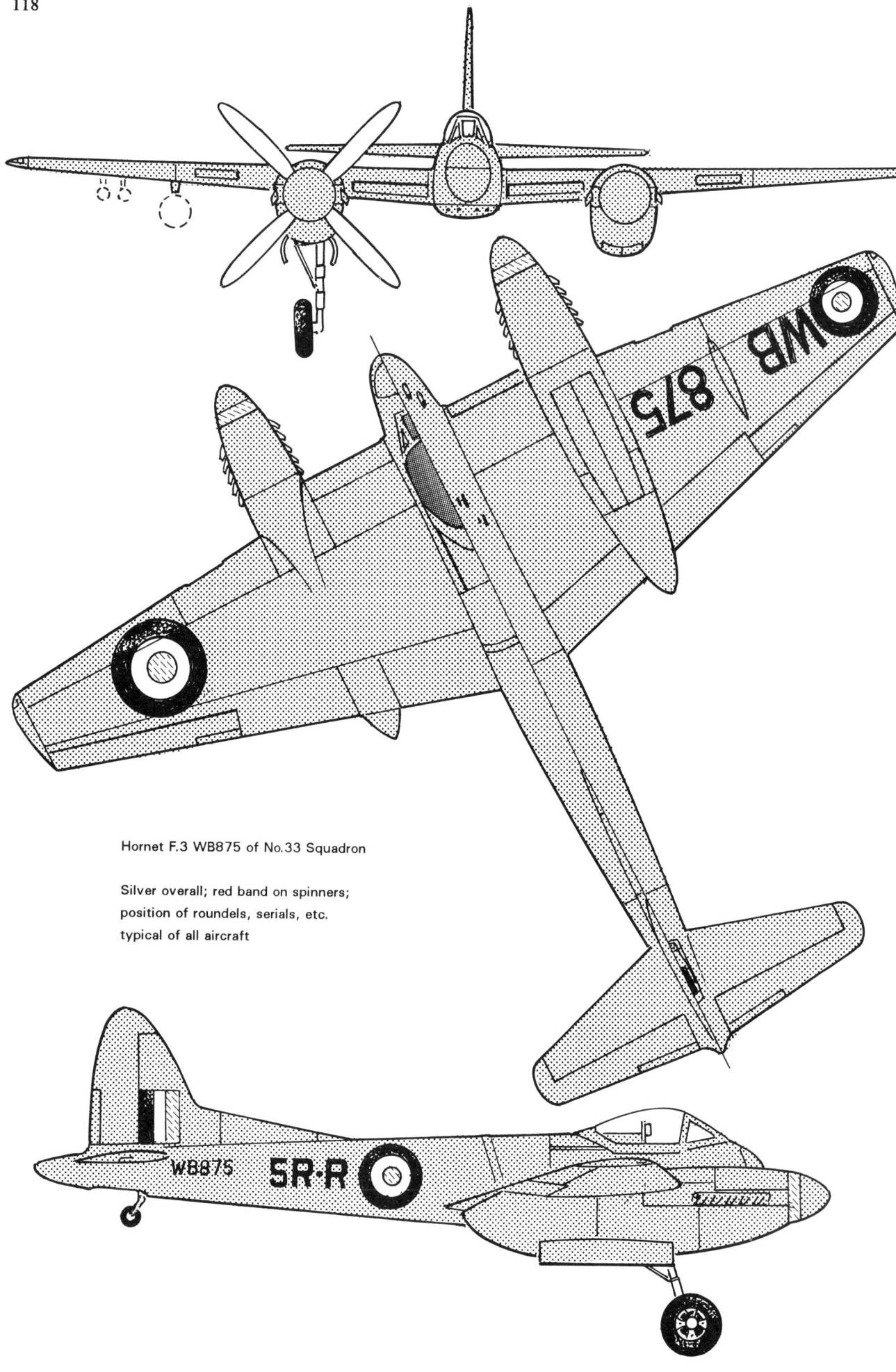

Hornet F.3 WB875 of No.33 Squadron

Silver overall; red band on spinners;
position of roundels, serials, etc.
typical of all aircraft

Production

Hornet F.I

Serial batches: PX210 - PX253; PX273 - PX288. Total production: 60

Cancelled: VB132 - VB135; VB154 - VB196; VB213 - VB257; VB280 - VB299; VB324 - VB358; VB379 - VB394; VB409 - VB436; VB452 - VB497; VB525 - VB558; VB584 - VB596; VB621 - VB653; VB682 - VB699; VB716 - VB748; VB764 - VB793; VB808 - VB849.

Hornet PR.II

Serial batches: VA962 - VA966. Total production: 5

Cancelled: VA967 - VA997, VB108 - VB131

Hornet F.III

Serial batches: PX289 - PX315; PX328 - PX369; PX383 - PX389; WB870 - WB889; WB897 - WB912; WF954 - WF962; WF966 - WF967. Total production: 121

Cancelled: PX399 - PX425; PX440 - PX487; PX501 - PX530

Hornet F.4

Serial batch: WF968 - WF979. Total production: 12

Sea Hornet F.20

Serial batches: TT186-TT213, TT247-TT248, VR837-VR864, VR891-VR892, VZ707-VZ715*, WE235-WE242*.
Total production: 79
*Built at Chester

Cancelled: VR611 - VR620; VR894 - VR912

Sea Hornet NF.21

Serial batches: VV430-VV441, VW945-VW950, VW951-VW980*, VX245-VX252*, VZ671-VZ682*, VZ690-VZ699*. Total production: 80
*Built at Chester

Sea Hornet PR.22

Serial batches: VW930-VW939, VZ655-VZ664*, WE245-WE247*. Total production: 23
* Built at Chester

Note: VW934 PR.22, VW945 NF.21, VW946 NF.21 and VW947 NF.21 partly built at Hatfield, completed at Chester.

WF957 landing on a wet runway at Butterworth after a strike

Hornets of No.33 Squadron lined up in the wet at Butterworth

Hornet F.1 PX216 of the Yorkshire Sector with the personalised code of Wg Cdr "Tiny" Neale

Production Aircraft Histories

60 Hornet F.Is produced under Contract No. 3235/ C23 by de Havilland, Hatfield
f/f = First flight dates where known.

PX210: 1.2.45, f/f. 9.2.45, to A & AEE 28.2.45, allocated to Controller R & D at A & AEE for service trials. 16.5.45, returned to Hatfield under DH charge. 8.10.46, to RAF Halton for instructional airframe as 6149M. 10.12.46, declared scrap and SOC.

PX211: 21.3.45, allocated to Controller R & D at DH. 27.7.45, delivered to A & AEE 23.8.45, Cat.A with repairs on site by DH working team. General trials aircraft. Sept/Oct 1945, DH and A & AEE for brief handling and manoeuvrability trials.

PX212: 18.4.45, f/f. Delivered to Heston Aircraft Co. for part naval conversion to Sea Hornet F.20 (non-folding wings. 19.4.45, first flight from Heston. 10.5.45, delivered to RAE for trials of arrester gear during ADDL. 15.6.45, to Hatfield for modifications to ailerons. 27.7.45, returned to RAE. 4.8.45, Flown to Arbroath for ADDLs. 6.8.45, to Ayr in preparation for forthcoming carrier deck landing trials. 10/11.8.45, deck landing trials aboard HMS *Ocean*. After trials aircraft returned to RAE, eventually returning to DH Hatfield. 2.10.45, displayed to the press at Heston with PX214. 4.2.46, to RAE. 6.2.46, to A & AEE. 6.2.46, to A & AEE for tests of arrestor hook installation. Then period with R-R. 25.3.46, to 778 STU RNAS Ford. Returned to R-R for inspection of 'Corliss' throttles. 16.4.46, to 778 Sqn for service trials. 11.9.46, flown to Hatfield for special investigation. 28.2.47, SOC by C.S.(A).

PX213; 27.4.45, f/f. 12.5.45, DH Propeller development. 12.5.47, a/c ferried to 10 MU Hullavington. 12.1.51, to instructional airframe. 25.5.47, surplus to requirements. 18.1.51, S.S. to International Alloys

PX214; 2.10.45, first public showing. DH to Heston. Converted to Sea Hornet F.20 (folding wings) with arrestor hook and accelerator gear pick-up points. 12.1.46, flown to RAE for accelerator trials at light load. 23.1.46, catapult proving trials. 29.1.46, returned to Hatfield for fitment of Corliss throttles and larger tailplane. 17.4.46, to 778 Sqn RNAS Ford. for pilot familiarisation and sundry trials. 20.11.46, allocated to NAFDU at West Raynham for pilot training. 9.1.47, allotted to 787 Sqn. 3.10.47, retired to Fleetlands.

PX215: 26.4.45, DH 5.5.45, trial installation of mods. CRD. Used for spares. 25.11.46, SOC. 12.12.46, on scrap dump.

PX216: 24.4.45, allotted to Controller R & D for development as PR prototype. 30.10.45, delivered to PRDU Benson in overall PRU finish, coded 'R'. 6.9.46, DH Hatfield for Cat.B repairs. 3.11.47, to HQ Linton-on-Ouse, Yorkshire Sector as personal aircraft, coded WA-TN, of W/Cdr. W.A. Nel, Wing Commander Ops., flown on occasions by squadron pilots for air tests and collection from various bases. 26.7.49, to ground instructional airframe 6685M. 25.9.49, SOC. 5.12.49, classified as scrap.

PX217: 26.4.45, to A & AEE for intensive flying trials. 17.9.45, del. FU Pershore. 30.8.46, 10 MU. 26.6.48, A & AEE and CFE. 18.1.51, S.S. to Int. Alloys.

PX218: 19.6.45, f/f. Allotted to A & AEE next day. 3.7.45, flown to A & AEE for intensive flying trials. 17.7.45, Cat.A at Boscombe Down. 14.3.46, approval for retention at A & AEE for hood jettison tests in wind tunnel. 11.6.47, 37 MU Burtonwood. 26.6.48, A & AEE. 3.11.48, to 10 MU for storage. 18.1.51, S.S. to International Alloys.

PX219: 1.1.46, A.W. Delivered unassembled to Heston Aircraft Ltd. for naval conversion (folding wings). 13.12.46, DH. 3.3.47, to A & AEE for handling trials with RPs. 20.3.47, tailplane struck by rocket which rolled off lorry after been unloaded from aircraft. 20.8.47, to Heston for trials of 'Hot Dog'. 26.4.48, to Hatfield for additional trials of 'Cord'. 12.10.48, ret. to ATDU Gosport for trials of 'Highball', later transferred to Vickers-Armstrong, Weybridge for removal of secret equipment. 9.3.49, to Arbroath as ground instructional airframe.

PX220: 3.7.45, allocated Controller R & D at Hatfield. 2nd PR.2 prototype. 29.1.46, trials at A & AEE. 28.2.46, CRD at DH. 8.3.46, to A & AEE. 30.11.47, arr. 37 MU for storage. 3.7.48, CRD DH. 3.11.48, 10 MU. 18.1.51, S.S. to International Alloys.

PX221: 20.6.45, DH. 6.7.45, preparations for instrumentation for impending tropical trials. 18.9.45, arr. A & AEE for brief tropical suitability trials. 30.11.45, at Boscombe Down principally for weight/loading data tests. 27.5.47, allocated to 10 MU as surplus to requirements, this subsequently being cancelled. 22.7.47, despatched by road to Hatfield for Cat.B repairs. 7.8.47, R.I.W. DH but cancelled. 30.9.47, declared surplus. 24.7.48, CFE. 31.8.49, SOC.

PX222: 21.9.45, allocated R.& D., Hatfield. 11.4.46, transferred to Hatfield. 22.8.46, Ret. to A & AEE. 18.12.46, A & AEE. Fitted with flame dampers by DH. 3.3.47, ret. to Hatfield for flame damper investigation. 14.8.47, transferred to Admiralty charge. 30.10.47, to Worthy Down as instructional airframe. 15.11.47, arr. by road at Arbroath.

PX223: 20.7.45, f/f. 11.8.45, awaiting collection at Hatfield. 22.8.46, A & AEE for GGS installation. 11.10.46, A & AEE for armament trials. 13.10.46, 37 MU. 26.10.48, 10 MU. 10.1.51, S.S.

PX224: 3.10.45, allocated to 27 MU. 19.2.46, issued to CFE West Raynham although flown to Hatfield on that date from Shawbury for hood jettison tests. Flight tests on hydraulic system prior to fitting of reversible pitch propeller tests at A & AEE. Also used for comparison of G flaps and Fowler flaps. 27.8.46, on loan to DH. 31.8.46, entered in High Speed Handicap Race at Lympne, Kent, reaching 3rd place at average speed of 343.5 m.p.h. 27.6.47, allocated to 37 MU. 30.6.47, allocation cancelled. 4.9.47, at DH for Cat.B repairs. 16.9.47, repairs stopped, a/c taken off contractor's charge. 3.10.47, 27 MU. 17.3.49, re-Cat.E.2. 31.9.49, S.S.

PX225: 7.9.45, to ECFS, Handling Sqn. 26.2.46, to 65 Sqn coded 'C'. 18.3.47, canopy broke away in dive; repaired on site by team from DH 3.4.47 to 8.5.47 and ret'd to 65 Sqn. 23.6.48, to 27 MU for storage. 22.1.51, S.S. to Enfield Rolling Mills.

PX226: 14.9.45, 10 MU. 1.8.46, 65 Sqn coded 'S'. 11.7.47, damaged by birdstrike on approach, Linton-on-Ouse. 21.8.47, 65 Sqn. 18.3.48, repaired on site by DH. 8.4.48, 65 Sqn. 23.6.48, 27 MU. 19.11.48, 10 MU. 18.1.51, S.S.

PX227: 7.9.45, del. 1 FU Pershore. 30.5.46, arr. MAAF. 1.7.46, Mauripur, India for tropical trials. 31.7.49, SOC

PX228: 7.9.45, f/f. 13.9.45, AW/CN. 7.2.46, 1 FU Pershore. 30.5.46, arr. MAAF 4.7.46, damaged undercarriage taxying on soft ground, Mauripur; Cat.A. 8.7.46, Mauripur for tropical trials. 13.2.47, Khartoum. 22.1.48, 109 MU Egypt. 14.4.49, to UK. 7.49, DH for examination after tropical trials; airframe completely dissected. 19.12.49, SOC as scrap.

PX229: 25.9.45, 27 MU. 15.2.46, DH. 16.3.46, 27 MU. 7.6.46, RAE. 12.11.46, flew into high ground near Charterhouse, Somerset. 9.1.47, SOC

PX230: 9.7.45, f/f. To RN as NF.21 Prototype. 8.8.45, RNAS Ayr. 12.3.47, Lasham scrap dump. 12.8.47, SOC.

PX231: 3.10.45, attempted delivery flight abandoned, u/c leg failed to retract. 8.10.45, 65 Sqn from 27 MU coded 'P'. 23.6.48, 226 OCU. 6.6.48, 41 Sqn. 1.10.48, to 34 MU. 29.9.48, SOC. Became 6612M. 7.1.50, cut up for scrap.

PX232: 26.10.45, f/f. 16.11.45, 10 MU. 13.8.46, 65 Sqn coded 'R'. 25.8.47, ground accident; engine repairs. 18.3.48, DH. 15.4.48, 65 Sqn. 6.6.48, 41 Sqn coded 'X'. 9.11.48, 10 MU. 18.1.51, S.S. Int. Alloys.

PX233: 26.10.45, 10 MU. 17.7.46, 64 Sqn. 10.10.46, to DH. 24.10.46, 64 Sqn. 30.10.46, 19 Sqn coded 'K'. 14.1.47, 19 Sqn. Church Fenton. 21.11.47, stalled following single-engine overshoot and crashed, Church Fenton; pilot killed.

PX234: 16.11.45, 27 MU. 16.5.46, 64 Sqn. 10.10.46, 19 Sqn coded 'C' and 'D'. 3.3.48, Cat.B. 18.3.48, DH. 15.4.48, 19 Sqn. 6.11.48, 10 MU. 18.1.51, S.S.

PX235: 3.10.45, f/f. From 5.10.45 to 26.11.45, aircraft u/s with port engine and propeller faults. 4.10.45, AW/CN. 29.1.46, cleared for delivery. 27.3.46, 10 MU. 18.1.51, S.S. to Int. Alloys.

PX236: 26.10.45, 10 MU. 18.6.46, 27 MU. 17.7.46, 64 Sqn coded 'T'. 22.1.51, S.S. to Enfield Rolling Mills.

PX237: 18.10.45, f/f. 29.10.45, shown at Farnborough. 6.11.45, collected from Farnborough and flown to Hatfield. 1.1.46, 10 MU. 27.10.46, RAE. 16.1.47, Eastern Sector, Horsham St.Faith. 17.12.47, 12 Group Comm. Flight. 2.2.48, bounced on landing, engine cut and undercarriage collapsed, Linton-on-Ouse; Cat B. 14.2.48, DH for repair. 7.4.48, 10 MU. 9.2.49, S.S. to Min of Supply.

PX238: 16.10.45, 10 MU. 17.10.46, 226 OCU. 17.6.48, Cat.AC. 4.7.48, ROS by DH. 26.7.48, 226 OCU coded 'BB-D' and 'XL-D'. 15.8.49, Cat.B. 25.8.49, to Henlow as 6696M.

PX239: 1.1.46, To RN (See Sea Hornet Conversions)

PX240: 16.11.45, 27 MU. 20.6.46, 65 Sqn coded 'L'. 23.6.48, 27 MU. 22.1.51, S.S. to Enfield Rolling Mills.

PX241: 28.11.45, 10 MU. 13.5.46, 64 Sqn coded 'N'. 17.1.47, canopy broke away; Cat.AC. 27.1.47, DH for repair. 12.1.47, 64 Sqn coded N. 8.5.48, 27 MU. 22.1.51, S.S. to Enfield Rolling Mills.

PX242: 1.11.45, f/f. 27.11.45, 27 MU. 26.9.46, 65 Sqn coded 'G'. 16.6.48, 41 Sqn coded 'X'. 25.4.49, Cat.B. 4.7.49, re-cat E and SOC.

PX243: 28.11.45, 10 MU. 9.5.46, bounced on landing and undercarriage collapsed, Hullavington; caught fire. 22.5.46, SOC

PX244: 10.11.45, DH flight tests. 10.1.46, 27 MU. 28.3.46, 64 Sqn. 30.10.47, Cat.AC. 8.5.48, 64 Sqn coded 'P'. 1.7.48, 41 Sqn coded 'T'. 4.11.48, both engines cut; force-landed 6 miles NW of Derby; DBR. 19.11.48, SOC as Cat.E2

PX245: 27.11.45, 27 MU. 22.5.46, to Malcolms Ltd. White Waltham for installation of retractable GGS mounting. 18.11.46, investigation into fitting of pilot ejection system. 5.2.48, aircraft crashed; Cat.E. 6.2.48, SOC.

PX246: 27.11.45, 27 MU. 13.6.46, 64 Sqn coded S. 10.10.46, DH 7.11.46, 19 Sqn coded 'A' and 'M'. 17.8.48, 37 MU. 14.12.48, 10 MU. 18.1.51, S.S. to Int. Alloys.

PX247: 28.11.45, 10 MU. 16.5.46, 64 Sqn coded 'Q'. 3.3.48, Cat.AC. 14.3.48, ROS by DH. 18.3.48, 64 Sqn. 8.5.48, 27 MU. 22.1.51, S.S. to Enfield Rolling Mills.

PX248: 1.1.46, 10 MU. 29.5.46, 64 Sqn coded 'DLR'. 10.10.46, 19 Sqn. coded 'D' and 'E'. 4.2.48, swung on landing and port undercarriage leg collapsed, Church Fenton; Cat.B. 8.3.48, 10 MU for storage. 10.2.49, S.S. to Min of Supply.

PX249: 13.12.45, CRD Hatfield. 3rd PR.2 Prototype. 30.1.46, A & AEE. 1.4.46, ECFS. 24.5.46, 10 MU. 24.8.46, arr. DH Hatfield for firm's spinning trials. 11.12.47, arr. A & AEE for check on spinning characteristics. 29.4.48, 10 MU. 24.8.49, S.S. to W. Lamont.

PX250: 27.11.45, f/f. 1.1.46, 10 MU. 30.5.46, 64 Sqn coded 'H'. 14.5.47, 19 Sqn coded 'G'. 19.4.48, stalled on to runway on landing and undercarriage collapsed, Church Fenton; Cat B. 16.6.48, 10 MU. 24.8.49, S.S. to W. Lamont.

PX251: 10.1.46, 10 MU. 10.5.46, 64 Sqn coded 'M'. 25.8.46, Cat.AC. 8.9.47, a/c req'd. for Battle of Britain display. 18.3.48, 64 Sqn. 26.5.48, 27 MU. 22.1.51, S.S. to Enfield Rolling Mills.

PX252: 10.1.46, 10 MU. 29.7.46, 65 Sqn coded 'H'. 6.9.46, landed too fast; braked and swung into totem pole, Linton-on-Ouse; Cat A. to DH for repair. 5.12.46, 65 Sqn. 20.8.47, flying accident Cat.AC. 20.4.48, hit by ricochet during air-to-ground firing near Acklington; Cat AC. 6.5.48, DH for repair. 9.6.48, 65 Sqn. 16.6.48, 41 Sqn coded 'H' and 'Z'. 17.11.48, 226 OCU coded 'BB-T', 'XL-T' and 'XL-V'. 8.1.49, dived into ground on overshoot, Bentwaters. Pilot killed.

PX253: 15.1.46, 27 MU. 21.3.46, 64 Sqn. 7.5.46, port engine broke away; crashed, High Green, Norfolk. Pilot killed.

PX273: 13.12.45, f/f. 15.1.46, 27 MU. 8.3.46, Horsham St.Faith as Sector Leader's aircraft coded 'PM-CLB'. 30.9.46, flew into hill in cloud 4 miles E. of Penderyn. Pilot killed. Cat.E. 8.11.46, SOC

PX274: 11.12.45, f/f. 10.1.46, 27 MU. 16.5.46, 64 Sqn coded 'G'. 8.9.47, a/c req'd for Battle of Britain exhibition. 22.12.47, flew into hill in cloud near Bacup, Lancs. Pilot killed. Cat.E2. 12.1.48, SOC

PX275: 28.1.46, 27 MU. 19.2.46, CFE West Raynham coded

Hornet I PX288 taxies in after a demonstration flight at Radlett, 10 February 1946 (via P. Jarrett)

'GO-F'. 16.10.47, DH for repair. 8.1.48, CFE. 18.3.48, 12 Group Comm. Flt. 1.3.49, 27 MU. 22.1.51, S.S. to Enfield Rolling Mills.

PX276: 10.1.46, 27 MU. 14.5.46, 64 Sqn coded 'P'. 17.10.46, 19 Sqn coded 'F' and 'H'. 17.8.48, 27 MU. 3.11.48, 10 MU. 18.1.51, S.S. to Int. Alloys.

PX277: 30.12.45, f/f. 24.1.46, 10 MU. 13.5.46, 64 Sqn coded 'O'. 10.10.46, 19 Sqn coded 'B'. 16.1.47, 27 MU. 13.2.47, 19 Sqn coded 'E', 'F' and 'P'. 29.1.48, 19 Sqn. 9.6.48, 41 Sqn coded 'W'. 11.1.49, hit by PX307 while parked, Church Fenton; Cat AC, later Cat B. 5.5.49, to Leconfield as 6658M. 29.3.50, SOC

PX278: 30.12.45, f/f. 24.1.46, 10 MU. 7.10.46, 65 Sqn. 10.10.46, 19 Sqn coded 'F' and 'E'. 3.3.48, Cat.B. 30.4.48, 19 Sqn. 9.6.48, 41 Sqn. 20.12.48, 27 MU. 22.1.51, S.S. to Enfield Rolling Mills.

PX279: 2.1.46, f/f. 28.1.46, 27 MU. 16.2.46, 64 Sqn coded 'A'. 20.6.46, hydraulics failed; belly-landed at Horsham St.Faith; Cat.B. 5.7.46, DH for repair on site. 3.5.48, 27 MU. 22.1.51, S.S. to Enfield Rolling Mills.

PX280: 8.1.46, DH flight tests. 28.1.46, Heston. 11.9.46, 65 Sqn coded 'A'. 6.12.48, 10 MU. 18.1.51, S.S. to Int. Alloys.

PX281: 12.1.46, f/f. 30.1.46, 10 MU. 5.11.46, 226 OCU coded 'BB-E' and 'XL-E'. Cat.2. 30.6.49, 27 MU. 30.3.50, SOC as scrap.

PX282: 1.2.46, 10 MU. 20.8.46, 65 Sqn coded 'B'. 22.5.47, Church Fenton. 29.10.47, 64 Sqn. 10.12.47, stalled on approach, Linton-on-Ouse; caught fire. Pilot killed. 11.12.47, SOC

PX283: 17.1.46, f/f. 4.2.46, 27 MU. 8.3.46, 64 Sqn. 20.3.46, hit trees low flying near Wroxham, Norfolk. Pilot killed. 28.3.46, SOC.

PX284: 31.1.46, AW/CN. 4.2.46, 27 MU. 19.3.46, 64 Sqn coded 'B'. 28.11.46, 19 Sqn coded 'H' and 'K'. 11.11.47, collided with Lancaster TW647, Stanford, Norfolk. Pilot killed. 20.4.48, SOC.

PX285: 27.1.46, f/f. 4.2.46, 27 MU. 21.3.46, 64 Sqn coded 'E'. 20.8.47, DH Cat.B. 31.8.49, S.S. to Coley.

PX286: 27.1.46, f/f. 1.2.46, 27 MU. 15.5.46, Ftr.Cmd. Comm.Sqn. 19.8.47, 10 MU. 20.7.49, National Air Races, Elmdon. 10 MU. 18.1.51, S.S. to Int. Alloys.

PX287: 1.2.46, wheels-up landing at Hatfield. Repaired on site by DH. 19.2.46, DH flight tests. 4.3.46, CRD Hatfield. 3.6.46, 27 MU. 27.6.46, 64 Sqn. 8.5.48, 27 MU. 22.1.51, S.S. to Enfield Rolling Mills.

PX288: 26.3.46, DH flight tests. 4.4.46, to Rolls-Royce for engine development. Fitted large drop tanks. 17.2.50, 27 MU. 22.1.51, S.S. to Enfield Rolling Mills.

* * * * * * * * * *

85 Hornet F.IIIs produced under Contract 3235/C23 by de Havilland, Hatfield

PX289: 12.1.46, AW/CN. 7.2.46, to DH for trial installation of outboard wing fuel mountings and zero length RPs. 13.5.46, TI of revised fuel system. 30.4.47, a/c taxied over to MRO for repairs, Cat.B and engines. 9.12.47, 10 MU. 11.5.50, 41 Sqn coded 'W'. 9.2.51, 27 MU. 28.5.53, FEAF via Benson. 15.6.53, MB Seletar. 3.10.53, 33 Sqn coded 'Y' and 'T'. 25.3.55, 45/33 Sqn. 26.4.55, SOC

PX290: 1.5.46, To DH Hatfield for TI of Merlin 132/133 engines fitted with reversible pitch propellers. 16.2.46, DH Propeller Division. A/c towed across from A/c Div. 19.9.46, development testing of braking propellers, regularising action only. 30.6.47, crashed due to swing on landing and collapse of undercarriage, Hatfield. 11.11.47, delivered to 54 MU as Cat.E.2.

PX291: 27.2.46, f/f. 10.7.46, 10 MU. 24.5.50, damaged by fire in hangar, Hullavington; Cat 3R. A & AEE. 24.10.52, 27 MU. 4.9.53, arr. Marshalls, Cambridge for TI of 'Rebecca'. 5.11.53, returned to 10 MU. 29.6.54, ferried FEAF via Benson. 12.7.54, MB Seletar for storage. 27.5.55, SOC

PX292: 19.7.46, 27 MU. 11.11.49, Station Flt. Linton-on-Ouse coded 'MS-K' and painted PR blue. Used by Hornet Conversion Flight. 3.1.51, undercarriage collapsed in heavy landing, Linton-on-Ouse; Cat.3R. 16.1.51, DH for repairs. 4.2.52, 27 MU. 30.6.52, ferried FEAF. 28.8.52, FETS. 9.3.53, undercarriage not locked down; collapsed on landing, Seletar. 12.3.53, 390 MU. 22.5.53, FETS. 26.2.55, 80 Sqn coded 'H'. 18.5.55,

SOC

PX293: 8.3.46, f/f. 14.8.46, 27 MU. 18.11.47, 19 Sqn coded 'A'. 17.5.51, 27 MU. 4.6.52, converted to F.4 by Airwork 29.1.53, 10 MU. 25.5.54, ferried FEAF via Benson. 9.6.54, 33 Sqn coded 'V'. 25.3.55, 45/33 Sqn. 27.5.55, SOC

PX294: 8.3.46, f/f. 3.7.46, 10 MU later 64 Sqn coded 'F'. 6.7.49, 19 Sqn. coded 'C'. 24.10.49, port undercarriage leg collapsed during single-engine landing, Church Fenton. 9.2.50, 41 Sqn coded 'E'. 19.4.51, 27 MU. 10.3.53, ferried FEAF via Abingdon. 31.5.53, 390 MU Seletar. 6.11.53, Kai Tak store. 20.4.54, 80 Sqn coded 'H' and 'M'. 29.3.55, SOC.

PX295: 14.8.46, 27 MU. 21.8.50, 64 Sqn. 30.3.51, FCCS Bovingdon. 14.6.51, 27 MU. 24.4.53, ferried FEAF via Abingdon. 20.5.53, MB Seletar store. 30.11.53, FETS. 28.12.53, tyre burst on landing; swung and undercarriage leg collapsed, Seletar; Cat.3R. 28.1.54, MB Seletar. 27.5.54, overstressed. 31.8.54, FETS. 30.5.55, SOC.

PX296: 23.7.46, 10 MU. 16.9.49, 64 Sqn coded 'N'. 21.3.51, 10 MU. 12.3.52, 27 MU. 7.5.52, conv. F.4 by Airwork 30.10.52, 27 MU. 28.5.53, ferried FEAF via Benson. 24.6.53, MB Seletar. 27.5.55, SOC.

PX297: 12.8.46, 27 MU. 6.7.50, 41 Sqn. 15.8.51, 27 MU. 13.2.53, ferried FEAF via Abingdon. 20.2.53, 390 MU. 16.3.53, 80 Sqn coded 'V'. 28.5.55, SOC.

PX298: 25.3.46, f/f. 21.8.46, 10 MU. 14.9.48, 41 Sqn coded 'V'. 22.7.49, cowlings deformed due to engine flexing. 13.9.49, DH. 27.2.50, 27 MU. 13.10.50, 64 Sqn coded 'H'. 9.2.51, 10 MU. 10.3.53, ferried FEAF via Abingdon. 19.3.53, 390 MU. 1.4.53, 33 Sqn coded 'G'. 11.2.54, SOC.

PX299: 8.7.46, 10 MU. 11.2.51, Yorkshire Sector/Linton-on-Ouse/Hornet Conversion Flt coded 'MS-C' and 'MS-G'. 9.2.51, 27 MU. 3.7.52, conv. F.4 by Airwork 5.2.53, 10 MU. 24.6.54, ferried FEAF via Benson. 13.7.54, Seletar store. 27.5.55, SOC.

PX300: 2.4.46, f/f. 12.7.46, 10 MU. 20.9.49, 41 Sqn coded 'Y' and 'Z'. 15.2.51, 10 MU. Storage. 10.6.54, ferried FEAF via Benson. 24.6.53, MB Seletar. 27.5.55, SOC

PX301: 4.4.46, f/f. 12.8.46, 27 MU. 18.10.49, 65 Sqn. 7.11.49, 19 Sqn coded 'D' and 'C'. 2.7.51, 27 MU. 16.5.52, conv. F.4 by Airwork 29.1.53, 10 MU. 23.10.53, ferried FEAF via Benson. 22.5.55, SOC

PX302: 12.7.46, 10 MU. 19.5.49, 41 Sqn coded 'D'. 15.2.51, 10 MU. 8.3.54, ferried FEAF via Benson. 27.5.54, 33 Sqn coded 'G'. 29.7.54, swung on take-off, collided with WF971, Butterworth. DBR

PX303: 20.7.46, DH flight tests. 14.8.46 27 MU. 22.12.48 arr. DH Hatfield for RP & bomb mechanism tests, F.52 camera and fitting of 2-stage day/night equipment. 14.1.49, a/c exchanged for PX393. 17.1.49, 64 Sqn coded 'T'. 20.6.49 Cat.A. 4.7.49, to DH for repair as Cat.B. 27.2.50, 27 MU. 9.8.50, 65 Sqn. 5.9.50, collided with PX359 on take-off, Linton-on-Ouse. DBR.

PX304: 28.8.46, 10 MU. 26.1.49, 12 Group Comm. Flight, Newton. 28.9.49, 65 Sqn coded 'A'. 9.2.51, 10 MU. 27.5.52, conv. F.4 by Airwork 3.11.52, 27 MU. 11.1.54, FEAF. 9.2.54, MB Seletar. 27.5.55, SOC.

PX305: 21.8.46, 10 MU. 13.6.49, 65 Sqn coded 'B'. 23.11.50, gun bay panel blown off during air-sea firing; Cat.3R. 18.4.51, Linton Hornet Conv. Flt. 29.6.51, 27 MU. 20.5.53, DH. 8.7.53, 27 MU. 25.5.54, ferried FEAF via Benson. 9.6.54, 33 Sqn coded 'P' and 'A'. Modified for T.T. 28.10.54, engine cut and brake pressure lost; belly-landed at Butterworth. DBR

PX306: 18.4.46, f/f. 21.8.46, 10 MU. 27.9.48, 19 Sqn coded 'G'. 20.2.51, 27 MU. 21.11.53, ferried FEAF via Benson. 30.11.53, MB Seletar. 19.8.54, 33 Sqn coded 'J'. 25.3.55, 45/33 Sqn. 16.5.55, SOC.

PX307: 12.8.46, DH flight tests. 28.8.46, 10 MU. 6.10.48, 41 Sqn coded 'X'. 11.1.49, jumped chocks and hit PX277, Church Fenton.

PX308: 26.4.46, f/f. 3.9.46, 10 MU. 9.11.48, 41 Sqn coded 'B'. 8.1.51, hit pole on approach, Linton-on-Ouse, and

caught fire.

PX309: 6.9.46, 10 MU. 30.11.50, RAFFC Manby. 9.3.51, 10 MU. 14.12.53, ferried FEAF via Benson. 30.12.53, MB Seletar. 15.7.54, FETS. 21.3.55, MB Seletar. 27.5.55, SOC

PX310: 1.5.46, f/f. 12.9.46, 10 MU. 22.3.50, arr. at DH Hatfield for TIs of G.4F compass, twin VHF and improvements to drop tank push system. 5.2.53, despatched to 27 MU. 4.6.54, ferried FEAF via Benson. 4.12.54, 45 Sqn coded 'M'. 25.3.55, 45/33 Sqn. 27.5.55, SOC

PX311: 11.5.46, DH Hatfield and allotted for TIs. Believed with 41 Sqn coded 'C'. 8.5.47, CFE. 5.7.48, 27 MU. 26.9.49, DH. 15.6.50, Linton-on-Ouse, Hornet Conv. Flt. 31.7.50, undercarriage prematurely retracted on take-off; belly-landed, Linton-on-Ouse. 22.9.50, DH. 28.3.51, 10 MU. 12.1.53, ferried FEAF via Abingdon. 28.1.53, 390 MU Seletar. 19.2.53, 33 Sqn coded 'Q'. 14.10.54, engine cut; belly-landed at Butterworth. DBR.

PX312: 8.5.46, f/f. F.3 Prototype. 14.5.46, awaiting collection at Hatfield for Heston Aircraft for conversion to Sea Hornet. 30.6.47, arr. A & AEE for drop tank trials, including jettison tests, official full load handling and stability trials with bombs, RPs and drop tanks. 1.12.47, Transferred to naval charge. 10.3.48, damage to tail dorsal and fin, port elevator and fuselage caused by disintegration of cockpit canopy. Cat.AC. 12.4.48, completion of full handling trials. 30.6.48, 37 MU. 26.10.48, 10 MU. 12.7.51, to DH for mods. 18.9.51, 27 MU. 31.3.53, FEAF via Abingdon. 20.4.53, 390 MU. 19.10.54, 45 Sqn. 23.3.55, 45/33 Sqn. 26.4.55, SOC

PX313: 11.5.46, DH flight tests. 8.10.46, 10 MU. 31.12.48, Church Fenton Station Flt. 15.2.51, 10 MU. 9.3.53, ferried FEAF via Abingdon. 21.3.53, 390 MU. 22.4.53, FETS. 10.5.54, belly-landed in error, Seletar. 26.6.54, SOC

PX314: 10.5.46, f/f. 23.9.46, 10 MU. 19.11.48, 41 Sqn coded 'C' and 'F'. 19.2.51, 27 MU. 19.11.53, ferried FEAF via Benson. 30.11.53, MB Seletar. 31.7.55, SOC; to GI airframe.

PX315: 6.9.46, overshot landing at Hatfield before delivery.

PX328: 15.5.46, f/f. 6.9.46, 10 MU. 13.6.49, 65 Sqn coded 'D'. 16.1.50, damaged by birdstrike; Cat.3. 2.3.50, 65 Sqn coded 'K'. 9.2.51, 27 MU. 19.4.54, ferried FEAF via Benson. 30.4.54, MB Seletar. 9.11.54, 33 Sqn coded 'X'. 25.3.55, 45/33 Sqn. 28.4.55, SOC.

PX329: 26.7.46, 10 MU. 10.1.51, 1 OFU Chivenor. 19.2.51, OFU Abingdon. 9.5.52, conv. F.4 by Airwork 3.11.52, 27 MU. 28.5.53, ferried FEAF via Benson. 15.6.53, MB Seletar. 27.5.55, SOC

PX330: 22.5.46, f/f. 19.7.46, 27 MU. 31.8.46, 41 Sqn coded 'Z', 'X', 'Y'. 22.7.49, 65 Sqn. 7.6.50, overshot landing at night, Church Fenton. 27.6.50, re-Cat. Scrap.

PX331: 19.7.46, 10 MU. 12.6.50, damaged by fire in hangar, Hullavington. DBR

PX332: 27.5.46, f/f. 23.7.46, 10 MU. 12.4.49, 19 Sqn coded 'D'. 15.3.51, 27 MU. 26.5.54, ferried FEAF via Benson. 27.6.54, MB Seletar. 4.1.55, 45 Sqn. 16.2.55, canopy shattered during tail chase; airframe DBR.

PX333: 2.7.46, 10 MU. 17.8.49, 41 Sqn. 23.8.49, belly-landed and slid into river, Acaster Malbis, Yorks.

PX334: 4.7.46, 10 MU. 26.9.49, 64 Sqn coded 'P'. 21.3.51, 10 MU. 21.5.52, conv. F.4 by Airwork. 3.11.52, 27 MU. 25.1.54, ferried FEAF via Benson. 9.2.54, MB Seletar. 26.2.55, 80 Sqn coded 'C'. 18.5.55, SOC.

PX335: 17.6.46, f/f. 8.7.46, 10 MU. 22.2.50, 65 Sqn coded 'H'. 9.2.51, 27 MU. 23.4.54, FEAF. 10.5.54, MB Seletar. 4.1.55, 33 Sqn coded 'A'. 25.3.55, 45/33 Sqn. 27.5.55, SOC

PX336: 10.7.46, 10 MU. 6.7.49, arr. DH Leavesden for installation of bombs and RPs. 26.9.49, allocated Boulton Paul. 3.10.49, arr. Boulton Paul for preliminary target towing equipment. 11.5.50, despatched to CFE West Raynham via Cosford. 6.10.50, arr. Boulton Paul for repositioning of target towing hook to enable towing

Hornet F.3 PX388 of No.65 Squadron (M.P.Marsh)

of winged target. Oct 1951 - Feb 1952, at A & AEE for
trials of RFD winged target and 30 ft. banner. 19.3.52,
to Hatfield for TI of radio compass. 31.10.52,
despatched to 27 MU. 8.4.53, ferried FEAF via
Abingdon. 30.4.53, 390 MU Seletar. 27.5.55, SOC

PX337: 19.6.46, f/f. 28.6.46, 10 MU. 4.10.49, 65 Sqn coded
'E'. 23.11.50, gun bay panel blown off during air-sea
firing; Cat.3R. 5.6.51, 10 MU. 3.7.52, conv. F.4 by
Airwork. 29.1.53, 10 MU. 23.10.53, ferried FEAF via
Benson. 30.11.53, MB Seletar. 27.5.55, SOC

PX338: 25.6.46, f/f. 3.7.46, 10 MU. 12.10.49, 19 Sqn coded
'B'. 14.10.50, hit trees during low-level sortie; Cat.3R.
11.12.50, to DH for repairs. 6.6.51, 10 MU. 6.11.52,
ferried FEAF via Abingdon. 1.12.53, 33 Sqn coded
'H'. 11.3.53, u/c failed to lower, belly-landed,
Butterworth. DBR

PX339: 15.7.46, 10 MU. 18.6.48, 65 Sqn coded 'A'. 14.6.49,
DH. 5.7.49, 64 Sqn. 5.4.50, 27 MU. 16.11.50, 64 Sqn.
9.2.51, 10 MU. 2.2.53, ferried FEAF via Abingdon.
7.2.53, 390 MU Seletar. 4.3.53, FETS. 13.3.53, SOC.

PX340: 10.7.46, f/f. 15.7.46, 10 MU. 16.6.48, 65 Sqn coded B.
5.7.49, 64 Sqn coded W. 21.6.51, 10 MU. 26.10.51,
conv. F.4 by Airwork. 21.3.52, 10 MU. 31.3.53,
ferried FEAF via Abingdon. 20.4.53, 390 MU Seletar.
30.6.53, FETS. 5.2.54, undercarriage collapsed while
taxying, Seletar. 12.11.54, SOC

PX341: 18.7.46, DH flight tests. 19.7.46, 10 MU. 4.9.49, 64
Sqn coded 'S'. 11.8.49, Gun bay panel detached during
firing practice; Cat.AC. 5.10.49, 64 Sqn. 9.2.51, 27
MU. 31.10.55, SOC. Used for fire-fighting practice.

PX342: 16.7.46, f/f. 23.7.46, 27 MU. 24.3.48, 19 Sqn coded
'E' and 'F'. 20.2.51, 27 MU. 17.9.54, ferried to FEAF.
19.10.54, MB Seletar. 10.12.54, 33 Sqn coded 'W'.
25.3.55, 45/33 Sqn. 16.5.55, ferried to Seletar for
scrapping. 27.5.55, SOC

PX343: 25.7.46, 27 MU. 24.3.48, 19 Sqn coded 'B'. 12.1.49,
lost radio aids on navex and force-landed on disused
airfield, Borizzo, Sicily. 8.5.50, 10 MU. 16.6.50,

Airwork, Gatwick. 18.5.51, 10 MU. 2.12.52, ferried
FEAF via Abingdon. 22.12.52, 80 Sqn coded 'C'.
16.9.54, MB Seletar. 30.11.54, HKACE. 16.9.54,
FEAF store. 14.4.55, SOC.

PX344: 22.7.46, f/f. 9.8.46, 27 MU. 7.4.48, 64 Sqn coded 'P'.
7.10.49, 10 MU. 19.6.50, 27 MU. 20.11.51,
despatched to Hatfield from Airwork for investigation
into rogue characteristics. 10.12.51, arr. Airwork for
F.4 conversion. 16.1.52, 10 MU. 13.2.53, ferried FEAF
via Abingdon. 20.2.53, 390 MU Seletar. 11.3.53,
FETS. 1.4.53, crashed during bad weather 14 miles E.
of Malacca. Pilot killed.

PX345: 12.8.46, 27 MU. 7.4.48, 64 Sqn coded 'V'. 27.9.50,
jack penetrated wing during lifting, Linton-on-Ouse.
14.2.51, DH. 18.9.51, 27 MU. 12.1.53, ferried FEAF
via Abingdon. 10.2.53, 80 Sqn coded 'G'. 6.5.55, SOC

PX346: 12.8.46, f/f. 20.8.46, 27 MU. 24.3.48, 19 Sqn coded
'C'. 13.3.49, hit trees during low-level attack on
Abbotsinch. 27.5.49, 65 Sqn coded 'E' and 'F'. 16.6.50,
Cat.3R. 21.6.50, 60 MU. 1.11.50, 64 Sqn coded 'M'.
10.7.52, conv. F.4 by Airwork. 29.1.53, 10 MU.
8.3.54, ferried FEAF via Abingdon. 26.7.54, 33 Sqn
coded 'Y'. 24.3.55, 45/33 Sqn. T.T. Mods. 26.4.55,
SOC

PX347: 9.9.46, 27 MU. 24.3.48, 19 Sqn coded 'D'. 14.2.49,
damaged. 28.3.49, DH for repair. 2.1.50, DH
Leavesden. 6.1.50, arr. Hatfield from Leavesden for TI
of F.52 Camera. 30.8.50, arr. at A & AEE for brief
handling trials with F.52 camera and I.F.F. check.
29.12.50, to Hatfield for TI of P.4F compass, AVF and
other equipment. 10.4.51, retained on permanent
C.S.(A) charge in exchange for PX393. 24.2.53, 27
MU. 17.9.53, ferried to FEAF via Benson. 30.11.53,
MB Seletar. 27.5.55, SOC.

PX348: 24.6.46, f/f. 19.12.46, CFE West Raynham & A & AEE
2.10.47, undercarriage jammed; belly-landed at West
Raynham; Cat.AC. 5.2.48, CFE. 25.8.49, DH. 1.5.50,
10 MU. 25.9.50, 65 Sqn. 26.2.51, 1689 Flt. 29.3.54,

ferried FEAF. 6.4.54, MB Seletar. 30.8.54, 33 Sqn coded 'G'. 25.3.55, 45/33 Sqn. 27.5.55, SOC.

PX349: 23.9.46, 10 MU. 29.6.48, 19 Sqn coded 'G', 'H'. 20.8.48, tyre burst in heavy landing; undercarriage leg collapsed, Newton; Cat.AC. 26.4.49, 19 Sqn. 7.9.49, DH. 21.2.50, 65 Sqn. 26.2.50, DH. 12.2.51, 10 MU. 17.12.53, ferried FEAF via Benson. 30.12.53, MB Seletar. 27.5.55, SOC

PX350: 23.9.46, 10 MU. 28.7.48, 41 Sqn coded 'Z'. 9.8.49, wheel link sheared; ground-looped and undercarriage collapsed, Church Fenton; Cat.B; repaired by DH. 22.1.51, 27 MU. 10.12.52, ferried FEAF via Abingdon. 20.10.52, 45 Sqn coded 'S'. 2.4.55, collided with PX362 during run over airfield, Butterworth. Pilot killed.

PX351: 26.9.46, 10 MU. 3.4.48, 64 Sqn coded 'Y' and 'M'. 12.1.50, stalled on approach, Linton-on-Ouse. Pilot killed. Cat.Scrap.

PX352: 16.10.46, 27 MU. 15.4.48, 65 Sqn coded 'J' and 'C'. 3.12.49, undercarriage leg collapsed on landing, Acklington; Cat 3. 17.5.50, conv. F.4 by Airwork. 7.5.52, 10 MU. 24.11.52, ferried FEAF via Abingdon. 1.12.52, 45 Sqn coded 'R'. 22.3.55, 45/33 Sqn. 27.5.55, SOC.

PX353: 10.10.46, 27 MU. 16.4.48, 64 Sqn coded 'SH-K'. 65 Sqn coded 'K'. 11.5.49, both engines lost power on take-off from Linton-on-Ouse; belly-landed on runway; Cat.AC. 16.6.49, ROS by 58 MU. 16.12.49, 65 Sqn. 29.6.50, damaged. 22.9.50, to DH for repair. 17.4.51, 27 MU. 15.10.52, ferried FEAF via Abingdon. 20.10.52, 45 Sqn. 27.5.55, SOC.

PX354: 11.10.46, 27 MU. 19.10.48, 10 MU. 20.5.49, Station Flight Linton-on-Ouse. 25.8.49, undercarriage leg collapsed on landing, Church Fenton. 4.1.50, 19 Sqn coded 'J' and 'M'. Linton-on-Ouse Station Flight, coded 'MS-A'. 1.5.50, cat as "rogue" aircraft. 12.6.50, to Airwork. 8.5.51, 10 MU. 2.12.52, ferried FEAF via Abingdon. 13.12.52, 390 MU Seletar. 5.1.53, 45 Sqn coded 'S'. 26.4.55, 45.33 Sqn. 2.5.55, SOC

PX355: 11.10.46, 27 MU. 13.6.49, 65 Sqn coded 'G'. 12.10.50, hit tree during low-level attack on Martlesham Heath; Cat.3R. 7.12.50, 65 Sqn. 9.2.51, 27 MU. 13.3.53, ferried FEAF via Abingdon. 6.11.53, Kai Tak store. 20.1.54, 80 Sqn.coded 'F' later 'G'. 6.5.55, SOC

PX356: 17.10.46, 37 MU. 15.10.48, 10 MU. 20.1.49, 65 Sqn. 6.3.49, hit water, Firth of Tay and belly-landed 4 miles E. of Newburgh, Fife. Cat.E.2. 10.3.49, SOC

PX357: 14.10.46, DH flight tests. 17.10.46, AW/CN. 24.10.46, 37 MU. 15.10.48, 10 MU. 18.1.49, 41 Sqn coded 'X'. 14.6.50, allotted to DH from Church Fenton for examination and report on spar attachment to fuselage. 23.6.50, arr. DH Leavesden via Hatfield. 13.10.50, despatched to 27 MU. 16.10.50, Abingdon. 13.12.52, ferried FEAF via Abingdon. 20.12.52, arr. FEAF. 23.12.52, 390 MU. Repairs. 3.2.53, 80 Sqn coded 'G'. 12.10.54, Prov. Cat.5(C). 7.1.55, SOC.

PX358: 18.10.46, f/f. 25.10.46, AW/CN. 6.12.46, 37 MU. 10.12.46, 37 MU. 5.5.47, jack collapsed and damaged wing, Hawarden; Cat.AC. 6.9.47, 48 MU. 24.11.47, 27 MU. 18.10.48, 10 MU. 19.1.50, 64 Sqn coded 'Y'. 10.10.50, hit ground recovering from dive and crash-landed during Exercise 'Emperor', Odiham. 11.10.50, Cat.Comp. 49 MU Re-Cat.Scrap.

PX359: 31.10.46, AW/CN. 18.12.46, 37 MU. 19.10.48, 10 MU. 18.12.48, 41 Sqn. 29.3.49, Cat.B. 9.5.49, 10 MU. 29.11.49, DH. 5.7.50, 65 Sqn. 4.9.50, collided with PX303 on take-off, Linton-on-Ouse. 5.9.50, confirmed Cat.3R. 6.10.50, re-Cat. Scrap.

PX360: 28.10.46, f/f. 31.10.46, AW/CN. 6.12.46, 37 MU. 10.12.46, 27 MU. 1.1.47, 37 MU. 26.10.48, 10 MU. 28.7.50, 19 Sqn. 9.5.51, 10 MU. 10.3.53, ferried FEAF via Abingdon. 21.3.53, 390 MU. 22.4.53, FETS. 16.11.53, undercarriage collapsed on landing, Changi. DBR and SOC.

PX361: 15.11.46, AW/CN. 26.11.46, 37 MU. 18.10.48, 10 MU. 22.1.49 65 Sqn coded 'A'. 13.4.49, swung on landing and tipped up. 1.9.49, cowling buckled during aerobatics; Cat.AC. 19.10.49, re-Cat.3A. 18.1.51 re-Cat.4R. 5.2.51, DH for repair. 17.7.51, 10 MU. 8.9.52, undercarriage leg collapsed in heavy landing; overshot and belly-landed, Hullavington; Prov. Cat.3R. 21.11.52, Airwork. 5.2.53, 10 MU. 24.4.53, FEAF. 26.6.53, MB Seletar for storage. 27.5.55, SOC.

PX362: 18.10.46, f/f. Crashed on test due to aileron lock. 6.11.46, flutter checks. 9.1.47, cleared for del. 10.1.47, AW/CN. 25.6.47, 37 MU. 16.4.48, 65 Sqn coded 'C'. 26.1.49, DH for investigation into rogue characteristics. 25.7.49, Station Flight, Linton-on-Ouse coded 'MS-H'. 29.6.51, 27 MU. 8.7.52, Airwork for F.4 conversion. 28.1.53, 10 MU. 8.3.54, ferried FEAF via Benson. 31.3.54, MB Seletar. 8.10.54, 45 Sqn. 13.10.54, MB for repair. 19.10.54, 45 Sqn. 2.4.55, collided with PX350 during run over airfield, Butterworth. Pilot killed. Cat.5(S). 30.4.55, SOC.

PX363: 28.11.46, AW/CN. 2.12.46, 37 MU. 12.10.48, 41 Sqn coded 'B' later 'Y'. 15.8.49, flew into ground during loop, Gütersloh. Pilot killed.

PX364: 7.2.46, AW/CN. 17.12.46, 10 MU. 7.3.50, 64 Sqn coded 'U'. 14.3.51, engine cut; undercarriage leg collapsed on landing, Waddington. Cat.4R. 3.4.51, Airwork. 13.12.51, re-Cat.5(S).

PX365: 7.12.46, AW/CN. 23.1.47, 37 MU. 19.10.48, 10 MU. 11.8.50, Hornet Conversion Flt, Linton-on-Ouse. 29.6.51, 27 MU. 2.2.53, ferried FEAF via Abingdon. 7.2.53, 33 Sqn. 23.11.54, MB Seletar repair. 14.12.54, 33 Sqn coded 'P'. 21.3.55, S.H.Q. Tengah. 27.5.55, SOC.

PX366: 6.46, shown at Farnborough. 2.1.47, AW/CN. 16.1.47, 37 MU. 12.10.48, 41 Sqn coded 'A' and 'Z'. 25.6.49, hit roof of building druing attack on Trimley Heath. 15.3.51, 27 MU. 13.2.53, ferried FEAF via Abingdon. 20.2.53, 390 MU Seletar. 16.3.53, 80 Sqn coded 'E'. 18.5.55, SOC.

PX367: 2.2.47, AW/CN. 20.3.47, 37 MU. 23.5.50, 19 Sqn coded 'J'. 15.2.51, 10 MU. 10.3.53, ferried FEAF via Abingdon. 20.5.53, MB Seletar, prep. for storage. 18.9.53, 45 Sqn. 22.3.55, 45/33 Sqn. 26.4.55, sank back after take-off, Butterworth. Cat.3 Prov., re-Cat. Scrap.

PX368: 2.1.47, AW/CN. 16.5.47, 37 MU. 1.11.48, 10 MU. 25.9.50, 65 Sqn. 9.2.52, 27 MU. 12.1.53, ferried FEAF via Abingdon. 28.1.53, 390 MU Seletar. 12.3.53, FETS. 30.3.53, swung on landing and hit Beaufighters RD814 and RD763, Seletar. Cat.4R. 2.4.53, 390 MU for repair. 23.9.53, FETS. 26.2.55. 80 Sqn. 26.4.55, flying accident, Cat.5R. [PX367 details in error?] 13.5.55, SOC

PX369: 17.1.47, AW/CN. 29.4.47, 37 MU. 5.7.50, 64 Sqn coded 'B'. 20.3.51, Bovingdon. 1.6.51, 27 MU. 21.1.53, ferried FEAF via Abingdon. 28.1.53, 390 MU Seletar. 24.3.53, 45 Sqn. 20.8.54, MB Seletar for repair. 11.10.54, 45 Sqn. 6.12.54, undercarriage jammed; belly-landed, Tengah. Cat.3R., re-Cat. scrap, 18.4.55, SOC.

PX383: 5.3.47, arr. DH Hatfield for TI of mods. 18.4.47, AW/CN. 29.5.47, C.S.(A) Hatfield. Tested NF.21 nose. 28.6.48, A & AEE for flight trials for clearance of 200-gallon wing drop tanks. 8.9.48, desp. to DH. 25.2.49, engine cut on take-off, Hatfield; abandoned near Royston, Herts. Cat. E1. 4.4.49, Cat. scrap. 28.4.49, at 58 MU. SOC Cat. E2

PX384: 15.4.47, f/f. 18.4.47; AW/CN. 9.5.47, 37 MU. 5.9.47, A.M. Unit, Hallam. 20.7.48, 37 MU. 20.10.48, 10 MU. 7.12.50, 65 Sqn. 8.1.51, Hornet Conversion Flt. Linton. 11.4.51, engine mountings distorted in spin; Cat.4R. 8.6.51, DH for repair. 16.1.52, 10 MU. 12.1.53, ferried FEAF via Abingdon. 23.1.53, arr. FEAF. 3.2.53, 33 Sqn coded 'E' and 'F'. 25.3.55, 45/33 Sqn. 27.5.55, SOC.

PX385: 3.5.47, f/f/. 4.6.47, 37 MU. 3.4.48, 64 Sqn coded 'Z'. 21.3.51, 10 MU. 3.4.51, DH. 27.7.51, arr. A & AEE for trials with drop tanks used as Napalm bombs.

Hornet PR.2 VA964 after engaging the crash barrier during trials at Farnborough (via Capt. E.M. Brown)

6.11.51, trials with 3" RPs with cut-down fins & excluding saddles. 21.11.51, accident at Boscombe, Cat.2. 14.1.52, despatched to 27 MU. 24.2.53, DH. 14.1.52, 27 MU. 5.10.53, ferried FEAF via Benson. 5.11.53, RAF Maintenance Base for storage. 27.5.55, SOC

PX386: 30.5.47, AW/CN. 19.6.47, loaned to DH for flights by Major Weiss of Argentine Air Force from 2-10th June. 8.7.47, A & A.E.E. for radio trials. 17.11.47, 10 MU for storage. 30.6.48, arr. DH Hatfield for fitting of tail parachute in preparation for spinning trials at A & AEE. 28.10.48, accident at Hatfield, u/c collapsed. Cat.B. 10.2.49, repairs completed at Hatfield. 4.49, spinning trials. 1.9.49, arr. at A & AEE. 19.10.49, authority given for a/c to enter National Air Races at Elmdon, 30.7.49-1.8.49. 27.11.50, a/c exchanged for PX310. 6.12.50, desp. to 10 MU. 15.6.53, to FEAF. 26.6.53, MB Seletar for storage. 22.8.54, 33 Sqn coded 'R'. 21.3.55, repair and prep. for MTS. 27.5.55, SOC

PX387: 30.6.47, AW/CN. 23.7.47, 10 MU. 2.7.48, 19 Sqn coded 'H'. 9.2.51, 27 MU. 29.1.54, arr. Hatfield for TI of mods. to introduce additional inspection covers in highly stressed areas. 25.4.54, a/c damaged. 5.5.55, 71 MU. 16.11.55, S.S. to W. Ashton & Son.

PX388: 25.7.47, AW/CN. 4.9.47, 37 MU. 16.4.48, 65 Sqn coded 'F' and 'H'. 17.1.50, flew into ground in cloud, Remscheid, W.Germany. Pilot killed.

PX389: 11.9.47, DH Hatfield. 17.9.47, allotted to DH for development of landing brake propellers and AV51 Constant Speed Units. 25.11.47, desp. to 10 MU. 18.3.48, 19 Sqn coded 'A'. 3.4.50, hit by PX338 while parked, Acklington; Cat.3R. 21.6.50, Airwork. 8.2.52, 27 MU. 15.10.52, ferried FEAF via Abingdon.

20.10.52, 45 Sqn. 21.5.53, swung on landing into ditch, Tengah. Cat.5C. 1.7.53, SOC

PX390: 29.9.47, f/f. 1.10.47, DH flight tests. 2.10.47, AW/CN. 16.10.47, 10 MU. 24.3.48, 19 Sqn coded 'D' and 'F'. 23.6.50, arr. at DH Leavesden via Hatfield for examination and report on spar attachment to fuselage. 12.10.50, del. to 27 MU. from Leavesden. 3.12.52, ferried FEAF via Abingdon. 11.12.52, arr. FEAF. 22.12.52, 80 Sqn coded 'R'. 14.2.55, SOC.

PX391: 29.10.47; AW/CN. 26.11.47, 10 MU. 30.3.48, 64 Sqn coded 'R'. 9.2.51, 27 MU. 19.9.53, ferried FEAF via Benson. 1.10.53, MB Seletar for storage. 30.4.54, FETS 15.11.54, Cat.3R. MB for repair. 18.12.54, FETS. 21.3.55, SHQ Tengah. 18.5.55, MB Seletar. 27.5.55, SOC.

PX392: 18.11.47, AW/CN. 19.12.47, 10 MU. 3.4.48, 64 Sqn coded 'X'. 2.6.50, overshot landing and undercarriage raised to stop, Linton-on-Ouse. Cat.Scrap.

PX393: 2.12.47, f/f. 16.1.48, 10 MU. 30.3.48, 64 Sqn Linton-on-Ouse. 14.1.49, arr. Hatfield for RP and bomb mechanism tests, TI of F.52 camera, 2 stage day and night equipment. (exchanged for PX303). 1.7.49, arr. at A & AEE for clearance trials of RPs and bombs. 12.1.50, accident at Boscombe Down, Cat.1. 21.2.50, arr. Hatfield for investigation into aileron flutter. 19.6.50, arr. Boscombe from Hatfield for completion of original handling and clearance trials. 26.10.50, accident at Boscombe, slight damage to starboard leading edge, Cat.2. 15.11.50, clearance obtained for use of bombs and RPs. 10.4.51, aircraft exchanged for PX347. 24.6.53, ferried FEAF via Abingdon. 1.10.53, MB for storage. 27.5.55, SOC

PX394: 22.1.48, AW/CN. 27.1.48, 10 MU. 23.6.48, 65 Sqn

coded 'G'. 20.4.49, overturned on landing, Linton-on-Ouse. Cat.E1. 21.4.49, SOC.

PX395: 18.2.48, 10 MU. 16.2.48, undershot landing and starboard leg collapsed in hitting rim of runway, Aston Down; Cat.AC. 30.3.48, DH. 1.4.48, re-Cat.B. R.I.W. DH. 6.9.49, AW/CN. 8.9.49, 41 Sqn coded 'W' and 'X'. 19.4.51, 27 MU. 23.7.53, to DH Hatfield for TI of 'Rebecca'. 20.8.53, C.S.(A) free loan for 6 months, arr. at Marshalls of Cambridge. 22.12.53, to DH Hatfield for TI of modified Vampire drop tanks for use with napalm. 13.5.54, desp. to 27 MU. 31.10.55, RAF Shawbury as scrap, for fire fighting.

PX396: 4.3.48, DH flight tests, aircraft u/s. 19.3.48, AW/CN. 24.3.48, 64 Sqn coded 'O'. 15.7.48, overshot landing and hit hedge, Linton-on-Ouse. Cat.E1. 16.7.48, confirmed Cat.E and SOC.

PX397: 30.4.48, AW/CN. 19.5.48, 10 MU. 25.7.48, 41 Sqn coded 'V'. 23.9.48, overshot landing, hit ditch and overturned, Church Fenton. Cat.E. 24.9.48, SOC.

PX398: 28.5.48, AW/CN. 9.6.48, 65 Sqn coded 'H'. 25.3.49, canopy detached and hit tail; Cat.AC. ROS by 58 MU. 3.6.49, 65 Sqn. 17.10.49, gun panel blown off during air-ground firing. 9.2.50, overshot landing and overturned, Leeming. Cat.4R. 22.4.50, re-Cat.Scrap.

PX399 to PX425: Cancelled
PX440 to PX487: Cancelled
PX501 to PX530: Cancelled

* * * * * * * * *

Five Hornet PR.IIs produced by de Havilland, Hatfield

VA962: 12.1.46, CRD at DH. 19.7.46, PRDU Benson. 20.9.46, 10 MU. 8.3.48, SOC Scrap

VA963: 5.2.46, f/f. 16.2.46, AW/CN. 27.3.46, 10 MU. 8.3.48, SOC Scrap.

VA964: 7.2.46, f/f. 16.2.46, AW/CN. 10.3.46, 10 MU. 24.6.47, allotted to RAE for crash barrier trials. 16.6.47, arr. from CFS Handling Sqn at RAE. 11.5.48, SOC & released to DH on loan. 8.3.48, DBR & SOC as scrap. Broken up at RAE.

VA965: 21.2.46, demonstrated at Horsham St. Faith. 27.3.46, CFS Handling Sqn. 24.6.47, allotted to RAE for crash barrier trials. 12.11.48, arr. CTU Lee-on-Solent. 4.5.49, authority for a/c to be SOC complete with engines at CTU.

VA966: 30.3.46, f/f. 17.11.46, CFS Handling Sqn. 11.6.47, RAE for barrier trials. 12.11.48, arr. CTU. 9.2.49, RAE barrier trials. 29.9.49, Cat.E2. 6.12.49, SOC.

VA967 to VA997: Cancelled
VB108 to VB135: Cancelled
VB154 to VB196: Cancelled
VB213 to VB257: Cancelled
VB280 to VB299: Cancelled
VB324 to VB358: Cancelled
VB379 to VB394: Cancelled
VB409 to VB436: Cancelled
VB452 to VB497: Cancelled
VB525 to VB558: Cancelled
VB584 to VB596: Cancelled
VB621 to VB653: Cancelled
VB682 to VB699: Cancelled
VB716 to VB748: Cancelled
VB764 to VB793: Cancelled
VB808 to VB849: Cancelled

* * * * * * * * *

36 Hornet F.3s produced by de Havilland, Chester

WB870: Del. 24.11.50, 27 MU. 18.4.51, ferried FEAF via Abingdon. 28.4.51, 33 Sqn coded 'M'. 10.8.51, Pilot lost control during aerobatics, aircraft crashed near Bedok, 5 miles S of Changi. Pilot killed.

WB871: Del. 24.11.50, 10 MU. 2.4.511, ferried FEAF via Abingdon. 9.4.51, 33 Sqn coded 'P'. 26.1.53, engine

cowling detached during aerobatics causing undercarriage to jam; pilot baled out over sea near Butterworth.

WB872: Del. 7.12.50, 10 MU. 18.4.51, ferried FEAF via Abingdon. 28.4.51, 33 Sqn coded 'S'. 14.5.53, A/c rolled after making dummy attack and dived into ground near Kroh, Malaya.

WB873: Del. 12.12.50, 27 MU. 2.4.51, ferried FEAF via Abingdon. 28.4.51, 33 Sqn coded 'X'. 10.54, DBR after towing hook attachment bracket was driven upwards during wheels-up landing at Butterworth. 15.10.54, SOC.

WB874: Del. 12.12.50, 27 MU. 10.5.51, ferried FEAF via Abingdon. 21.5.51, 33 Sqn coded 'W'. 6.11.53, SOC.

WB875: Del. 11.1.51, 10 MU. 16.5.51, ferried FEAF via Abingdon. 21.5.51, 33 Sqn coded 'R'. 22.7.53, 45 Sqn coded 'N'. 31.7.54, SOC

WB876: Del. 11.1.51, 10 MU. 18.5.51, ferried FEAF via Abingdon. 16.6.51, 33 Sqn coded 'D'. 25.10.51, damaged by bomb splinters during strike; Cat.3. 2.11.51, undercarriage jammed; bellylanded at Changi; Cat.3. 3.7.52, 45 Sqn coded 'O' and 'E'. 27.5.55, SOC.

WB877: Del. 9.1.51, 27 MU. 23.5.51, ferried FEAF via Abingdon. 31.5.51, 33 Sqn coded 'B'. 25.3.55, 45/33 Sqn. 16.5.55, SOC.

WB878: Del. 31.1.51, 27 MU. 23.5.51, ferried FEAF via Abingdon. 31.5.51, 33 Sqn coded 'D'. 28.3.55, SOC.

WB879: Del. 26.1.51, 10 MU. 4.7.51, ferried FEAF via Abingdon. 23.10.51, 390 MU store. 6.12.51, 80 Sqn. 27.2.52, swung while taxing and hit WB880, Kai Tak. 28.4.52, 390 MU for repair. 14.8.53, FETS. 6.10.53, undercarriage leg collapsed while taxying, Seletar. 24.4.55, 45/33 Sqn coded 'T'. 27.5.55, SOC.

WB880: Del. 12.2.51, 10 MU. 22.11.51, ferried FEAF via Abingdon. 4.12.51, 80 Sqn coded 'C'. 27.2.52, hit by WB879 while parked, Kai Tak. 28.4.52, 390 MU. 20.11.53, FETS. 7.4.54, undercarriage retracted prematurely on take-off and damaged; belly-landed, Seletar. 8.4.54, MB Seletar. 13.7.54, FETS. 16.3.55, SOC.

WB881: Del. 16.2.51, 10 MU. 15.6.51, ferried FEAF via Abingdon. 29.6.51, 33 Sqn coded 'E'. 26.6.52, swung on landing at Butterworth and hit drain. SOC as Cat 5C.

WB882: Del. 19.3.51, 10 MU. 4.12.51, ferried FEAF via Abingdon. 6.12.51, 80 Sqn coded 'R'. 4.6.52, throttles jammed, belly-landed at Kai Tak. SOC.

WB883: Del. 16.2.51, 10 MU. 4.7.51, ferried FEAF via Abingdon. 19.10.51, 33 Sqn coded 'J'. 3.7.52, 45 Sqn. 27.5.55, SOC.

WB884: Del. 9.3.51, 27 MU. 28.6.51, ferried FEAF via Abingdon. 7.7.51, 390 MU Seletar. 31.7.51, FETS. 28.9.51, damaged. 1.10.51, SOC.

WB885: Del. 27.3.51, 10 MU. 11.7.51, ferried FEAF via Abingdon. 23.10.51, 390 MU Seletar. 20.11.51, FETS. 18.2.53, brake pressure lost; belly-landed at Butterworth. 12.3.53, 390 MU. 18.5.53, 33 Sqn coded 'S'. 3.2.54, following loss of power on both engines after taking off, overshot and overturned, Butterworth. Pilot killed.

WB886: Del. 20.3.51, 10 MU. 18.5.51, ferried FEAF via Abingdon. 11.6.51, 33 Sqn coded 'F'. 18.4.52, canopy shattered and airframe damaged. 14.5.52, 390 MU. 3.6.52, 33 Sqn. 14.7.53, lost fairing and upper area of upper wing skin during dive attack; returned safely to Butterworth but found DBR. 6.10.53, SOC.

WB887: Del. 8.5.51, 27 MU. 9.11.51, ferried FEAF via Abingdon. 15.11.51, 390 MU store. 1.12.51, 80 Sqn. 3.12.51, abandoned in bad weather near Clark Field, Philippines whilst on delivery to 80 Sqn.

WB888: Del. 13.4.51, 10 MU. 28.6.51, ferried FEAF via Abingdon. 10.8.51, FETS. 24.1.52, 80 Sqn coded 'A' and 'L'. 24.11.52, damaged by debris during practice RP attack. 12.3.53, SHQ Kai Tak. 27.4.53, 80 Sqn

Hornet F.3 WF962 of No.80 Squadron at Kai Tak (80 Squadron archives)

coded 'L'. 30.1.54, canopy shattered during dive and damaged airframe. 12.10.54, 80 Sqn coded 'L'. 14.4.55, SOC.

WB889: Del. 1.5.51, 27 MU. 15.6.51, ferried FEAF via Abingdon. 29.6.51, 33 Sqn coded 'A'. 11.2.54, SOC.

WB897: Del. 1.5.51, 27 MU. 4.12.51, ferried FEAF via Abingdon. 6.12.51, 80 Sqn coded 'X'. 26.10.54, tyre burst on landing; skidded and tipped up, Kai Tak. Repaired by HKACE. 16.1.55, 80 Sqn. 15.3.55, SOC.

WB898: Del. 8.5.51, 27 MU. 15.12.51, ferried FEAF via Abingdon. 28.1.52, 45 Sqn coded 'A'. 15.7.53, dived into the ground during gunnery practice 10 miles NW of Butterworth. Pilot killed.

WB899: Del. 1.5.51, 27 MU. 11.7.51, ferried FEAF via Abingdon. 20.10.51, FETS. 24.1.52, 80 Sqn coded 'T'. 6.5.55, SOC.

WB900: Del. 18.5.51, 10 MU. 15.12.51, ferried FEAF via Abingdon. 27.12.51, 80 Sqn. 4.1.52, missing in rain cloud during delivery to Kai Tak 85 miles E of Seletar. Pilot killed.

WB901: Del. 30.5.51, 27 MU. 9.11.51, ferried FEAF via Abingdon. 15.11.51, SHQ Seletar. 21.4.52, FETS. 28.3.55, SOC.

WB902: Del. 5.6.51, 27 MU. 5.11.51, ferried FEAF via Abingdon. 1.12.51, 80 Sqn. 3.12.51, flew into high ground during bad weather approach to Clark Field, Philippines, on ferry flight to Kai Tak. Pilot killed.

WB903: Del. 4.6.51, 27 MU. 22.11.51, ferried FEAF via Abingdon. 4.12.51, 80 Sqn coded 'A'. 25.8.52, collided with WF958 during formation flying and crashed in sea off Hong Kong. Pilot killed.

WB904: Del. 6.6.51, 10 MU. 4.12.51, ferried FEAF via Abingdon. 6.12.51, 80 Sqn coded 'Z'. 18.5.55, SOC

WB905: Del. 29.6.51, 10 MU. 14.9.51, Colerne for display. 17.9.51, 10 MU. 22.11.51, ferried FEAF via Abingdon. 6.12.51, 80 Sqn coded 'D'. 24.1.52, belly-landed in error, Seletar. 1.5.52, FETS. 25.6.53, swung on landing and undercarriage collapsed, Seletar.

26.6.53, Cat 5C and SOC.

WB906: Del. 25.6.51, 27 MU. 5.11.51, ferried FEAF via Abingdon. 1.12.51, 80 Sqn coded 'F'. 16.10.52, canopy shattered and damaged airframe. 24.2.53, Kai Tak store. 12.3.53, 80 Sqn. 17.1.54, blown back on to runway by leader's slipstream and ditched in Kai Tak harbour.

WB907: Del. 29.6.51, 10 MU. 22.11.51, ferried FEAF via Abingdon. 6.12.51, 80 Sqn. 20.5.52, dived into the sea out of cloud, 1 mile W of Stanley Point, Hong Kong.

WB908: Del. 3.7.51, 10 MU. 22.2.52, ferried FEAF via Abingdon. 28.2.52, 45 Sqn coded 'L'. 28.1.54, MB Seletar. 6.4.54, 45 Sqn. 29.9.54, a/c swung on landing, u/c collapsed, Tengah.

WB909: Del. 3.7.51, 10 MU. 11.9.51, Aston Down fro display. 17.9.51, 10 MU. 4.12.51, ferried FEAF via Abingdon. 6.12.51, 80 Sqn coded 'N', 'W', 'F' and 'L'. 30.4.52, propellers hit sea during attack on HMS *Ocean*. 17.10.52, canopy shattered and damaged airframe. 2.5.55, SOC.

WB910: Del. 10.8.51, 10 MU. 11.1.52, ferried FEAF via Abingdon. 18.1.52, FETS. 7.3.52, overshot runway and overturned during single-engine approach to Butterworth. DBR

WB911: Del. 8.8.51, 10 MU. 22.2.52, ferried FEAF via Abingdon. 28.2.52, 45 Sqn coded 'B'. 14.9.54, undercarriage jammed; belly-landed at Tengah. 17.9.54, SOC as DBR.

WB912: Del. 29.8.51, 10 MU. 25.4.52, ferried FEAF via Abingdon. 1.5.52, 45 Sqn coded 'C'. 28.8.52, stalled recovering from dive and hit trees 6 miles E of Seremban. Pilot killed.

* * * * * * * * *

11 Hornet F.3s and 22 F.4s produced by de Havilland, Chester

WF954: Del. 11.9.51, arr. Hatfield for investigation into fuel tank failures in FEAF. 21.11.51, TI to prevent damage to tailplane by ejected ammunition links during air strikes. 29.11.51, arr. A & AEE for check gunnery shoot. 10.3.52, ret. to Hatfield for repairs to gun door and jettison trials of S.C. 250 lb. Type G Mk.5. 25.6.52, desp. to 10 MU. 15.10.52, ferried FEAF. 20.10.52, 45 Sqn coded 'Q'. 25.8.53, swung on landing and hit ditch; undercarriage collapsed, Tengah. To MB Seletar for repair. 30.11.53, 45 Sqn. 1.9.54, undershot landing and undercarriage leg broke off; caught fire, Butterworth; Cat.5S and SOC

WF955: Del. 18.9.51, 10 MU. 18.6.52, a/c lost during ferry flight to FEAF. Undercarriage jammed up and loss of power caused aircarft to ditch in Persian Gulf off Kalak, Iran.

WF956: Del. 10.10.51, 10 MU. 25.4.52, ferried FEAF. 1.5.52, 45 Sqn coded 'N'. 30.9.54, overshot landing at Tengah and hit ditch. DBR.

WF957: Del. 23.10.51, 27 MU. 8.2.52, allotted to FEAF. 20.2.52, 1 OFU: stalled on landing and undercarriage collapsed, Abingdon. Repaired and ferried to FEAF. 19.3.53, 390 MU Seletar. 1.4.53, 33 Sqn coded 'H'. 25.3.55, 45/33 Sqn. 27.5.55, SOC

WF958: Del. 18.10.51, 27 MU. 15.12.51, ferried FEAF. 27.12.51, 80 Sqn coded 'M'. 25.8.52, collided with WB903 and crashed in sea off Hong Kong. Pilot killed.

WF959: Del. 30.10.51, 27 MU. 11.1.52, ferried FEAF. 1.2.52, 45 Sqn coded 'K'. 25.3.55, 45/33 Sqn. 27.5.55, SOC.

WF960: Del. 2.11.51, 27 MU. 11.1.52, ferried FEAF. 18.1.52, FETS. 4.1.54, SOC.

WF961: Del. 21.11.51, 10 MU. 16.6.52, ferried FEAF. 5.7.52, 45 Sqn coded 'D'. 25.3.55, 45/33 Sqn. 27.5.55, SOC.

WF962: Del. 7.12.51, 10 MU. 28.7.52, ferried FEAF. 15.8.52, 80 Sqn coded 'A'. 26.8.54, hit sea during roll off Hong Kong. Pilot killed.

WF966: Del. 7.12.51, 10 MU. 26.6.52, ferried FEAF. 5.7.52, 45 Sqn coded 'N'. 27.5.55, SOC

WF967: Del. 28.12.51, 10 MU. 13.12.52, ferried FEAF. 20./12.52, 45 Sqn coded 'H'. 17.2.53, lost hydraulic fluid and belly-landed, Tengah. 14.5.53, 45 Sqn. 31.7.55, SOC as GI airframe 7230M

WF968: Del. 4.1.52, 10 MU. 2.7.52, ferried FEAF. 22.7.52, engine caught fire during ferry flight; dived into sea 20 miles E of Muharraq, Bahrein. Pilot killed.

WF969: Del. 12.2.52, 10 MU. 11.8.52, ferried FEAF. 18.9.52, 80 Sqn coded 'D'. 15.1.55, HKACE repairs. 18.2.55, 80 Sqn. 6.5.55, SOC

WF970: Del. 8.2.52, 10 MU. 13.6.52, ferried FEAF. 7.7.52, 33 Sqn coded 'E', 'O' and 'J'. 20.3.52, belly-landed in error, Butterworth. 16.8.53, MB Seletar. 22.9.53, 33 Sqn. 25.3.55, 45/33 Sqn. Modified for P.R. 27.5.55, SOC.

WF971: Del. 29.2.52, 27 MU. 13.6.52, ferried FEAF. 7.7.52, 33 Sqn coded 'J'. 29.7.54, hit by PX302 on take-off, Butterworth. SOC as DBR.

WF972: Del. 4.3.52, 27 MU. 26.6.52, ferried FEAF. 7.7.52, 33 Sqn coded 'T'. 29.1.54, force-landed in padi field after losing top of starboard radiator while pulling out of 45 degree dive. Repaired. 28.6.54, canopy shattered; force-landed, Singkir Darat, Malaya. DBR.

WF973: Del. 7.3.52, 27 MU. 16.6.52, ferried FEAF. 7.7.52, 33 Sqn coded 'O'. 11.10.54, 45 Sqn. 25.3.55, 45/33 Sqn. 27.5.55, SOC

WF974: Del. 3.4.52, 10 MU. 28.7.52, ferried FEAF. 15.8.52, 80 Sqn coded 'M'. 28.4.53, Kai Tak store. 9.2.54, 80 Sqn. 12.4.54, airframe DBR during spinning. SOC.

WF975: Del. 28.4.52, 10 MU. 15.9.52, ferried FEAF. 4.10.52, 390 MU Seletar. 30.12.52, 33 Sqn coded 'C'. 25.3.55, 45/33 Sqn coded 'N'. 31.5.55, SOC.

WF976: Del. 9.4.52, 27 MU. 16.8.52, ferried FEAF. 18.9.52, 80 Sqn coded 'P' and 'Q'. 18.5.55, SOC

WF977: Del. 6.5.52, 27 MU. 11.8.52, ferried FEAF. 3.11.52, 80 Sqn coded 'B'. 6.5.55, SOC

WF978: Del. 22.5.52, 27 MU. 15.9.52, ferried FEAF. 24.10.52, 80 Sqn coded 'Q'. 6.5.55, SOC

WF979: Del. 4.6.52, 27 MU. 24.11.52, ferried FEAF. 1.12.52, 33 Sqn coded 'Q'. 26.1.53, lost power during take-off from Butterworth; undercarriage raised to stop. DBR.

WF972 bellylanded in a padi field, 29 January 1954

Sea Hornet TT202 flying over the New Forest (D.H. photo)

Sea Hornets

Prototypes:

PX211 General trials a/c. 19.4.45, converted to Sea Hornet F.20 (non-folding wings). Sept/Oct. A&AEE for brief manoeuvrability trials. 25.7.46, Cat.B. 6.2.47, SOC. 15.9.47, sent to Leconfield.

PX212 RAE 25.3.46, 778 STU Ford. 13-16.8.46, trials on HMS *Illustrious*. 4.5.46, Rolls-Royce then retd to 778 Sqn. 28.2.47, SOC.

PX214 Converted to Sea Hornet F.20 (folding Wings). Flown from Hatfield to RAE for accelerating trials with light load. Ret. DH for fitting of Corliss throttles and larger tailplane prior to undergoing deck landing trials, 17.4.46. Ford for pilot familiarisation and further deck landing trials. 20.11.46, to West Raynham for re-sighting. 3.10.47, to Fleetlands.

PX219 Converted to Sea Hornet (folding wings) by Heston Aircraft Ltd. 20.8.47, with Heston Aircraft for trials of "Hot Dog". 26.4.48, DH for flight trials of "Cord". Gosport/Vickers-Armstrongs for extra trials of "Cord". 12.10.48, ATDU Gosport for trials of "Highball". 20.10.48, Vickers-Armstrongs, Weybridge for removal of special equipment and Class "G" (Guard) symbol. 9.3.49, Arbroath.

PX222 PR.22; 18.12.46, A&AEE. Fitted with flame dampers at DH. 3.3.47, DH for flame damper investigation. 30.10.47, ASU Worthy Down as ground instructional airframe. 15.11.47, Arbroath.

PX230 8.8.45, to Ayr for month's ship trials from 4.9.45. 26.10.45, to DH for night fighter conversion. 24.4.47, To A&AEE for handling trials. 16.5.47, aircraft crashed near Boscombe Down; port engine detached in dive. 12.8.47, despatched by 49 MU to Lasham dump. 16.10.47, surplus to requirements.

PX239 Second NF.21 Prototype. 30.4.47, Hatfield for trial installation of AN/APS 13. 24.3.48, A&AEE for handling trials. 26.8.48, force-landed due to failure of port engine. 25 10.48, trials on HMS *Illustrious*. 17.1.49, surplus to requirements and allotted to Yeovilton as instructional airframe A2059, del. 7.1.49.

* * * * * * * * * *

32 Sea Hornet F.20/FR.22 produced by de Havilland, Hatfield

TT186 13.3.46, f/f. 22.8.46, TI of FR Camera. 1.9.46, C.S.(A) Charge Hatfield. 9.46, displayed SBAC Show Radlett. 10.46, with No.703 Sqn for trials. 7.5.47, ARDU Culham. 22.5.47, desp. 787 Sqn NAFDU West Raynham. 4.2.48, from C.S.(A) charge to RN. 28.4.48, surplus to C.S.(A) requirements and allotted to NAFDU. 27.4.48, with No.787 Sqn West Raynham. 24.5.48, to Stretton. 4.7.49, arr. Boscombe from West Raynham for position error measurement and RP trials. With 'C' Flt. A&AEE. 25.7.49, arr. ARDU Culham for on site repair. 7.51, Airwork, Gatwick for re-conditioning.

4.10.51 ret. Culham ARDU for LTS. 15.2.53, out of LTS to Lossiemouth AHU. 30.5.53, further storage. 10.53, AHU Lossiemouth Aerobatic Team. Retd. to LTS. 1.7.54, out of LTS and desp. to Hal Far, arr. 7.7.54. 31.7.54, to 728 Sqn coded HF/532. 20.4.55, heavy landing, repaired on site. 27.10.55, towing accident, removed to Hal Far AHU. 9.1.56, WOC for fire fighting practice. Remains 1957.

TT187 (Prototype PR.22) 13.11.46, DH Flight trials. 1.12.46, C.S.(A). charge for intensive flight trials. 23.11.46, DH preparation for armament trials & "Uncle Tom" handling. 3.5.47, retained for TI of PR cameras. 30.6.48, arr. A&AEE for handling & clearance trials. 11.10.48, release trials for 4-5" Photoflashes. 3.11.48, Hatfield for investigation into rudder control loads. Converted to PR.22 Prototype. 1.4.49, Culham ARDU as surplus to requirements. 15.6.49, Stretton AHU SOC. 1952, to RNEC Manadon as ground instructional airframe. Used by St. Eval fire section during Roborough Air Display 22.6.54. Broken up by Civil Defence during rescue instruction. Remains reported at Paradise School, Plymouth during 1956.

TT188 15.1.47, C.S.(A).Charge. 1.47-5.47, DH as armament test aircraft. 7.5.47, A&AEE 'C' Flt. for trials with 1,000-lb bombs, followed by clean handling trials. 26.6.47, hood came off in dive; damaged Cat.AC. whilst at A&AEE. Aircraft replaced by TT205 for remainder of trials. 30.9.47, repaired on site by DH working party. 12.4.48, Del'd RDU Culham. By 1.49, RNAY Fleetlands. 13.12.50, SOC. Remains transported to Gosport as ground instructional airframe.

TT189 1.1.47, f/f. 22.1.47, Handling Squadron, Hullavington. 28.5.47, STU, CFS Handling Squadron. 8.1.48, arr. A&AEE from Hullavington for intensive flying trials. 11.11.48, a/c damaged on port aileron during rocket firing; Cat A. 18.3.49, starboard engine feathered after loss of oil. 14.7.49, surplus to C.S.(A) requirements. 15.7.49, arr. Culham for mods. and storage. By 1.51, Airwork for re-con. 14.11.51, Culham AHU. 3.12.51, LTS. 6.7.53, Lossiemouth AHU. 10.7.53, LTS. 8.4.57, S.S.

TT190 28.1.47, f/f. 1.3.47, TOC C.S.(A); test bed for exhaust shrouds. 1948, test bed for performance trials. DH for trials of "Hot Dog". 23.7.48, loaned to DH for flights by Mr. Lee Murray, Sales Director, DH Australia. 18.4.49, arr. A&AEE for cockpit ventilation and windscreen wiper assessment. 29.4.49, ret. DH for improvements. 14.12.49, ret A&AEE for further cockpit ventilation and windscreen wiper tests, followed by trials with modified cockpit insulation. 20.1.50, on landing at Boscombe, torsion link on starboard u/c failed, causing collapse. Cat 3R. 1.9.50, a/c despatched to Airwork, Langley. 14.11.51, Culham ARDU. 3.12.51, LTS 22.6.53, Lossiemouth AHU. 26.6.53, LTS. 8.4.57, S.S.

TT191 5.2.47, f/f. C.S.(A) Charge. 1.5.47, to RAE for radio trials and aerial checks. 8.1.47, arr. Hatfield for T.I. of revised V.H.F. aerial. 3.10.47, DH Leavesden for further radio trials. 19.12.47, RAE stores jettison trials. 3.48-4.48, with RAE. 10.3.48, arr. RAE. 20.10.48, A&AEE for further radio trials and rocket firing trials from 11.48. 8.12.48, armament acceptance trials. including depth charge and flare drops at 250-320 knots. 14.12.48, bomb dropping. 2.2.49, 8 Practice bomb drops. 10.2.49, bomb drops, 2 x 500 lb & 2 x 1,000 lb bombs. 2.49, drag measurement & performance trials with stores until 5.49. 19.7.49, surplus to C.S.(A) requirements. 15.7.49, arr. Culham for mods. and storage. 18.8.49, Culham ARDU for LTS. 29.11.49, removed from LTS. 24.3.50, dismantled for road transportation. 26.3.50, DH Leavesden. 6.2.51, Culham ARDU. 21.5.51, 736 Sqn Culdrose. 22.6.51, 759 Sqn also at Culdrose. 1.10.51, CW/456, all units operating as 52 TRAG. 18.2.53, Lossiemouth store. 1.57, SOC. 13.3.57, S.S.

TT192 24.4.47, f/f. DH Flight trials. 13.5.47, Deld Culham ARDU. 6.6.47, SAMSU Worthy Down. 23.2.48, TAM

Section Yeovilton. 14.7.51, LTS Yeovilton. 5.6.53, SAMSU, Worthy Down with occasional service at Lee-on-Solent. Circa 1957, remaining at Worthy Down with wings from VW960 in scarred condition as GI airframe A2294.

TT193 24.4.47, TOC CS(A) DH Hatfield. 26.4.47, prepared for winterisation trials by 47 MU. 11.7.47, crated for shipment to WEE Canada. 13.12.48, commencement of winterisation trials. 1.7.50, sold in Canada to Spartan Air Services. Became CF-GUO. 4.52, sold to Field Aviation Services. 11.7.52, crashlanded after engine fire, Terrace, B.C.; lack of spares led to scrapping.

TT194 25.4.47, f/f. 29.5.47, Culham ARDU. 1.7.47, booked to 801 Sqn Ford but returned on same day. 28.7.47, with 703 Sqn coded 'X'. NAFDU RAF Thorney Island. 25.5.48, Lee-on-Solent coded LP/009 by 6.49. 31.1.50, port engine failed to attain correct r.p.m., take-off being abandoned. Failed to stop on brakes and undercarriage retracted to avoid overrun. 17.2.50, Hatfield for Cat.B repairs. 12.9.50, in store at Culham. 22.2.52, AHU Hal Far. 29.2.52, joined No.728 Sqn FRU, Hal Far, Malta. coded HF531. 18.11.52, single-engine landing with one wheel not locked down; swung on to grass at Hal Far. 26.11.52, AHU Hal Far. 28.11.52, aboard HMS *Theseus*. 14.12.52, to MARU, Gosport for overhaul, less engines. 23.10.53, crashed during single-engine landing. 3.3.54, repairs completed by MARU Gosport. 11.3.54, a/c desp. AHU Lossiemouth. 10.4.54, LTS. 13.3.57, S.S.

TT195 15.4.47, DH flight trials. 1.5.47, TOC by RN. 20.5.47, ARDU Culham. 28.5.47, A&AEE for intensive flying trials. 21.12.48, explosion and fire on ground; Cat.E. 3.2.49, fuselage arrived at Yeovilton by road for use as instructional airframe.

TT196 26.4.47, f/f. DH flight trials. 1.5.47, ARDU Culham. 27.6.47, Culham. 2.7.47, 801 Sqn Ford coded 150/FD. 8.1.48, 801 Sqn Culdrose coded 450/C. 17.2.48, RN Aircraft Yard, Fleetlands. 19.3.48, starboard undercarriage collapsed on landing at Linton-on-Ouse. 17.8.48, by road to RNAY Fleetlands for repairs. 18.10.48, DH Leavesden. 5.7.50, ARDU Culham for LTS. 12.5.53, AHS Lossiemouth for LTS. 4.3.54, Airwork FRU Hurn. 13.10.55, a/c grounded. 31.12.55, WOC for fire practice. 10.1.56, Worthy Down. 6.6.56, SOC

TT197 1.5.47 f/f. DH flight trials. 1.6.47, To 703 Sqn. NASWU, Thorney Island as 'W'. 25.5.48, NASWU/STU Lee-on-Solent coded 'X'. Culham ARDU. By 1.49, Culham AHU. 7.49, No.738 Sqn Culdrose. 2.50, No.736 Sqn Culdrose. 7.10.50, Airwork for re-cond. 2.7.51 Culham ARDU. 29.7.51, LTS. 8.10.52, de-preserved and inspected. 10.3.53, overload tanks fitted. 16.3.53, aircraft despatched to Hal Far Test Flt. 13.5.53, No.728 Sqn coded HF/531. 25.5.54, heavy landing. 8.11.55, Hal Far AFU. 5.1.56 SOC. 1.2.56, disposed of at sea.

TT198 DH Flight trials. 1.6.47, TOC by RN. 13.6.47, Del. Culham ARDU by 778 Sqn pilot. 28.7.47, to 703 Sqn Thorney Island as 'F'. Used for RP trials. 4.48, used by 801 Sqn coded 456. A&AEE. 12.7.48, No.778 Sqn. NATU Lee-on-Solent as LP/007. 7.48, to 703 Sqn also at Lee as LP/007. 26.11.48, starboard undercarriage gave way on landing at Lee-on-Solent. 7.2.49, DH Hatfield for repairs. 19.5.49, RNAY Fleetlands. 9.12.49, Culham AHU for LTS 22.9.50, Out of LTS. 13.11.50, delivered to 801 Sqn at Lee-on-Solent coded C/456, later re-coded A/456. 14.3.51, Culham AHU for LTS. 9.7.53, removed from LTS after sustaining damage during towing. 14.7.53, Lossiemouth AHU for LTS. 8.4.57, S.S.

TT199 5.5.47, f/f. DH flight trials. 1.6.47, Culham ARDU. 1.7.49, still ARDU Culham. Arbroath. 5.10.49, ARDU Culham. 14.10.49, DH Leavesden for radio trials. 16.1.50, Lee-on-Solent No.801 Sqn coded 460/C. 17.5.50, collided with VR851 at 10,000 ft whilst flying from HMS *Implacable*.

Sea Hornet FR.20 TT197 531/HF of No.728 Squadron, Hal Far (via R.C. Sturtivant)

TT200 9.5.47, f/f. DH flight trials. 6.47, Culham ARDU. 7.47, with 801 Sqn Ford as FD/151. 30.8.47, aircraft crashed on single-engine overshoot into a cabbage patch 100 yds beyond airfield boundary.

TT201 14.5.47, f/f. DH flight trials. 15.5.47, TOC by RN Culham ARDU, being delivered by 778 Sqn pilot. 7.47, to 801 Sqn., Ford coded FD/153. 3.48, recoded C/453. 30.4.48, coded AO/453. 24.7.48, to Stretton AHU. 1.1.50, with 801 Sqn., Lee-on-Solent. 2.50, joined HMS *Implacable*. 31.3.50, Airwork, Gatwick for re-cond. 26.8.51, Culham ARDU for LTS. 29.10.52, out of LTS. 6.11.52, AHU Lossiemouth arr. 7.11.52. 4.12.52, LTS. 8.4.57, S.S.

TT202 22.5.47, f/f. 14.7.47, TOC by RN. 17.7.47, Arr. ARDU Culham. 7.47, A&AEE for dive performance tests. Culham ARDU. 3.3.48, Company trials aircraft for low Mach No. tests. 3.3.48, RAE. By 1.49, C.S.(A) charge at D.H., converted to PR.22. 26.4.49, Lee-on-Solent. 29.4.49, crash barrier trials. 4.6.49, Hatfield. 30.8.49, ret. Lee-on-Solent for further barrier trials aboard HMS *Implacable*. Transferred to RAE for yet more barrier trials. Stored until SOC. 13.6.54 broken up at Farnborough.

TT203 29.5.47, f/f. 19.6.47, ARDU Culham. 26.7.47, to 801 Sqn at Tangmere, coded 152. 9.47, at Ford coded FD/152. 12.11.47, repaired at Ford ARS. 10.12.47, repairs taken over by RNAY Fleetlands. 6.7.48, to Stretton AHU for storage. 19.7.49, Culham ARDU. 22.2.50, with 801 Sqn. HMS *Implacable* and *Indomitable*. 14.3.51, Culham ARDU. 21.6.51, to No.738 Sqn Culdrose. 12.12.51, Airwork Gatwick for re-cond. 2.5.52, to AHU Abbotsinch for LTS. 9.8.57, SOC as scrap.

TT204 4.6.47, f/f. 27.6.47, ARDU Culham. 1.9.47, to 801 Sqn., Ford coded FD/154. 30.4.48, at Arbroath coded AO. 1.50, with 801 Sqn at Lee-on-Solent, coded C/466. By 7.50, at Airwork Gatwick for re-cond. 23.8.51, AHU for LTS. 8.1.53, out of LTS. 26.5.53, to AHU Lossiemouth for LTS. 1.57, SOC

TT205 18.6.47, f/f. DH flight trials. 30.6.47, to No.778 Sqn

S.T.U. Ford. 8.7.47, deck landing trials aboard HMS *Illustrious*. 27.7.47, to AHU Abbotsinch, then returned for further deck landing trials aboard *Illustrious*. 18.8.47, from Ford to 'C' Sqn at A&AEE for handling and armament trials. 4.2.48, Culham ARDU. 21.1.49, to 801 Sqn Culdrose coded C/452, later aboard HMS *Implacable*. 24.11.49, to AHU Gosport. 7.9.50, Airwork, Gatwick for recond. 22.8.51, ARDU Culham for LTS. 28.1.53, out of LTS. 10.2.53, AHU Abbotsinch for further LTS. 22.7.57, S.S.

TT206 23.6.47, f/f. 1.7.47, ARDU Culham. 1.9.47, to 801 Sqn Ford coded FD/151, later re-coded in 4 Series. 8.1.48, with Sqn to Culdrose. 30.4.48, to Arbroath with sqn until 5.48. By 1.49, with AHU Stretton. 25.3.49, swung on landing and port undercarriage leg collapsed. 4.49, still at Stretton. 7.49, with DH until at least 1.50. 7.50, Culham AHU. 1.51, with 801 Sqn Lee-on-Solent. 29.1.51, whilst aboard HMS *Indomitable* during DLP veered to starboard striking gun.

TT207 DH flight trials. 1.7.47, ARDU Culham. 4.9.47, to 801 Sqn at Ford coded FD/156 later re-coded in 4 Series. 8.1.48, moved with squadron to Culdrose. 30.4.48, with sqn to Arbroath. 7.6.48, whilst at Arbroath struck the tail of VR857 during formation flying. 11.10.48, to CMU Arbroath. 26.6.49, to Anthorn AHU. 2.7.49, Culham ARDU. 15.12.49, to 801 Sqn at Lee-on-Solent coded 467. 17.5.50, barrier crash aboard *Implacable*. 5.9.50, to RAE to assist in automatic bridle and hold trials. 15.9.50, returned to Lee-on-Solent. Later to 1 CAG aboard HMS *Indomitable* as A/467. 17.10.50, involved in barrier crash; suffered fractured tail oleo. 4.2.51, arr. Abbotsinch AHU for STS. 26.5.51, sent to Airwork for recond. 3.3.52, arr. AHU Abbotsinch for LTS. 23.2.53, fully preserved. 9.8.57, SOC

TT208 2.7.47, f/f. 5.7.47, to ARDU Culham. 2.9.47, to Ford joining 801 Sqn coded FD/155. 8.1.48, sqn to Culdrose, became C/462. 30.4.48, sqn to Arbroath; became AO/462. 20.10.48, recoded again C/462 at Culdrose to at least 7.49. By 1.50, to AHU Culham presumably for LTS. 8.5.51, to Airwork Gatwick for re-cond. 10.1.52, rec'd. by Abbotsinch AHU. 24.4.52, into LTS. 3.2.53, preserved. 9.8.57, SOC & S.S. to Minworth Metals.

TT209 15.7.47, DH flight trials. 16.7.47, TOC by ARDU Culham. 10.9.47, to 801 Sqn at Ford coded FD/157; 8.1.48, to Culdrose and re-coded C/457. Selected for service with 806 Sqn N. American tour. 27.5.48, embarked aboard HMS *Magnificent* retaining code C/457. Returned briefly to 801 Sqn. 16.2.49, arr. Abbotsinch AHU for LTS. 27.5.50, to Airwork Gatwick for recond. 2.7.52, ret.to AHU Abbotsinch for preservation. 14.8.52, entered LTS. 9.8.57, S.S.

TT210 16.7.47, Hatfield for radio checks, u/s from 18-20.7.47. 24.7.47 cleared for del. 19.5.49, Hatfield from 703 Sqn, Lee-on-Solent for trial u/c. and additional deck landing trials. 8.6.49, ret. Lee-on-Solent. 9.50, Airwork, Gatwick. Coded 453 ex-801 Sqn./738 Sqn.

TT211 29.8.51, ARDU Culham. 801 Sqn Ford coded 158/FD. 20.4.53, Abbotsinch. 10.6.53, Airwork FRU Hurn. 10.1.56, Worthy Down.

TT212 24.7.47, f/f. DH flight trials. 21.8.47, to ARDU Culham. 4.10.47, to 801 Sqn at Ford coded FD/159. 8.1.48. recoded C/459 on sqn move to Culdrose. 30.4.48, sqn to Arbroath; became AO/459. 27.10.49, to AHU Abbotsinch for LTS. 26.9.50, to Airwork Gatwick for recond. 29.8.51, to AHU Culham FRU for LTS. 14.12.52, out of LTS. 20.4.53, a/c arrived AHU Abbotsinch where it was involved in slight landing mishap, necessitating some repairs. 10.6.53, a/c despatched to Airwork FRU Hurn. 13.10.55, a/c grounded. 6.6.56, SOC and WOC for fire fighting practice.

TT213 21.8.47, ARDU Culham. 12.10.47, C.S.(A) Hatfield. 7.11.47, prepared for forthcoming Tropical trials. 21.2.48, RAAF Point Cook, Victoria, for trials. Allocated serial A83-1. (Trials scheduled to last 12 months). Despatched to 47 MU. 11.6.48, arrived 1 AD, assembled and TOC (RAN). 10.9.48, ARDU Laverton, Victoria and flown to Darwin. 13/14.12.49, aircraft returned to Laverton via Mallala, Alice Springs and Oodnadatta, SA. for hot weather performance trials. 2.1.50, loan extended to 2.7.50 including trials at Woomera. 16.8.50, passed to DH Australia for strip-down inspection. (Further extension of loan to 23.7.51). 17.1.51, prepared for shipment to UK. 2.4.51, DH Hatfield. 2.1.52, flown to Airwork, Gatwick for recond. 7.52, TOC by RN to Abbotsinch. Later to Airwork FRU St. Davids, coded BY/421. 26.5.53, transferred to Airwork FRU Hurn, coded BQ/421. 1.55, still flying, although declared surplus. 1957, with AHU Lossiemouth.

TT247 21.8.47, f/f. 11.9.47, arr. ARDU Culham. 18.2.48, to AHU Stretton for LTS. By 1.49, TOC by C.S.(A) for trials. 6.5.49, SOC

TT248 15.7.49, to 10 MU. 17.9.49, arr ARDU Culham. 10.47, to A&AEE handling trials. 20.10.48, A&AEE Brief handling trials with 2 x 1,000 lb bombs. 22.10.48, A&AEE Brief handling trials with Window dispenser. 27.10.48, trials with 2 x 500 lb bombs. 22.11.48, A&AEE. Landing mishap when starboard propeller struck runway. 13.1.49, flare dropping trials. 18.1.49, port oleo leg collapsed while aircraft was being towed. By 1.50, at Culham AHU. By 1.51, 801 Sqn Lee-on-Solent coded A/459. By 3.51, Airwork until at least 7.52. 6.2.52, struck trench at end of runway, damaging undercarriage. By 1.53, Abbotsinch store. 28.1.55, SOC and broken up.

*   *   *   *   *   *   *   *   *   *

32 Sea Hornet F.20s produced by de Havilland, Hatfield

VR837 1.9.47, f/f. Appeared SBAC show at Radlett. 1.10.47, Culham ARDU. 28.10.47, 801 Sqn Ford as FD/161. 29.4.48, Culdrose as C/461. 10.4.48, 801 Sqn. Arbroath as AO/461. 20.10.48, to Culdrose as C/461. 12.10.49, starboard oleo collapsed during deck landings on HMS

Implacable. 28.10.49, Hatfield for Cat.B repairs. 13.11.50, Culham AHU . 11.1.51, 759 Sqn as CW/454. 10.51, to 738 Sqn as CU/454. 25.10.51, DH Hatfield. 7.2.52, Abbotsinch store. 22.7.57, S.S.

VR838 4.9.47, f/f. DH Flight trials. 9.47, Culham ARDU. 27.10.47, delivered to 801 Sqn, Ford coded FD/160. .47, suffered u/c collapse, possibly due to failure of torque link after heavy landing. By 1.49, Culdrose with 801 Sqn and re-coded C/460. 16.6.49, test flown at Culdrose by 809 Sqn. 1.7.49, Culham AHU to at least 1.52. By 4.52, Airwork Gatwick for recon. 23.7.52, Lossiemouth AHU for LTS comm. 24.9.52. 13.3.57, S.S.

VR839 DH flight trials. 10.10.47, Culham ARDU. 11.11.47, to 801 Sqn. Ford coded FD/152. 8.1.48, Culdrose recoded C/452. 9.3.48, crashed aboard HMS *Implacable* after undercarriage retracted on landing on. By 1.49, Lossiemouth AHU. 24.6.49, Anthorn ARDU. 1.10.49, Culham ARDU for short term storage. 18.8.50, del. 52 TRAG, Culdrose with 759 Sqn. 18.6.51, SOC

VR840 1.10.47, DH flight trials. 20.10.47, Culham ARDU. 2.12.47, to 801 Sqn. Ford coded FD/155. 8.1.48, to Culdrose re-coded C/455. 30.4.48, Arbroath re-coded AC/455. 1.49, aboard HMS *Implacable* coded C/455 until at least 7.49. By 1.50, DH to at least 7.50. By 1.51, Culham ARDU to at least 7.52. 8.5.53, Airwork FRU Hurn until 7.54. 1954, Lossiemouth AHU for LTS. 28.1.55, SOC

VR841 8.10.47, DH flight trials. 27.10.47, Culham ARDU. 17.12.47, to 787 Sqn. West Raynham for naval trials. 16.3.50, Culham ARDU for LTS until about 7.52. 2.1.53, at Airwork FRU St. Davids. 16.2.53, lost at sea off St.David's Head, Pembs.

VR842 16.10.47, DH flight trials. 28.10.47, Culham ARDU. 23.1.48, to 787 Sqn. West Raynham for naval trials. 17.3.50, Culham ARDU for LTS. 21.12.52, Lossiemouth AHU. Delivered by road, arrived 21.1.53. 29.3.54, Airwork Gatwick for recon. 19.1.55, arr. Lossiemouth AHU for LTS. 28.3.55, removed from LTS. 11.5.55, despatched to Airwork FRU, Hurn. 10.10.55, a/c grounded by DH/RN order. 10.1.56, desp. to SNATSU, Worthy Down for fire fighting practice. 6.6.56, WOC

VR843 DH flight trials. 19.12.47, Culham ARDU. 5.7.48, RNARY Fleetlands. 22.7.48, desp. to ARDU Stretton. 11.4.49, ret. to ARDU Culham. 17.10.49, with 801 Sqn., Culdrose coded C/454. 25.11.49, to Gosport. 31.3.50, to Lee-on-Solent. 3.4.50, to 801 Sqn at Lee as C/454. 24.4.51, Culham ARDU. 7.51, to Airwork Gatwick for maintenance. 1.52, Abbotsinch AHU. By 11.52, with Airwork FRU St. Davids coded BY/425. 4.53, transferred to FRU Hurn as BQ/425. 27.6.55, SOC

VR844 DH flight trials. 11.47, Culham ARDU. 6.48, to 703 Sqn., Lee-on-Solent coded LP/001. 7.7.48, a/c made heavy landing during ADDLs. By 10.48, to RNAY Fleetlands for repairs. 2.2.49, ret. to 778 Sqn Lee-on-Solent recoded LP/006. 3.2.49, Lee-on-Solent AHU for further repairs. 9.3.49, with 703 Sqn Lee-on-Solent remaining as LP/006. 9.12.49, SOC; to Yeovilton as GI airframe.

VR845 DH flight trials. 7.11.47, arr. ARDU Culham. 3.48, aboard HMS *Implacable* coded C/452. 6.5.48 attached to 806 Sqn at Eglinton for participation in N. American tour. 5.6.48, a/c crashed 200 yds south of McNabs light, Halifax Harbour, NS, after emerging from cloud in steep dive.

VR846 12.11.47, f/f. DH flight trials. 14.1.48, arr. Culham ARDU although officially TOC by RN on 17.11.47. 11.2.48, a/c damaged by exploding air bottle. 19.5.48, to RNAY Fleetlands for repairs. 18.10.48, to DH Hatfield for repairs. 2.12.49, arr. Culham ARDU for STS. 1.7.50, out of STS 1.7.50, to 801 Sqn at Lossiemouth coded C/467. 3.7.50, with No.1 CAG aboard HMS *Implacable* coded C/452. 14.3.51, to Culham ARDU for LTS from 17.12.51. 11.7.53,

Sea Hornet F.20 VR857 (via P. Jarrett)

removed from LTS. 15.7.53, a/c desp. to AHU Lossiemouth for preservation until 21.8.53. 8.4.57, S.S.

VR847 28.11.47, DH flight trials. 15.1.48, arr. ARDU Culham. (Officially TOC by RN on 11.12.47.) 13.4.48, to 801 Sqn, Culdrose coded C/461. 5.5.48, a/c suffered u/c collapse. 21.6.48, arr. workshops RNAS Arbroath. 25.8.48, arr. RNAY Fleetlands. 15.10.48, DH Hatfield for repairs. 3.4.50, arr. ARDU Culham for LTS from 20.6.50. 22.1.51, out of LTS. 23.1.51, arr. 801 Sqn at Lossiemouth coded 454, later C/454 aboard HMS *Implacable*. 24.4.51, arr. ARDU Culham for LTS from 21.8.53. 8.4.57, S.S.

VR848 27.11.47, f/f. 15.1.48, arr. ARDU Culham. 13.4.48, to RNAS Stretton AHU for LTS from 17.7.48 to 23.3.49. 6.7.49, ARDU Culham for further LTS from 12.9.49 until 4.7.50 and 11.7.50 until 17.5.51. 21.3.52, delivered to Hal Far. 24.3.52, 728 Sqn coded HF/533. To HF/153 by 6.53.14.9.54, ret. to UK via Lee-on-Solent. 15.9.54, AHU Lossiemouth for LTS comm. 17.9.54. 8.4.57, S.S.

VR849 15.12.47, DH flight trials. 19.1.48, arr. ARDU Culham. 22.9.49, to 801 Sqn aboard HMS *Implacable* coded C/462. 29.1.50 and 17.2.50, Two separate taxying accidents. 2.6.50, aircraft off-loaded to Lee-on-Solent for repairs. 8.9.50, re-joined HMS *Implacable*. 14.3.51, arr. Culham ARDU for LTS. 25.6.53, to AHU Lossiemouth for cocooning. 13.3.57, SOC

VR850 DH Flight trials. 1.48, ARDU Culham. By 8.48, with 801 Sqn coded C/456 until at least 8.49. By 1.50, at DH Leavesden. 30.10.50, Culham for LTS. 5.2.51, arr. aboard HMS *Indomitable* with 801 Sqn. 14.3.51, Culham AHU for LTS. 3.7.52, arr. Arbroath for

possible conversion to M/N airframe. 25.7.52, Airwork Gatwick for re-cond. 7.1.54, arr. AHU Lossiemouth. 15.1.54, into LTS. 25.6.54, emerged from LTS for use with Lossiemouth Aerobatic Team for unit's air day on 10.7.54. 12.7.54, ret. to LTS until 3.9.54. 20.9.54, STS until 13.10.54. 22.2.55, into further LTS until sold as scrap.

VR851 DH flight trials. 1.48, ARDU Culham. 23.3.48, del. to 801 Sqn at Culdrose coded C/450. Del. to 806 Sqn Eglinton on loan for tour of Canada and USA. 27.5.48, dep. for Halifax aboard HMCS *Magnificent*. 12.9.48, last recorded flight with 806 Sqn. 16.2.49, arr. AHU Abbotsinch. 10.12.49, del. from Culham to DH Leavesden for radio trials. 16.1.50, to RAE Farnborough. 23.1.50, to 801 Sqn Lee-on-Solent, coded C/459. 17.5.50, collided with TT199 at 10,000 ft., both a/c falling into sea westwards of Mull of Galloway.

VR852 DH flight Trials. 9.2.48, arr. ARDU Culham. 22.3.48, arr. ARDU Stretton. 10.4.48, joined 801 Sqn at Culdrose coded C/454. 1.3.50, port undercarriage collapsed on landing aboard HMS *Implacable*. 1.4.50, off-loaded to AHU Stretton via Lee-on-Solent, eventually arriving at Airwork Gatwick for repairs. 2.6.51, arr. ARDU Culham. 5.7.51 into LTS until 29.10.52. 12.11.52, arr. AHU Lossiemouth for additional period of LTS. 8.4.57, S.S.

VR853 DH flight trials. 9.2.48, arr. ARDU Culham. 12.4.48, with 801 sqn. at Culdrose coded C/451. 8.6.48, with AHU Lee-on-Solent. By 10.48, ret. to 801 Sqn. Arbroath coded AO/451, later on board HMS *Implacable* coded C/451, later C/454. 30.3.50, SOC

VR854 5.2.48, DH flight trials. 18.2.48, Culham ARDU.

3.11.48, with 801 Sqn. Culdrose. 7.6.49, RNAY Fleetlands. To 771 Sqn Lee-on-Solent. 11.49, 801 Sqn to at least 7.50. 1.51, to Airwork Gatwick for record. 11.6.51, ret. to Culham AHU for LTS comm. 13.7.51. 20.8.52, emerged from LTS. 16.9.52, del. to Hal Far then to LTS comm. 25.9.52. 24.11.52, joined 728 Sqn coded HF/533. 3.3.53, minor taxying accident. 29.3.54, to AHU Hal Far for LTS on 5.4.54 until 24.6.55. 8.10.55, desp.to Lee-on-Solent as rogue aircraft. 12.1.56, SOC for fire fighting duties. 6.6.56, remains SOC and broken up.

VR855 DH flight trials. 2.48, Culham ARDU. 11.5.48, 801 Sqn at Culdrose. 7.49, loaned to 809 sqn. for pilot practice. 11.1.50, re-joined 801 Sqn.aboard HMS *Implacable* coded C/452. 7.2.50, crashed after bouncing following fast approach, starboard wing striking two Bofors guns, finishing up in deck park and WOC

VR856 8.3.48, TOC at DH Hatfield for trials on engine controls. 6.10.48, to DH Propellers for flight strain gauging of propellers. 11.12.49, damaged. .50, with 801 Sqn coded C/454. 12.5.50 to RAF Manby. 5.50-6.50 with 771 Sqn possibly Arbroath. 1.51, at Ford with 703 Sqn. 7.51, to Airwork Gatwick for record. 12.12.51, to AHU Abbotsinch for LTS from 8.1.52 until 14.2.52. 19.3.52, arr. Hal Far AHU. 22.3.52, joined 728 Sqn coded HF/534. 22.3.54, ran off runway on touchdown. 18.6.55, ret. to Hal Far AHU. 24.6.55, ret. to UK at Lee-on-Solent. 11.7.55, to AHU Lossiemouth for LTS on 15.7.55 until declared Cat.ZZ and used for fire fighting practice.

VR857 DH flight trials. 12.3.48, to ARDU. 11.5.48, joined 801 Sqn at Culdrose coded C/457. 7.6.48, tail struck by TT207 during formation flying. 10.11.49, barrier crash and consequently SOC 13.12.49.

VR858 DH flight trials. 1.6.48, to ARDU Culham. 13.8.49, to 739 Sqn at Culham. 23.9.50, joined 738 Sqn Culdrose coded CW/457. 17.10.51, to Airwork Gatwick for record. 22.4.52 to AHU Abbotsinch for LTS. 9.8.57 S.S.

VR859 DH flight trials. 25.5.48, arr. ARDU Culham. 3.49, to 801 Sqn coded C/455 aboard HMS *Implacable*. 23.1.50, to Abbotsinch AHU. 7.50, at Airwork Gatwick for record. 31.5.51, ret. to ARDU Culham for LTS. 21.3.52, arr. Hal Far AHU. 23.5.52, joined 728 Sqn Hal Far until around 7.53. 12.1.54, flying accident, 10.54 hrs. While making practice approach, a/c struck ground short of runway; u/c collapsed.

VR860 DH flight trials. 9.6.48, to ARDU Culham. By 11.48, to 801 Sqn HMS *Implacable* coded C/453. 29.1.50, tail hit round-down and snapped; a/c bounced and skidded on the deck hitting No.1 Barrier stanchion with port wing and SOC

VR861 DH flight trials. 9.6.48, arr. ARDU Culham. 24.1.50, joined 703 Sqn. Lee-on-Solent coded LP/006. 7.7.50, to AHU Lee-on-Solent for STS. 12.9.50, passed to 801 Sqn at Lee. 11.3.51, aircraft suffered starboard u/c collapse. 28.3.51, a/c despatched to Gosport for repairs. 28.11.51, del. to AHU Abbotsinch for LTS. 18.3.52, desp. to AHU Hal Far. 22.3.52, 728 Sqn Hal Far. 8.5.52, aircraft made heavy landing. 21.5.52, to Hal Far AHU. 6.52, ferried to UK via HMS *Vengeance*. 7.52, at Airwork Gatwick for repairs. 23.10.52, del. to AHU Lossiemouth for storage. 8.4.57, S.S.

VR862 DH flight trials. 6.7.48, ARDU Culham. 11.48, del. to 801 Sqn at Culdrose coded C/460. 3.12.48, belly-landed on airfield after starboard u/c failed to lock down. (Repaired). By 7.49, with Culham AHU eventually returning to 801 Sqn. 12.6.50, port wing folded after take-off; crashed in sea off Kilda. 15.6.50, SOC.

VR863 14.6.48, DH flight trials. 30.6.48, arr. ARDU Culham. 17.1.49, joined NAMDU at Lee-on-Solent. 10.10.49, passed over to AHU Culham, suffering damage in landing accident on arrival. Repairs carried out by DH working party at Culham. 5.7.50, into LTS until 13.8.52. 30.1.53, del. to AHU Lossiemouth for further LTS from 12.2.53. 8.4.57, S.S.

VR864 DH flight trials. 21.7.48, arr. ARDU Culham. By 12.48, with 801 Sqn. By 7.49, to AHU Culham. By 8.49, based at St.Merryn. By 1.50, with 801 Sqn Lee-on-Solent coded A/461 until at least 7.50. By 1.51, at Airwork Gatwick for record. 14.11.51, ret. to ARDU Culham for period of LTS commencing 5.12.51. 8.2.53, emerged from storage. 27.3.53, passed to Airwork FRU at Hurn. 12.10.55, aircraft grounded. 10.1.56, taken to SNATSU Worthy Down for fire fighting practice. 6.7.56, SOC

VR891 12.7.48, f/f. 11.8.48, to ARDU Culham. 17.9.48, joined 801 Sqn at Arbroath coded 459. 13.10.48, undercarriage retracted after landing during ADDLs, Milltown. 20.10.48, to Lossiemouth for STS awaiting transfer. 20.12.48, arr. DH Hatfield for repairs. 2.3.50, to ARDU Culham into LTS. 4.12.50, removed from LTS. 10.1.51, arr. 801 Sqn at Lee-on-Solent coded 450. 14.3.51, a/c ret. to Culham for LTS. 16.7.53, desp. to Lossiemouth for further LTS on 24.7.53. 8.4.57, S.S.

VR892 DH flight trials. 9.48, appeared at SBAC Show at Farnborough. 30.9.48, TOC by RN at ARDU Culham. 18.9.49, Lossiemouth AHU. By 10.49, with 801 Sqn at Lee-on-Solent. 4.11.49, lost power on take-off from *Implacable* and ditched.

* * * * * * * * * *

12 Sea Hornet NF.21 produced by de Havilland, Hatfield.

VV430 1st Production NF.21, taken on charge 13.7.48. To RAE for radio trials; with Airwork FRU Hurn.

VV431 21.7.48, TOC C.S.(A). Test bed for fuselage static vent. 19.1.49, RAE for catapult trials. 25.3.49, DH Hatfield for static vent trials. 11.1.51, to RAE. 30.1.51, to DH. 27.3.51, RAE radio trials. 10.4.51, DH for TI. 17.11.52, a/c transferred to Marshalls of Cambridge for TI for target towing, a/c remaining on DH charge. 12.6.53, DH Leavesden Division for basic research into propeller noise & propeller development. 6.5.55, despatched to Lossiemouth. 24.3.58, SOC.

VV432 5.8.48, DH flight trials. 19.11.48, to ARDU Culham. 24.5.49, joined 809 Sqn at Culdrose coded 486/CW until about late Sept. By 1.51, to Airwork at Gatwick for record. 3.10.51, to Culham ARDU for future LTS. 24.11.52, out of LTS. 16.3.53, del. to Airwork FRU at Hurn. 13.10.55 withdrawn from service. 31.12.55, handed over to SNATSU at Worthy Down for fire fighting duties. 10.1.56, WOC

VV433 DH flight trials. 16.9.48, to ARDU Culham. By 11.48, with 703 Sqn. 2.2.49, with 787 Sqn West Raynham to at least 8.50. By 1.51, at AHU Culham until at least 7.52. By 2.53, with Airwork FRU at Hurn coded 481. By 7.53, Lossiemouth. 1.4.54, to Airwork, Gatwick for record. 19.1.55, at AHU Lossiemouth. 2.2.55, into LTS. 8.4.57, S.S.

VV434 29.10.48, 703 Sqn Lee-on-Solent. 4.11.48, RAE for catapulting tests. 23.12.48, Cat.A.C. due to movement at rear attachment bracket, wing to fuselage. 26.7.49, surplus to C.S.(A) requirements. 18.7.49, Hullavington for compilation of Pilot's Notes. 29.8.49, ARDU Culham. 5.6.52, to 809 Sqn marked J/487. 22.7.53, to Airwork, Gatwick. 18.1.54, Lossiemouth. 7.10.54, Airwork FRU St. Davids coded BY/454. 13.10.55, a/c grounded following minor inspection. 18.1.56, Southern NATSU. To Culdrose for fire-fighting practice.

VV435 DH flight trials. 19.11.48, to ARDU Culham. 11.3.49, joined 809 Sqn at Culdrose, coded Q/483. 10.1.51, to Airwork at Gatwick for repairs and record. 3.10.51, to AHU Culham. 11.10.51, entered LTS. 12.11.52, removed from LTS. 11.2.53, to Airwork FRU at Hurn. 10.1.56, SOC for fire fighting duties and removed to SNATSU, Worthy Down.

VV436 DH flight trials. 14.12.48, to ARDU Culham. 7.49, Del. to 787 Sqn at West Raynham. 2.2.50, to AHU Culham for LTS until at least 1.53. By 5.53, with Airwork FRU at Hurn coded 423. 1.7.54, to AHU Lossiemouth for

First production Sea Hornet PR.22 VW930 is wheeled out on a jury undercarriage (BAe photo)

LTS. 24.3.58, SOC and scrapped.

VV437 DH flight trials. 17.12.48, to ARDU Culham. 25.3.49, joined 809 Sqn at Culdrose coded CW/484. 28.11.49, a/c crashed on landing after u/c failed to lower; being repaired on site. 6.52, with 809 Sqn aboard HMS *Vengeance* coded Q/484. 7.52, to AHU Abbotsinch to at least 7.53. 1.12.53, with Airwork FRU St. Davids coded BY/423. By 7.55, at AHU Lossiemouth for LTS. 24.3.58, S.S.

VV438 DH flight trials. 14.12.48, to ARDU Culham. 17.2.49, to 809 Sqn at Culdrose coded CW/481, later Q/481. 11.10.50, to Culham AHU for LTS. 12.10.51, canopy blew off and struck fin. 2.7.52, del. to Airwork FRU at St. Davids. 17.9.53, to Airwork for recon. 25.1.54, del. to AHU Lossiemouth. 3.2.54, a/c preserved. 7.9.54, a/c de-preserved. 14.9.54, a/c returned to FRU St. Davids coded 423. 31.12.55, WOC for fire fighting practice. 18.1.56, TOC by SNATSU Worthy Down. 6.6.56, SOC

VV439 DH flight trials. 9.12.48, TOC at ARDU Culham. 11.3.49, to at least 1.51, with 809 Sqn coded Q/482. By 7.51, Airwork Gatwick. 12.12.51, Abbotsinch store. 24.3.53, Airwork FRU St. Davids, coded BQ/420. 13.10.55, a/c grounded. By 7.56, Lossiemouth AHU. 19.12.56, S.S.

VV440 DH flight trials. 10.2.49, ARDU Culham. 26.11.52, Culdrose. 8.12.52, 809 Sqn marked CW/486 and J/486. 23.7.53, Airwork, Gatwick for Cat.4 repair. 29.4.54, Lossiemouth store. 24.3.58, SOC.

VV441 DH flight trials. 23.2.49, to ARDU Culham. 3.49, Out to 809 Sqn at Culdrose coded Q/487. 3.10.50, to AHU Culham for LTS. 18.7.52 despatched to Airwork FRU St. Davids coded BY/416. 12.3.54, sent to Airwork at

Gatwick for recond. 20.9.54, to AHU Lossiemouth for LTS. 24.3.58, S.S.

* * * * * * * * * *

Ten Sea Hornet PR.22s produced by de Havilland, Hatfield. VW934 completed at Chester

VW930 1st Production PR.22. 30.9.48, f/f. 30.9.48, A&AEE for drop tank jettison trials. 3.3.49, TOC by RAE, Farnborough (Compass check). 12.7.49, to Handling Sqn Hullavington (Pilot's notes). 23.9.49, Hatfield for Trial Installation of AYF. 29.9.50, DH propellers for investigation into propeller overspeeding. 21.3.51, trial installations. 9.2.53, TI of Jury aircraft (sic). 1.9.53, Lossiemouth for survey. 11.9.53, SOC.

VW931 5.7.49, TOC ARDU Culham. 5.5.50, 738 Sqn Culdrose, coded 450/CW. 8.6.51, 1833 Sqn Bramcote (40 mins flying recorded). 2.2.52, ARDU Abbotsinch. 14.6.50, Airwork, Gatwick. 30.10.52, AHU Lossiemouth. 13.3.57, sold for scrap.

VW932 12.5.49, ARDU Culham. 16.5.50, 738 Sqn Culdrose. 21.8.51, to 759 Sqn Culdrose coded CW/452. 2.2.52, loaned 703 Sqn Ford, coded FD/009. 5.3.52, 759 Sqn Culdrose, recoded CW/452. 9.9.52, Abbotsinch store. 30.6.52, Lossiemouth store. 3.3.57, S.S.

VW933 30.6.49, ARDU Culham. 29.3.50, damaged by exploding air bottle. 14.6.50, Airwork, Gatwick. 27.3.53, Abbotsinch store. 6.7.54, Lossiemouth.

VW934 6.5.49, ARDU Culham. 22.6.50, Abbotsinch store. 22.7.57, S.S.

VW935 4.5.49, ARDU Culham. 15.6.49, 787 Sqn West

Raynham 3.10.49, Culham AHU. 10.1.50, Abbotsinch. 22.7.57, S.S.

VW936 DH flight trials. 18.5.49, to ARDU Culham. 16.6.50, Joined 738 Sqn at Culdrose coded 453/CW. 7.7.50, port oleo failed to lower, landed with starboard u/c only which collapsed after landing. 22.7.50, SOC

VW937 13.5.49, to ARDU Culham but belly-landed there after engine failure. 6.7.49, belly-landed. 27.4.53, to Lossiemouth AHU. 8.4.57, S.S.

VW938 11.4.49, DH flight trials. 10.5.49, to ARDU Culham. 28.6.49, to 759 Sqn at Culdrose. 10.7.50, passed to 703 Sqn at Ford coded FD/006. 15.11.50, suffered heavy deck landing on board HMS *Indomitable*. Repaired on site, returning to 703 Sqn. 13.9.51, to Airwork for recond. 11.1.52, del. to AHU Abbotsinch. 24.4.52, into LTS. 10.2.53, emerged from LTS. 6.11.53, further attention by Airwork for rectification of defects. 7.1.54, del. to AHU Lossiemouth for LTS. 8.4.57, S.S.

VW939 DH flight trials. 14.6.49, to ARDU Culham until at least 7.50. 8.50, joined 738 Sqn at Culdrose. 25.8.50, emergency landing after coolant leak. 15.5.51, spun into the sea 3-5 miles SW of Porthleven.

* * * * * * * * * *

36 Sea Hornet NF.21s produced by de Havilland, Hatfield, except for VW945, VW946 and VW947 completed at Chester

VW945 Hatfield a/c completed by DH Chester. 9.5.49, Culham AHU. 14.1.52, Abbotsinch store. 10.6.53, Culdrose. 21.7.53, to 809 Sqn/HMS *Eagle* coded CW/488. 9.4.54, Lossiemouth store. 13.3.57, WOC

VW946 Hatfield a/c completed by DH Chester, 20.11.48, f/f. 19.5.49, ARDU Culham. 6.49, to 809 Sqn at Culdrose coded CW/481. 1.4.49, to ARDU Culham until at least 7.52. By 11.52, with 809 Sqn coded J/481 by 11.52-6.53. Eventually desp. to Airwork, Gatwick. 11.5.54, to AHU Lossiemouth for LTS comm. 13.5.54. 24.3.58, S.S.

VW947 Hatfield a/c completed by DH Chester. Del. 23.5.49. 29.8.49, to 787 Sqn at West Raynham for trials. 6.2.50, passed to AHU Culham for storage until around 7.51. By 1.52, with 809 Sqn at Culdrose coded CW/482 later A/482 remaining until at least 7.53. 5.2.54, to Airwork, Gatwick for recond. 7.7.54, rec'd by AHU Lossiemouth for LTS. 13.7.54, LTS. 24.3.48, S.S.3 with 809 Sqn Culdrose. A/c at Hal Far. 18.6.54, Airwork, Gatwick.

VW948 DH flight trials. 6.5.49, to ARDU Culham. 8.6.49, to Culdrose to join 809 Sqn Culdrose coded CW/488. 15.7.49, a/c crashed in circuit during night flying.

VW949 DH flight trials. 28.2.49, 20.5.49, to 809 Sqn at Culdrose coded CW/485. 11.1.50, ret. to AHU Culham. By 5.50, with 809 Sqn coded Q/485. 1.7.50, with 813 Sqn at Eglinton. 26.9.50, to Airwork, Gatwick for recond. 7.9.51, ret. to ARDU Culham for LTS comm. 27.11.51. 3.12.51, emerged from LTS. 18.3.53, arr. Airwork FRU at Hurn. 13.10.55, a/c grounded. 10.1.56, arr. SNATSU Worthy Down for fire fighting practice at Westhampnett. 1968, scrapped at Chichester. +

VW950 DH flight trials. 6.5.49, to ARDU Culham until about 8.7.49. 8.49, arr. Lee-on-Solent, presumably with 809 Sqn. to at least 1.50. 7.50, a/c at Gosport. 24.8.51, desp. to RNAY Donibristle for recond. 12.9.51, to ARDU Culham. 11.11.52, to AHU Abbotsinch for LTS 5.3.53, passed to Airwork FRU at Hurn. 19.5.53, transferred to Airwork FRU St. Davids coded BQ/418. 17.9.53, arr. Airwork, Gatwick for recond. 12.3.54, to AHU Lossiemouth for LTS. 3.4.57, SOC

VW951 17.3.49, DH flight trials. 31.5.49, del. ARDU Culham. 31.5.49, into LTS. 8.5.52, removed from LTS. 1.7.52, Airwork FRU St. Davids. 30.6.54, Lossiemouth store for LTS. 24.3.58, S.S.

VW952 23.2.49, f/f. DH flight trials. 8.6.49, del. ARDU Culham for LTS at least to 1.51. By 4.51, with 809 Sqn Culdrose coded CW/485, later Q/485 then A/485. 30.3.53, SOC

VW953 DH flight trials. 6.7.49, del. ARDU Culham for LTS until 7.51. 8.51, 809 Sqn aboard HMS *Vengeance* coded Q/484, later A/484. Passed to Airwork, Gatwick for record. 18.3.53, to AHU Lossiemouth for period of LTS. 6.53, with 809 Sqn aboard HMS *Eagle* coded J/484. 28.1.54, floated into barrier on *Eagle*. 5.54, noted at Airwork, Gatwick for repairs. Eventually del. to AHU Lossiemouth. 20.5.55, SOC

VW954 DH flight trials. 21.7.49, arr. ARDU Culham for storage until at least 7.51. By 7.51, at Lee-on-Solent with 809 Sqn coded Q/484. 1.52, at AHU Culham. 7.52, ret. to Lee-on-Solent. 9.1.53, to Airwork, Gatwick for record. 16.3.53, to ARDU Lossiemouth. 21.5.53, arr. AHU Culdrose. 11.6.53, rejoined 809 Sqn coded CW/487, later J/487. 9.4.54, to Airwork FRU St. Davids coded 414. 13.10.55, grounded. 22.1.57, broken up on site.

VW955 6.4.49, f/f. DH flight trials. 18.7.49 to ARDU Culham for storage. 6.50, noted with 792 Sqn at Culdrose. 16.8.50, Joined 809 Sqn at Culdrose coded CW/493. By 1.51, with AHU Culham. By 7.51, TOC by C.S.(A) prior to trials. 1.52, noted at Culham AHU for long term storage. 13.5.53, 809 Sqn aboard HMS *Eagle* coded J/483. 10.2.54, a/c rolled overboard. 15.2.54, SOC.

VW956 6.4.49, DH flight trials. 15.6.49, ARDU Culham. 17.8.49, with No.809 Sqn coded CW/488, later Q/488. 17.6.50, a/c crashed landing at Arbroath. By 1.51, at Airwork, Gatwick for repairs. 3.6.52. to AHU Abbotsinch for LTS comm. 1.9.52. 22.7.57, S.S.

VW957 20.6.49, ARDU Culham. 17.1.51, to 809 Sqn Culdrose. 18.3.53, Lossiemouth. 21.8.53, Culdrose. 2.9.53, to 809 Sqn coded CW/481, later J/481. 19.1.54, hydraulic failure. 9.4.54, to Airwork FRU St.Davids coded BQ/415. 19.12.56, S.S.

VW958 6.6.49, ARDU Culham. 2.50, to 771 Sqn Lee-on-Solent coded LP/001, later FD/001, later LP/552 to at least 7.52. By 3.53, Airwork, Gatwick. 16.3.53, AHU Lossiemouth. 30.3.53, to 809 Sqn coded CW/485, later J/485. 9.4.56, Airwork FRU St.Davids coded BQ/411. 19.12.56, S.S.

VW959 2.6.49, ARDU Culham. 22.5.51, C Sqn A&AEE for trials of ASR Type G. Surplus to C.S.(A) requirements. 28.6.51, RDU Culham for rectification and storage. By 1.52, 809 Sqn coded Q/481, later A/481, then J/489. 30.10.53, SOC.

VW960 2.6.49, ARDU Culham. 24.4.52, Culdrose. 28.4.52, 809 Sqn coded CW/483, later Q/483 then A/483. 31.3.53, deck crash on HMS *Indomitable*. To Airwork, Gatwick for Cat.4 repairs. 28.5.54, AHU Lossiemouth. 8.4.57, S.S.

VW961 15.6.49, ARDU Culham. 1.53 with 809 Sqn Culdrose coded CW/488, later J/488. Later to Airwork, Gatwick until at least 7.52. 2.2.54, Lossiemouth store. 24.3.58, S.S.

VW962 23.6.49, ARDU Culham. 29.6.50, to Culdrose. 8.7.50, to 792 Sqn Culdrose. 1.51, with 809 Sqn Culdrose coded Q/489. 7.12.51, to Airwork, Gatwick, for reconditioning. 24.4.52, RAE for u/c vertical velocity measurement. 22.9.52, to 703 Sqn Ford for deck trials on HMS *Illustrious*. 8.10.52, RAE for further u/c vertical velocity measurements. 18.3.53, AHU Lossiemouth for survey. 5.10.54, preserved. 13.3.57, S.S.

VW963 18.7.49, ARDU Culdrose. 13.12.49, to 809 Sqn Culdrose coded Q/485. 5.12.51, aircraft crashed whilst on approach after starboard engine caught fire. 21.12.51, SOC.

VW964 24.6.49, ARDU Culham. 10.7.52, Airwork FRU St. Davids coded BY/415. 26.5.54, Lossiemouth Store. 24.3.58, SOC.

VW965 15.8.49, ARDU Culham. 10.4.51, RAE for u/c tests, vertical velocity measurements. 18.8.52, a/c landed wheels up at Ford following damage to u/c after colliding with carrier's gun turret during deck landings on HMS *Illustrious*. 31.3.52, Airwork, Gatwick for Cat.4 repairs. Found DBR. 25.5.52, SOC

Sea Hornet NF.21 VW949 of No.809 Squadron at Culdrose

VW966 29.6.49, DH flight trials. 5.8.49, ARDU Culham. 8.7.52, Airwork FRU St.Davids. 26.5.54, Lossiemouth store. 13.3.57, S.S.

VW967 2.9.49, ARDU Culham. 2.50, No.771 Sqn., Lee-on-Solent coded LP/553. 30.10.52, C.S.(A) charge - not req'd. 27.1.53, Lee-on-Solent. 11.3.53, to AHU Lossiemouth. 17.12.53, Airwork, Gatwick for reconditioning. 31.8.54, AHU Lossiemouth. 3.12.54, Airwork FRU St. Davids coded BY/424. 13.10.55, a/c grounded. 22.1.57, WOC

VW968 6.9.49, ARDU Culham. 1.50, No.809 Sqn coded A/481, then CW/481, later Q/488. 24.4.51, landed heavily during ADDL and on next landing starboard oleo collapsed, the a/c swinging off runway. By 7.52, Abbotsinch store. By 4.53, Airwork, Gatwick. 29.4.53, AHU Abbotsinch. 21.8.53, Culdrose. 2.9.53, 809 Sqn Culdrose coded CW/486. 13.4.54, AHU Abbotsinch. 14.6.54, AHU Lossiemouth. 2.4.57, S.S.

VW969 5.9.49, ARDU Culham. 16.5.50, No.792 Sqn Culdrose marked CW/494. 22.8.50, 809 Sqn coded CW/494. 3.10.50, AHU Culham. 23.1.51, 809 Sqn coded CW/489, recoded Q/482 whilst aboard HMS *Vengeance*. 11.6.51 AHU Culham for LTS. 4.5.53, Airwork FRU Hurn. 20.7.54, Lossiemouth store. 24.3.58, S.S.

VW970 10.9.49, ARDU Culham. 3.50, No.809 Sqn coded CW/480, later Q/480. 20.7.50, 809 Sqn. Precautionary landing at Wunstorf due to fuel shortage. 9.51, recoded Q/487. By 7.52, recoded A/487. By 7.53, Airwork, Gatwick. 8.7.53, AHU Lossiemouth. 20.11.53, NARU Gosport, 29.3.55, Lossiemouth store. 24.3.58, S.S.

VW971 24.8.49, DH flight trials. 26.9.49, ARDU Culham. 26.2.50, AHU Abbotsinch for LTS. 27.7.51, after inspection ret. LTS. 1.9.52, inspected & ret. to LTS on 24.10.52. 26.2.56, Abbotsinch store. 22.7.57, S.S.

VW972 23.8.49, DH flight trials. 14.9.49, ARDU Culham. 25.2.50, del.Abbotsinch AHU for LTS 16.2.51-2.6.51 & 15.3.52-24.9.52. Aircraft inspected. Remainder of life spent in storage. 22.7.57, S.S.

VW973 3.10.49, ARDU Culham. 26.2.50, AHU Abbotsinch 27.3.50, LTS stored (various periodic inspections). 22.7.57. S.S.

VW974 5.10.49, ARDU Culham. 2.5.50, AHU Abbotsinch for LTS stored. 22.7.57, S.S.

VW975 13.10.49, ARDU Culham. 25.2.50, AHU Abbotsinch. for LTS stored. 9.8.57, S.S.

VW976 28.10.49, ARDU Culham. 26.2.50, AHU Abbotsinch LTS stored. 22.7.57, S.S.

VW977 10.11.49, ARDU Culham. 26.2.50, AHU Abbotsinch. for LTS. 22.8.57, S.S.

VW978 16.1.50, ARDU Culham. 17.3.50, AHU Abbotsinch for LTS. 22.8.57, S.S.

VW979 14.12.49, ARDU Culham. 2.4.50, AHU Abbotsinch for LTS. 9.9.53, Airwork FRU Hurn. 13.10.55, a/c grounded. 10.1.56, SNATSU Worthy Down for fire fighting practice. 1.6.56, Fleetlands. 6.6.56, SOC

VW980 11.1.50, ARDU Culham. 21.4.50, AHU Abbotsinch. 21.5.52, Marshalls, Cambridge for TI of target marking equipment. 10.4.53, DH u/c work. 19.10.53, A&AEE Hood jettison test in blower tunnel. 3.11.53, Marshalls, Cambridge. 31.8.54, AHU Lossiemouth for LTS. 24.3.58, S.S.

*   *   *   *   *   *   *   *   *   *

Eight Sea Hornet NF.21s produced by de Havilland, Chester

VX245 DH flight trials. 17.1.50, ARDU Culham. 2.4.50, AHU Abbotsinch. 3.5.50, into LTS. 13.4.51, de-preserved and inspected. 9.7.51, re-preserved. 25.7.52, de-preserved. 28.11.52, inspected and re-preserved. 22.7.57, S.S. Remains to AWRE Foulness.

VX246 DH flight trials. 16.1.50, ARDU Culham. 2.4.50, AHU Abbotsinch. 24.7.51, for LTS. 25.8.52, out of LTS. 25.8.52, inspected. 24.10.52, re-preserved. 22.8.57, S.S.

VX247 DH flight trials. 27.2.50, ARDU Culham. 29.6.50, into STS. 4.2.52, AHU. 7.2.52, into LTS. 16.1.54, out of LTS Abbotsinch for LTS. 10.4.54, to AHU Lossiemouth. 13.3.57, S.S.

VX248 DH flight trials. 27.2.50, ARDU Culham. By 6.50, 792 Sqn marked CW/491. 2.6.50, observer's hatch blown off on landing. By 10.50, Airwork for repairs until at least 3.51. By 7.51, to AHU Culham until at least 7.52. By 7.53 Airwork FRU St. Davids. 28.1.55, AHU Lossiemouth. SOC

VX249 DH flight trials. 14.3.50, ARDU Culham. 18.8.50, into LTS. 6.3.52, AHU Abbotsinch for period of LTS. 22.7.57, S.S.

VX250 DH flight trials. 6.3.50, ARDU Culham. By 5.50, with 792 Sqn Culdrose coded CW/486. 10.50, 809 Sqn coded CW/486. 2.2.51, port oleo collapsed whilst a/c was making emergency landing, slewed off runway. Culdrose. 4.51, HMS *Vengeance* coded Q/486. 7.52 Aboard HMS *Indomitable* coded A/486 to at least 1.53 and then to Airwork. 29.4.53, AHU Lossiemouth. 2.9.53, with Airwork FRU St. Davids marked BY/425. 19.12.56, scrapped on site. Remains still at St. Davids up to at least 1970, small piece of fuselage with Mosquito Museum, London Colney.

VX251 DH flight trials. 14.3.50, ARDU Culham to at least 7.51. 6.7.50, LTS. By 1.52, AHU Abbotsinch. By 10.53, Airwork St. Davids. 18.1.55, WOC

VX252 DH flight trials. 6.3.50, rec'd. ARDU Culham. 6.7.50, LTS. 29.1.52, DH Leavesden for trials. 19.5.52, AHU Abbotsinch, to LTS. 22.7.57, S.S.

*　*　*　*　*　*　*　*　*　*

Ten Sea Hornet PR.22s produced by De Havilland, Chester

VZ655 DH flight trials. 17.8.49, ARDU Culham. 5.7.50, 703 Sqn coded FD/005 Ford. 24.10.50, bounced on ADDLs, tailwheel collapsed. Went round again, landed on mainwheels and tail cone. 7.4.51, aileron problem after take-off. 13.9.51, Culham. 14.1.52, Storage. 14.1.53, de-preserved. 8.6.53, Lossiemouth store. 8.4.57, S.S.

VZ656 13.7.49, DH flight trials. 17.8.49, ARDU Culham. 26.7.50, Abbotsinch AHU. 22.7.57, SOC 9.8.57. S.S.

VZ657 6.8.49, DH flight trials. 18.8.49, ARDU Culham. 23.10.49, LTS. 23.10.50, Abbotsinch. 16.1.51, preserved. 22.7.57, S.S.

VZ658 DH flight trials. 6.9.49, ARDU Culham. 9.49, exhibited at Farnborough Air Display. 13.12.49, 801 Sqn Lee-on-Solent marked LP/465. 23.1.50, No.1 CAG on HMS *Indomitable* marked A/465. 23.1.50 Abbotsinch for preservation. 22.7.57, S.S.

VZ659 DH flight trials. 5.9.49, ARDU Culham. 10.12.49, 801 Sqn marked LP/463 later A/463 with No.1 CAG Lee-on-Solent. 10.1.50, slight taxying accident. 23.1.50, Culham, AHU for minor repairs. 31.7.50, Abbotsinch store. 22.7.57, S.S.

VZ660 19.9.49, DH flight trials. 16.10.49, ARDU. 19.10.49, Stretton RDU. 20.10.49, Culham. 10.12.49, 801 Sqn Lee-on-Solent, marked LP/464. 17.3.50, in store Abbotsinch. 22.7.47, S.S.

VZ661 18.11.49, DH flight trials. 6.12.49, ARDU Culham. 18.12.49, Abbotsinch AHU for storage. 22.7.57, S.S.

VZ662 28.11.49, DH flight trials. 6.1.50, ARDU Culham. 16.3.50, Abbotsinch AHU for storage. 22.7.57, S.S.

VZ663 8.12.49, DH flight trials. 11.1.50, ARDU Culham. 13.2.50, Abbotsinch AHU for storage. 22.7.57, S.S.

VZ664 DH flight trials. 23.2.50, ARDU Culham to at least 1.51. 6.5.51, to 738 Sqn Culdrose. 10.51, to 759 Sqn. marked CW/451 until at least 7.52. By 1.53 Abbotsinch AHU. 6.9.54, during gentle pull out from 400 knot dive at 4,000 ft. the canopy shattered, requiring mods. Used as ground instruction airframe. 17.9.54, SOC

*　*　*　*　*　*　*　*　*　*

22 Sea Hornet NF.21s produced by de Havilland, Chester

VZ671 DH flight trials. 31.3.50, ARDU Culham. 1.7.50, LTS. 10.12.51, AHU Abbotsinch. 25.11.52, inspected. 9.12.52, preserved. 22.7.57, S.S.

VZ672 DH flight trials. 1.4.50, ARDU Culham. By 6.50, No.792 Sqn Culdrose coded CW/491. 10.8.50, No.809 Sqn Culdrose, marked CW/481. 9.51, personal a/c for C.O. marked Q/481 on board HMS *Vengeance*. 3.12.52, AHU Abbotsinch. STS. 9.12.52, AHU Lossiemouth. 11.3.53, Airwork FRU Hurn/St. Davids. 5.12.53, Airwork, Gatwick. 27.10.54, WOC

VZ673 DH flight trials. 1.4.50, ARDU Culham. 30.5.50, No.792 Sqn Culdrose, coded CW/482. 10.8.50, No.809 Sqn. 11.10.50, AHU Culham. 26.1.51, No.809 Sqn. HMS *Vengeance* coded Q/482. 21.11.51, AHU Culham. 17.12.51, 809 Sqn marked 482?. 19.3.52, Hal Far, collected same day by HMS *Vengeance*. 2.4.52, ferried to Gosport. 16.4.52, Airwork, Gatwick for repairs. 25.7.52, AHU Abbotsinch. 22.7.57, S.S.

VZ674 9.3.50, DH flight trials. 1.4.50, ARDU Culham. 7.6.50, Lossiemouth for flight tests. 21.9.50, AHU Culham. Preservation. 5.2.52, AHU Abbotsinch via Renfrew. 22.9.54, AHU Lossiemouth. LTS. 8.4.57, WOC

VZ675 DH flight trials. 21.4.50, ARDU Culham. 22.6.50, LTS. 4.3.52, AHU Abbotsinch LTS. 22.7.57, S.S.

VZ676 DH flight trials. 21.4.50, ARDU Culham. By 6.52 Airwork, Gatwick, reconditioning. 24.7.52, AHU Lossiemouth. LTS. 27.1.53, de-preserved. 12.2.53, Airwork FRU Hurn. 13.10.55, a/c grounded. 10.1.56, SNATSU Worthy Down. 6.6.56, WOC

VZ677 DH flight trials. 26.4.50, ARDU Culham. 10.50, with 809 Sqn Culdrose coded CW/488. 18.2.52, hit fire extinguisher while being marshalled, Hal Far. By 6.53, Airwork, Gatwick. 1.9.53, AHU Lossiemouth. 15.2.54, Airwork FRU Hurn. 10.1.56, Worthy Down. 7.56, destroyed in fire-fighting demonstration, Anthorn.

VZ678 DH flight trials. 12.5.50, ARDU Culham. 7.2.52, AHU Abbotsinch store. 8.1.54, 809 Sqn Culdrose coded J/482. 9.4.54, AHU Abbotsinch store. 24.3.58, S.S.

VZ679 DH flight trials. 26.4.50, ARDU Culham. 15.1.52, Abbotsinch. 30.10.53, No.809 Sqn. 31.5.54 coded Q/435. Lossiemouth store. 24.3.58, S.S.

VZ680 DH flight trials. 10.5.50, ARDU Culham. 22.1.52, AHU Abbotsinch, then Culham to at least 3.52. 26.5.52, drifted to starboard after cut and wing hit island; flew off and landed safely, Culdrose. 6.7.52, 809 Sqn. Culdrose coded A/484, later J/484. 1.5.53, starboard oleo collapsed on landing (USMC pilot) after engaging barrier. 18.6.53, force-landed, Culdrose. 16.8.53, to Airwork, Gatwick for repair. 25.1.54, AHU Lossiemouth. 24.3.58, S.S.

VZ681 DH flight trials. 1.6.50, ARDU Culham. 18.5.54, AHU Lossiemouth. 13.3.57, S.S.

VZ682 DH flight trials. 5.6.50, ARDU Culham. 29.1.52, AHU Abbotsinch. 7.10.53, No.809 Sqn Culdrose coded J/484. 9.4.54, Airwork FRU Hurn. 10.1.56, Worthy Down for fire-fighting practice.

VZ690 DH flight trials. 9.6.50, arr. ARDU Culham. 17.10.50, to A.H.U Abbotsinch. 21.10.50, into LTS. 9.11.51, removed from LTS and inspected. 2.7.52, ret. to LTS. 22.7.57, S.S.

VZ691 DH flight trials. 9.6.50 arr. ARDU Culham. 15.7.50, placed into LTS. 4.2.52, passed to AHU Abbotsinch, 5.2.52, re-preserved. 3.9.53, de-preserved. 16.7.54, Rec'd. Airwork FRU Hurn. 13.10.55, a/c grounded. 10.1.56, rec'd. by SNATSU Worthy Down. 6.6.56, SOC. 2.59, remains finally burnt at Bramcote.

VZ692 DH flight trials. 26.6.50, TOC by ARDU Culham. 15.1.52, AHU Abbotsinch store. 24.7.53, Airwork FRU St. Davids coded BY/421. 19.12.56, S.S.

VZ693 DH flight trials. 4.7.50, TOC at ARDU Culham. 1.8.50, into LTS. 8.2.52, passed to AHU Abbotsinch for LTS. 26.2.52, re-preserved. 30.6.54, rec'd AHU Lossiemouth

Sea Hornet NF.21 VW947 lands at Hal Far after a test flight

for further period of LTS. 28.3.55, removed from LTS, inspected and prepared for service. 7.10.55, re-preserved. 24.3.58, S.S.

VZ694 DH flight trials. 10.7.50, TOC by ARDU Culham. 22.8.50, preserved. 23.1.52, de-preserved. 4.2.52, to AHU Abbotsinch. 7.2.52, preserved. 14.7.53, de-preserved. 2.9.53, into STS. 9.9.53, TOC by Airwork FRU St.Davids coded BY/427. 13.10.55, a/c grounded. 19.12.56, S.S. Remains at St. Davids during 1970.

VZ695 DH flight trials. 25.7.50, TOC by ARDU Culham. 22.9.50, AHU Abbotsinch for LTS. After inspection re-preserved 27.9.51. 1.10.52, de-preserved. 5.3.53, TOC by Airwork FRU St. Davids coded BY/417. 13.10.55, a/c grounded. 19.12.56, S.S.

VZ696 DH flight trials. 27.7.50, ARDU Culham. 18.9.50, AHU Abbotsinch. 10.4.51, into LTS. 1.7.52, a/c fully cocooned. 22.7.57, S.S.

VZ697 DH flight trials. 29.8.50, ARDU Culham. 6.10.50, to AHU Abbotsinch. 25.1.52, to Hal Far, possibly with 809 Sqn. 22.3.52, ret. to UK with 809 Sqn coded 489. 5.52, aboard HMS *Indomitable* coded A/489. 1.7.52, a/c suffered tailwheel collapse on landing. 29.9.52, arr. Culdrose ARS for repairs, returning to 809 Sqn. 30.3.53, SOC

VZ698 DH flight trials. 13.9.50, TOC by ARDU Culham. 23.10.50, into LTS. 8.2.52, AHU Abbotsinch. 26.2.52, re-preserved until 8.8.53. 12.3.54, joined Airwork FRU St. Davids coded BY/416. 13.10.55, a/c grounded. 19.12.56, S.S.

VZ699 (Final production NF.21). DH flight trials. 3.11.50, ARDU Culham. 5.2.51, into LTS. 4.2.52, removed from storage. 4.3.52, AHU Abbotsinch AHU. 13.3.52, further period of LTS. 22.7.57, S.S.

*   *   *   *   *   *   *   *   *   *

16 Sea Hornet F.20s produced by de Havilland, Chester:

VZ707 DH flight trials. 30.8.49, ARDU Culham. 18.9.49, Lossiemouth AHU. 18.10.49, 801 Sqn. Lee-on-Solent coded A/459, later C/458. 23.1.50, 801 Sqn in *Implacable*. 14.3.51, Culham. 29.6.53, Lossiemouth store.

VZ708 DH flight trials. 6.10.49, ARDU Culham. 1.12.49, 801 Sqn Lee-on-Solent coded 456 later re-coded 456/C when embarked on HMS *Implacable*. 14.7.50, whilst aboard *Implacable* it missed all arrestor wires and crashed into barrier. Transported to Culham shortly afterwards for repairs. 1.51, with Airwork Gatwick for further repairs and renewals. Repairs not considered practicable. 24.9.51, SOC

VZ709 DH flight trials. 27.10.49, ARDU Culham. 6.12.49, to 801 Sqn Lee-on-Solent coded C/450, later A/450, until at least 7.50. By 1.51, at Airwork Gatwick for re-cond. 19.5.52, AHU Abbotsinch for LTS. 22.7.57, S.S.

VZ710 DH flight trials. 6.12.49, ARDU Culham. 14.9.50, 801 Sqn Lee-on-Solent coded 463, later changed to C/456 by 9.50. 14.9.50, crashed when failed to pull out of loop at low altitude whilst giving aerobatic display to Argentinean cadets.

VZ711 DH flight trials. 21.11.49, ARDU Culham. 6.12.49, to 801 Sqn at Lee-on-Solent, coded 463. 9.50, Code changed to C/451 whilst aboard HMS *Implacable* until at least 1.51. By 7.51, Culham AHU until at least 7.52. By 1.53, with Airwork FRU St. Davids. 7.53, to Airwork at Gatwick. 4.10.54, loss of coolant in port engine. 4.11.54, to AHU Lossiemouth for LTS. 15.2.55, to Airwork FRU, Hurn. 13.10.55, aircraft grounded and subsequently handed over to fire fighting section. 10.1.56, remnants to SNATSU, Worthy Down.

VZ712 DH flight trials. 13.10.49, ARDU Culham. 14.12.49, TOC, ARDU Culham to at least 1.50. By 5.50, with 801 Sqn. 14.3.51, ret. to AHU Culham. 3.10.51, to 759 Sqn., Culdrose (Part of 52 TRAG) coded CW/453. 26.1.53, passed to ARS Culdrose. 26.2.53, storage at AHU Lossiemouth. 7.4.54, to Airwork, Gatwick for recond. 4.11.54, returned to AHU Lossiemouth for further storage. 2.6.55, removed from LTS. 14.6.55, to Hal Far AHU 21.9.55, taken on charge by 728 Sqn. 13.10.55, grounding order. 28.10.55, transferred to Hal Far AHU being received 1.11.55. 12.1.56, consigned to the sea off the stern of *Ark Royal*.

VZ713 DH flight trials. 26.1.50, ARDU Culham. 28.6.50, 801 Sqn. Crashed during steep turn near sea and exploded on impact.

VZ714 6.1.50, DH flight trials. 3.2.50, ARDU Culham. 21.3.50, ARDU for LTS. 3.9.50, removed from storage and prepared for squadron service. 13.9.50, to 801 Sqn, Lee-on-Solent, coded 457. Embarked on HMS *Implacable*, code changed to C/457. 14.3.51, AHU Culham. 5.10.51, LTS. 20.5.53, arr. AHU Lossiemouth for further LTS. 8.4.57 S.S.

VZ715 2.2.50, DH flight trials. 6.3.50, del. ARDU Culham. 24.5.50, arr. 801 Sqn Culdrose, coded CW/460, later C/460. 7.50, Aboard HMS *Implacable*. 6.12.50, crashed on flight deck. After repair aboard ship returned to 801 Sqn. 14.3.51, arr. AHU Culham. 2.7.53, at AHU Lossiemouth. 8.4.57, scrapped.

* * * * * * * * * *

Eight Sea Hornet F.20s produced by de Havilland, Chester

WE235 DH flight trials. 16.1.51, ARDU Culham. 31.1.51, passed to RNAY Belfast en route to join squadron. 5.2.51, to 801 Sqn in *Implacable*. Aircraft dived into sea 20 miles west of Mull of Kintyre.

WE236 DH flight trials. 22.1.51, ARDU Culham. 1.2.51, flying accident; aircraft broke up during test flight from Culham.

WE237 DH flight trials. 3.4.51, ARDU Culham. 24.3.51, LTS. 22.2.52, removed from LTS. During a routine test flight from Culham (prior to overseas ferrying) aircraft made-single engine landing. 19.5.52, RAE for tests. 17.6.52, to 703 Sqn Ford coded FD/009 for further tests. 27.9.52, aircraft suffered heavy landing, being repaired on site. 21.10.52, Lossiemouth AHU. 18.11.52, LTS. 8.11.57, S.S.

WE238 6.2.51, DH flight trials. 20.3.51, rec'd. ARDU Culham for storage. 21.2.52, at Hal Far with 728 Sqn coded HF/530. 16.9.53, at Hal Far AHU for checks. 11.53, ret. to UK aboard HMS *Perseus*. By 1.54, AHU Lossiemouth. By 3.54, with Airwork Gatwick. 12.5.54, ret. to AHU Lossiemouth for LTS. 30.8.54, removed from storage for service. 14.9.55, to Airwork FRU at Hurn. 13.10.55, grounded and WOC for fire fighting practice. 10.1.56, collected by SNATSU Worthy Down; delivered to AHU Abbotsinch. 6.6.56, SOC

WE239 15.3.51, DH flight trials. 21.5.51, ARDU Culham. 15.6.51, to 703 Sqn. Ford, coded FD/009. 1.9.51, ground accident. 5.11.51, arr. Airwork Gatwick for repairs. 21.7.52, arr. AHU Lossiemouth by road. 11.9.52, LTS. 6.11.53, de-preserved and prepared for service. 18.11.53, joined NARIU, Gosport for instruction. 24.5.54, returned to AHU Lossiemouth. 28.5.54, LTS 24.6.54, de-preserved for use with Lossiemouth Aerobatic Team. 10.7.54, flown during Open Day. 12.7.54, preserved. 3.9.54, de-preserved. 6.10.54, rec'd by Airwork FRU Hurn. 18.7.55, aircraft grounding order. 25.7.55, aircraft struck by lightning on cockpit window frame. 14.9.55, AHU Lossiemouth for storage. 13.3.57, SOC

WE240 DH Flight trials. 3.5.51, ARDU Culham. 14.6.51, LTS. 5.10.52, DH Leavesden for tests. 5.2.53, AHU Lossiemouth. 21.2.53, LTS. 26.10.53, removed from LTS forming part of Lossiemouth Aerobatic Team. 18.11.53, aircraft arr. Hal Far AHU. 13.1.54, to 728 Sqn Hal Far, possibly coded HF/535. Following bird strikes aircraft passed to AHU Hal Far. 14.2.55, SOC

WE241 DH flight trials. 29.5.51, ARDU Culham. 21.7.51, appeared at '50 Years of Flight' exhibition at RAF Hendon. 31.7.51, Culham AHU for LTS from 31.7.51-11.12.52. 5.11.52, arr. Lossiemouth for further period of LTS. 10.53, de-preserved for use with Lossiemouth Aerobatic Team. 16.6.54-8.9.54, returned to LTS. 8.4.57, S.S.

WE242 28.5.51, DH flight trials. 12.6.51, ARDU Culham. 24.8.51, LTS. 10.11.52, taken out of LTS. 31.1.53, arr. Hal Far AHU for LTS from 24.2.53-4.5.53, when inspected. 10.7.53, returned to LTS. 5.9.53, out of LTS. 15.9.53, to 728 Sqn Hal Far, coded HF/530. 13.10.55, grounding order. 1.11.55, aircraft rec'd by AHU Hal Far. 19.1.56, WOC for fire fighting. Survived until 1957.

* * * * * * * * * *

Three Sea Hornet PR.22s produced by De Havilland, Hatfield

WE245 8.9.50, DH flight trials. 18.9.50, Culham RDU. By 1.51, Gosport. By 6.51, DH Hatfield. 5.7.51, ret. AHU Culham. 8.9.51-8.7.53, LTS. 9.7.53, AHU Lossiemouth for further LTS. 8.4.57, S.S.

WE246 29.8.50, DH flight trials. 25.9.50, AHU Culham. 13.11.50, to 703 Sqn coded FD/008. 23.10.53, Lossiemouth AHU. 27.10.53, LTS. 13.3.57, S.S.

WE247 6.9.50, DH flight trials. 25.9.50, AHU Culham. 24.10.50-7.11.50, LTS. 14.11.50, to 703 Sqn Ford, coded FD/007. 26.2.53, AHU Lossiemouth for LTS from 15.6.53-4.5.54, inspected and ret'd to LTS same day. 13.3.57, S.S.

* * * * * * * * * *

VW959 shows off the radome of the NF.21
(via P. Jarrett)

TT213 with Airwork at St.Davids
(C. Bruce via RCS)

DE HAVILLAND HORNET F.3

Technical Details and Performance Figures

Wing Data:

Aerofoil Section   Thickness grading EC1240 Series Camberline:-

Constant load up to 0.4 C. and linear decrease at T.E.	
Span	45 ft
Chord at fuselage side (21 in from centre-line of fus.)	12 ft 2 in
Chord at tip (21 ft from centre-line of fuselage)	4 ft 2 in
Incidence	1½ degrees
Dihedral (Measured on top face of front spar)	1 degree 11 min
Sweep back at Rib No.4	6 1/4 degrees

Tail Unit Data:

Span	18 ft 1½ in
Chord at Root (including elevator)	5 ft 1½ in
Incidence	Neutral

Areas:

Wings (Total)	361 sq ft
Ailerons (Total)	17½ sq ft
Aileron Trim Tab (Starboard Side)	2.7 sq ft
Split Flaps (Hornet) Per side	17½ sq ft
Tailplane with elevators (Excluding fuselage width)	55 sq ft
Elevators (Total)	22.15 sq ft
Elevator Trim Tabs	1.08 sq ft
Fin	16.3 sq ft
Rudder (With Trim and Balance Tab)	12.1 sq ft
Rudder Trim and Balance Tab	1.397 sq ft

Fuselage Data:

Length	36 ft 8 in
Width (Maximum)	3 ft 2 in
Height (Maximum (Less Canopy)	4 ft 2 in

Range of movement of Control Surfaces:

Ailerons	Up and Down 15 degrees
Aileron Tabs	Up and Down 15 degrees
Elevators	Up 20 degrees Down 15
Elevator Tabs	Up 15 degrees Down 15
Rudder	30 degrees each way
Rudder Tab	20 degrees each way
Flaps	75 degrees Down.
Ground Angle (No load)	13 degrees 20 min

Weights:

Weight empty	12,880 lb
Weight loaded	20,900 lb
Max. Weights (Take-off and gentle manoeuvres)	19,550 lb
(All forms of flying)	17,880 lb
Wing loading (lb/sq.ft)	44.5
Power loading (lb/hp)	4.85
Max. Speed at 10,000 ft	438 m.p.h.
at 22,000 ft	472 m.p.h.
Max. Speeds with 100 gal drop tanks (IAS)	
Sea level to 10,000 ft	290 knots
10,000 ft to 20,000 ft	270 knots
20,000 ft to 30,000 ft	225 knots
Above 30,000 ft	195 knots
Initial Rate of climb	4,000 ft/min
Time to height (minutes) 10,000 ft	4.0
Service Ceiling	35,000 ft
Stalling Speed (Undercarriage and flaps up)	136 m.p.h.
(Undercarriage and flaps down)	105 m.p.h.
Final Landing Approach Speeds (at 16,100 lb AUW)	
Engine assisted (Flaps up)	144 m.p.h.
(Flaps down)	125 m.p.h.
Glide landing Approach (flaps in max. lift position)	160 m.p.h.
Single Engine Approach (flaps in max. lift position)	160 m.p.h.
Safety speed (Engine failure on take off) no external stores	165 m.p.h.
Maximum Range	3,000 miles

Fuel Tank Capacities:

Outer Wing Tanks, Port and Starboard	120 gal
Inner Wing Tanks, Port and Starboard	310 gal
Upper and lower Fuselage Tanks	108 gal
Total:	538 gal
Total with 2 x 100 gal drop tanks	738 gal
2 x 200 gal drop tanks	938 gal

Engine Data:

Merlin 130/131, 2,030 hp
Fuel, 100 Octane
Oil, D.E.D 2472

Max. Take off power	3,000 rev/min at +18 psi
Max. Continuous power	2,850 rev/min at +9 psi

Flying limitations:

Maximum diving speeds IAS

Below 5,000 ft	400 m.p.h.
5,000-10,000 ft	380 m.p.h.
10,000-20,000 ft	340 m.p.h.
20,000-30,000 ft	280 m.p.h.
Above 30,000 ft	240 m.p.h.
Undercarriage Down	200 m.p.h.
Flaps down	180 m.p.h.

A Sea Hornet in its element as H.M.S. Implacable butts into a heavy sea (via R.C. Sturtivant)

Glossary of Abbreviations

A. & A.E.E.	Aeroplane & Armament Experimental Establishment
A.D.D.L.	Airfield Dummy Deck Landing
A.F.S.	Advanced Flying School
A.H.U.	Aircraft Holding Unit
A.P.C.	Armament Practice Camp
A.P.S.	Armament Practice Station
A.R.D.U.	Aircraft Receipt and Despatch Unit
B.A.F.O.	British Air Forces of Occupation
B.O.A.C.	British Overseas Airways Corporation
C.A.P.	Combat Air Patrol
C.A.G.	Carrier Air Group
C.F.E.	Central Fighter Establishment
C.F.I.	Chief Flying Instructor
C.F.S.	Central Flying School
C in C	Commander-in-Chief
C.S.U.	Constant Speed Unit
C.S.(A)	Controller of Supplies (Aircraft)
C.T.U.	Carrier Trials Unit
D.B.R.	Damaged beyond repair
E.T.A.	Estimated time of arrival
F.E.A.F.	Far East Air Force
F.E.T.S.	F.E.A.F. Training Squadron
F.R.U.	Fleet Requirements Unit
F.O.S.M.	Flag Officer Submarines
G.C.A.	Ground Controlled Approach
G.C.I.	Ground Controlled Interception
G.G.S.	Gyro Gun Sight
I.A.S.	Indicated Air Speed
L.T.S.	Long-term Storage
M.B.	Maintenance Base
M.U.	Maintenance Unit
N.A.F.D.U.	Naval Air Fighting Development Unit
O.C.U.	Operational Conversion Unit
O.F.O.	Overseas Ferry Unit
P.R.D.U.	Photographic Reconnaissance Development Unit
R.A.A.F.	Royal Australian Air Force
R.A.E.	Royal Aircraft Establishment
R.A.F.F.C	Royal Air Force Flying College
R.N.A.R.Y	Royal Naval Aircraft Repair Yard
R.N.A.S.	Royal Naval Air Station
R.N.E.C.	Royal Naval Engineering College
R.O.C.	Royal Observer Corps
R.P.	Rocket Projectile
S.E.A.C.	South East Asia Command
S.T.S.	Short-term Storage
S.T.U.	Service Trials Unit
S.O.C.	Struck off charge
T.A.S.	True Air Speed
T.I.	Trial Installation
S.O.C.	Struck off Charge
S.S.	Sold as scrap
W.O.C.	Written off Charge (R.N.)

KEY

1 Glycol reservoir
2 Oxygen bottles
3 Nose armour
4 Instrument panel
5 Gunsight
6 Throttle/airscrew controls
7 Seat armour
8 I.F.F.
9 Magazines
10 Hydraulic tank
11 Four 20 mm cannon
12 Oil/intercooler radiators
13 Fuel filter
14 Fuel tanks
15 Split flaps
16 Composite ribs inboard
17 Oil tank
18 Motor intercooler
19 Rolls-Royce Merlin
20 Engine mounts
21 Main undercarriage
22 Cold air intake
23 Metal leading end ribs and skin
24 Front spar (both plywood with
25 Rear spar   metal reinforcements)
26 Wooden ribs outboard
27 Radio
28 Fuselage frame
29 Control cables
30 Ply/balsa/ply skin
31 Retractable tailwheel
32 Typical fin/tailplane skin
33 Plywood skin on wooden stringers

Cliff Minney f.f.a.i.

Acknowledgements:

The task of researching this classic fighter would have been difficult, if not impossible, without the assistance received from many quarters at home and abroad, including the Ministry of Defence, The Royal Air Force Museum at Hendon and British Aerospace at Hatfield and Chester.

My deep gratitude to Ray Sturtivant for providing invaluable help (at the drop of a hat) with Sea Hornet historical data and numerous "leads" for contacts within the retired echelon of the Fleet Air Arm and to Cliff Minney for producing the drawings, cut-away and cover artwork. Not forgetting timely advice and encouragement from Jim Halley, whose patience seems endless.

Special thanks are due to the following for material contributions:

Capt. E.M. Brown RN; Cdr. C.A. Brown; Capt. A.B.B. Clarke; Air Commodore W.H. Croydon C.B.E.; Peter Dalosso; Frank Dowson; Lt. Cdr. N.N. Ducker; A.J. Fairbrother (ex-D.H. Hatfield); Fred Farmer; Sydney Foster (ex-Heston Aircraft); Geoffrey Frost; Jim Froud; E.V. George; John Greenland; P. Godfrey; Rear Admiral H.C.N. Goodhart; J. Greenland; Wg. Cdr. N.P.W. Hancock O.B.E., D.F.C.; Air Vice Marshal W. Harbison C.B., C.B.E., A.F.C., F.B.I.M.; M. Hardman (B Ae Chester); Jim Hartley; S/Ldr C. Haw D.F.C., D.F.M., A.E., Order of Lenin; Dennis Hayward; Jesse Hanks; Sqn.Ldr. Harvey; Lt. Cdr. M.W. Henley; Bill Hunt (MoD); Wg. Cdr. W. Hoy; Peter James (A & AEE), David King; Capt. D.B. Law; Capt. H.A. Leahy; Capt. K. Lee-White; Gp. Capt. I. Madelin (Air Historical Branch); H. McKenzie; Roger de Mercado (B.Ae Chester); C.M.C. Mitchell; W. Morrison; S/Ldr. H.H. Moon; P.G. Murton (R.A.F. Museum); Jack Norman; S.B. "Olly" Oliver; Geoff Phillips; M. Retallack; S/Ldr. N.E. Rose A.F.C. & Bar; S/Ldr. C.J.D. Scholfield; R.H. Searle (R.A.E.); P.R. Sheppard; Jack Sherburn; Air Commodore I.S. Stockwell C.B.E., D.F.C, A.F.C. F.R.Ae.S; R.W. Stubbs; Derek Taylor; John Tipp; Mrs J. St. Vaughan; D. Watson; S. Watson; Anthony C. White; Mrs J. Williams; H.A. Wallace; S/Ldr J.H. Wilson; Bob Wolfendon; D.A. Wyldes.

Photographic credits to:

A.D. Beavor; F.D. Brownlie; Carl Cederberg (R.Swed.A.F.); L.T. Chamberlain; R. Clarke; Darryl Cott (B.Ae Hatfield); P. Cook; F. Farmer; S. Foster; E.V. George; K. Harding; J. Hartley; C. Haw; D.L. Hayward; M.W. Henley; L. Hook; Bill Hunt (MoD); Peter James (A. & A.E.E.); Philip Jarrett; D. King; F. King; D.B. Law; C.N.C. Mitchell; H.H. Moon; J. Norman; Bruce Robertson; N.E. Rose; Ray Sturtivant; R. Stynes; D. Taylor; Mrs. J. St.Vaughan; H.H. Wallace; S.H. Wheatley; Mrs. J.B. Williams.

Bibliography

Aircraft of the Royal Air Force since 1918 - Owen Thetford - Putnam
British Naval Aircraft since 1912 - Owen Thetford - Putnam
Squadrons of the Fleet Air Arm - Ray Sturtivant - Air-Britain
Squadrons of the Royal Air Force and Commonwealth - James J Halley - Air-Britain
De Havilland Hornet - Phillip Birtles - Profile Publications
De Havilland Aircraft since 1912 - A.J. Jackson - Putnam
Aeromilitaria - Air-Britain
Roundel - B.A.R.G.

AIR-BRITAIN - THE INTERNATIONAL ASSOCIATION OF AVIATION HISTORIANS - FOUNDED 1948

For forty-four years, Air-Britain has recorded aviation events as they have happened, because today's events are tomorrow's history. In addition, considerable research into the past has been undertaken to provide historians with the background to aviation history. Over 15,000 members have contributed to our aims and efforts in that time and many have become accepted authorities in their own fields.

Every month, *AIR-BRITAIN NEWS* covers the current civil and military scene.

Quarterly, each member receives *AIR-BRITAIN DIGEST* which is a fully-illustrated journal containing articles on various subjects, both past and present.

For those interested in military aviation history, there is the quarterly *AEROMILITARIA* which is designed to delve more deeply into the background of, mainly, British and Commonwealth military aviation than is possible in commercial publications and whose format permits it to be used as components of a filing system which suits the readers' requirements. This publication is responsible for the production of this volume and other monographs on military subjects. Also published quarterly is *ARCHIVE*, produced in a similar format to *AEROMILITARIA* but covering civil aviation history in depth on a world-wide basis. Both magazines are well-illustrated by photographs and drawings.

In addition to these regular publications, there are monographs covering type histories, both military and civil, airline fleets, Royal

Air Force registers, squadron histories and the civil registers of a large number of countries. Although our publications are available to non-members, prices are considerably lower to members who have priority over non-members when availability is limited. Normally, the accumulated price discounts for which members qualify when buying monographs far exceed the annual subscription rates.

A large team of aviation experts is available to answer members' queries on most aspects of aviation. If you have made a study of any particular subject, you may be able to expand your knowledge by joining those with similar interests. Also available to members are libraries of colour slides and photographs which supply slides and prints at prices considerably lower than those charged by commercial firms.

There are local branches of the Association in Bournemouth, Exeter, Gwent, Heston, London, Luton, Manchester, Merseyside, Rugby, Sheffield, Southampton, South-West Essex, Stansted and West Midlands.

If you would like to receive samples of Air-Britain magazines, please write to the following address enclosing 50p and stating your particular interests. If you would like only a brochure, please send a stamped self-addressed envelope to the same address (preferably 230 mm by 160 mm or over)

Air-Britain Membership Enquiries (HF), 1 Rose Cottages, 179 Penn Road, Hazlemere, High Wycombe, Bucks., HP15 7NE

MILITARY AVIATION PUBLICATIONS

Royal Air Force Aircraft series: (prices are for members/non-members and are post-free)

J1-J9999	(£8.00/£12.00)	K1000-K9999	(£2/50/£3.75)*	L1000-L9999	(£2.50/£3.75)
N1000-N9999(R)	(£4.00/£6.00)	P1000-P9999	(£2.00/£3.00)	R1000-R9999	(£2.50/£3.75)
T1000-T9999	(£3.00/£4.50)*	V1000-W9999	(£4.00/£6.00)*	X1000-Z9999	(£4.00/£6.00)
AA100-AZ999	(£6.00/£9.00)	BA100-BZ999	(£6.00/£9.00)	DA100-DZ999	(£5.00/£7.50)
EA100-EZ999	(£5.00/£7.50)	FA100-FZ999	(£5.00/£7.50)	HA100-HZ999	(£6.00/£9.00)
JA100-JZ999	(£6.00/£9.00)	KA100-KZ999	(£6.00/£9.00)	LA100-LZ999	(£7.00/£10.50)
MA199-MZ999	(£8.00/£12.00)	NA100-NZ999	(£8.00/£12.00)	SA100-VZ999	(£6.00/£9.00)
		WA100-WZ999	(£5.00/£7.50)*		

* Currently out of print; (R) Reprinted in limited numbers with slightly reduced quality of photographic reproduction

Type Histories

The Halifax File	(£6.00/£9.00)*	The Lancaster File	(£8.00/£12.00)	The Washington File	(£2.00/£3.00)
The Whitley File	(£4.50/£6.75)*	The Typhoon File	(£4.00/£6.00)*	The Stirling File	(£6.00/£9.00)*
The Anson File	(£15.00/£22.50)	The Harvard File	(£7.00/£10.50)	The Hampden File	(£11.00/£16.50)
		The Beaufort File	(£10.00/£15.00)		

Hardbacks

The Squadrons of the Royal Air Force and Commonwealth   (£18.00/£26.00)

The Squadrons of the Fleet Air Arm   (£14.00/£21.00)

Both the above cover the histories of all squadrons with precise tables of movements and equipment. Squadron badges are included for all units and both are profusely illustrated.

Royal Navy Shipboard Aircraft Developments 1912 - 1931 (£18.00/£27.00)

Royal Navy Aircraft Serials and Units 1911 - 1919 (£19.00/£28.50)

Individual Squadron Histories

Strike True - The History of No.80 Squadron, Royal Air Force (£4.00/£6.00)

With Courage and Faith - The History of No.18 Squadron, Royal Air Force (£5.00/£7.50)

The above are available from Air-Britain Sales Department, 5 Bradley Road, Upper Norwood, London SE19 3NT